D0330958

Mastering
Mule
Deer

Mastering Mule Deer

Hunter's Information Series™
North American Hunting Club
Minneapolis, Minnesota

Mastering Mule Deer

Copyright© 1988, Wayne van Zwoll

Library of Congress Catalog Card Number 88-62840
ISBN 0-914697-16-1

Printed in U.S.A.
7 8 9

Contents

Acknowledgments

Mastering Mule Deer is one of the most authoritative books on hunting mule deer in the Mountain West. It unveils the most proven techniques, and deciphers the technical information that will help you understand the habits and behavior of mule and black-tailed deer. Our congratulations to author Wayne van Zwoll.

Congratulations also to: NAHC Publisher Mark LaBarbera, Editor Bill Miller, Associate Editor Dan Dietrich, Member Products Manager Mike Vail and Special Products Coordinator Linda Kalinowski. Their efforts have provided us with another excellent book in the Hunter's Information Series™.

Steven F. Burke, President
North American Hunting Club

Photo Credits

Photos in this book were provided by the author. He has also included photos from Judd Cooney, the Washington Department of Wildlife and the Wyoming Game and Fish Department. Product photos were provided by the manufacturer whose product appears in the photo.

Dedication

To Alice.

About The Author

In Michigan's swamps and woodlots Wayne van Zwoll first came to know deer. He was a young hunter then, and inexperienced. They were white-tailed deer, adept at dodging hunters. In short order they taught Wayne that to hunt deer well he had to understand them. So Wayne studied deer.

He studied them on the hunt and in the off season, in the classroom as well as in the field. Earning a bachelor's degree at Michigan State University, Wayne went west for his graduate work. While earning a master's degree at Oregon State University, he hunted black-tailed deer in the Willamette Valley and Cascade Mountains, mule deer in eastern Oregon.

Deer and deer hunting have been Wayne's passion since, complementing his work as a range conservationist for the Bureau of Land Management, wildlife control agent for Washington's Department of Wildlife, editor of *Kansas Wildlife* and northwest field director for the Rocky Mountain Elk Foundation. An active outdoor writer, Wayne has shared what he's learned about deer in such magazines as *Sports Afield, Field & Stream* and *Petersen's Hunting*.

If Wayne has another interest as strong as deer, it is rifles. Since his earliest days in rimfire competition, Wayne has studied and experimented with sporting and target rifles, publishing his findings in *Rifle, Handloader, The American Rifleman* and other

journals. His practice on the firing line has given him two state smallbore championships and keeps him competitive on National Match and Metallic Silhouette courses as well. His treatment of deer rifles and cartridges in *Mastering Mule Deer* is as complete as you'll find in any book on deer hunting.

Wayne resides in Washington state with his wife, Alice, and two daughters.

Foreword

There are many books about deer hunting. Some are shallow, others are better. If you like to read about hunting you can enjoy even the shallow ones. You'll learn most from the books that took a long time to write, books that are tightly edited, books you must pay attention to as you read. As with exercise, you improve only when you stretch.

There's more to black-tailed and mule deer hunting than this book will tell you, but it will tell you more than most. Many people have contributed to this book. I've simply distilled what I've learned from them. My time with deer has taught me a lot too, and I pass that on. You'll learn more as you hunt and study deer, provided you're interested in more than just killing one.

Some people think you can hunt deer by following a set of rules or copying the latest technique. If procedure is hunting, and if the kill alone is a measure of the hunt, much of what I've written is of no use.

Still, there are others who think hunting a grand thing, beyond the scope of procedure and more than killing in the woods. I'm one of those people. I hope you are too.

This book will help you kill black-tailed and mule deer. It's supposed to. Maybe that's the reason you bought it. But there is more here than procedure, and you will find your view of deer hunting different at the end of this book than it is right now. You will know more about deer and getting close to deer, more about rifles and cartridges than perhaps you thought necessary. Better it will be, though, if here you glimpse something you want to learn more about.

Like the gleam of an antler tip in a mahogany thicket, this book offers you a promise. To read only procedure is to stare at the antler tip. Wanting to learn more and opening your mind to different perspectives is, like moving into the mahogany, the only way to better your position. It's the only way to find out what deer hunting is all about.

Once in a while you'll find a book that claims to be the last you'll have to read on the subject. That's a strange thing to say. If this book doesn't leave you with questions and ideas and a desire to read more, it is a poor book indeed.

What you do is only part of what you are. How you hunt is only part of what makes you a hunter. There are plenty of deer hunters busy being experts. Students are hard to find. This book is for students.

Wayne van Zwoll
Bridgeport, Washington

1

History:
How Deer Came To Be

Two million years ago nobody was around to record the evolution of deer. According to paleontologists, though, that's when deer of the genus *Odocoileus* arrived in North America. *Odocoileus* now includes two species: *O. virginianus*, white-tailed deer, and *O. hemionus*, black-tailed and mule deer. This book is about *O. hemionus*.

Even-toed hoofed animals are called ungulates, and belong to the order Artiodactyla. Nine families and 82 genera comprise this order. Ungulates occur naturally in most areas of the world, except Australia, New Zealand and Antarctica. They range in size from the 10-pound mouse deer to the 10,000-pound hippopotamus. One thing worth remembering about North American ungulates: upper canine teeth and incisors are either reduced or missing. The canines may be tusk-like, as in elk, but the upper palate in front lacks functional teeth.

One of the nine Artiodactyl families is Cervidae, represented by 17 genera and 53 species. Cervids are ruminants, or cud-chewing animals with four-chambered stomachs. This allows them to digest forage in stages and regurgitate hastily-cropped food for leisurely chewing in a safe place. That's an important benefit for a creature with no front uppers. All cervids except the musk deer lack a gallbladder.

Though all cervids are ruminants, not all ruminants are cervids.

To tell which is and which isn't you need only consider the antlers. All male cervids have bony antlers that are shed each year. Ruminants, like wild sheep and goats and African antelope wear permanent horns comprising a keratin sheath over a bony core. The American pronghorn is in that group too, though the keratin sheath of pronghorn is shed annually.

With most horned ungulates, the females as well as the males have horns. Almost all female cervids are antlerless, an exception being our caribou. Most cervid young are spotted.

Though most paleontologists agree that *O. hemionus* originated in the Old World, no mule or black-tailed deer live there now. *Odocoileus* does not occur in Europe at all. In order to trace the origins of our deer we must guess a lot, but we can make some pretty good guesses.

By the middle of the Cenozoic Era—which is the one we're in today—the earth consisted of scattered clumps of land jutting from the sea. Some of these islands were connected by isthmuses. Because the Cenozoic has been ticking away for about 63 million years, specific dates are irrelevant. But these land bridges probably began forming in the late Oligocene Epoch and continued in the more recent Miocene and Pliocene Epochs. By the end of the Tertiary Period (the end of the Pliocene, about 12 million years ago), North America, Eurasia and Africa had become united.

Among the land bridges linking continents at that time was the Bering-Chukchi platform. From its formation until the late Pleistocene Epoch this isthmus across the Bering Sea allowed animals to pass from Eurasia to North America and back. Alternately exposed and covered by water, the platform was last passable during the Wisconsin glacial stage of the late-Pleistocene, between 10,000 and 70,000 years ago. It is now 330 feet under water.

This land bridge varied in size according to the whims of the sea, but may have been nearly 1,000 miles wide during cold spells. Across it came many vertebrates. Deer-like creatures appear in fossil records in Eurasia dating from the Pliocene; by the Pleistocene these same kinds of animals were in North America. Migration across the isthmus was primarily a one-way movement from Eurasia to North America.

Because the accuracy of carbon dating is questionable beyond 50,000 years, tracing the evolution of deer during their early days in North America is hard. So let's dispense with the Pliocene and Miocene Epochs, as well as 900,000 years of the Pleistocene.

Mule and black-tailed deer are descendants from deer-like creatures that crossed a 1,000-mile wide land bridge that connected North America and Eurasia about 70,000 years ago.

Roughly 70,000 years ago the last of the great glacial periods, called the Wisconsin, was starting to make things cold. Under its chill large sections of what is now the western United States would, for 60,000 years, be iced in. Deer were limited by the glaciers to the desert Southwest and a narrow coastal strip that extended only a short distance north of Puget Sound. The Rockies were uninhabitable, as was the upper Canadian coast.

When the glaciers receded deer spread north. Into the mountains they went, and up the Pacific shores to southeastern Alaska.

Now, 10,000 years later, we classify what we see and speculate on how it got to be that way.

There are seven subspecies or races of *Odocoileus hemionus*: the Rocky Mountain mule deer, desert mule deer, California mule deer, southern mule deer, peninsula mule deer, Columbian black-tailed deer and Sitka black-tailed deer. Two other groups are considered subspecies by some taxonomists, but simply isolated populations by most. Both inhabit islands in the Gulf of California. They are the Tiburon Island mule deer of the desert race and the Cedros Island mule deer of the southern race.

At one time 11 subspecies of mule deer were proposed. Two, the burro deer of the desert southwest and the Inyo mule deer of eastern California, were later dropped.

The Rocky Mountain subspecies is by far the most common. Its range extends from central New Mexico north almost to Alaska, and from the Cascade crest east to the Kansas prairie and Dakota badlands. Rocky Mountain mule deer inhabit more territory, in fact, than all other subspecies combined.

Not that the other deer are scarce. Some, like the island races, occur only in small areas. But others, notably desert mule deer and Columbian blacktails, are widespread, their ranges overlapping that of the Rocky Mountain subspecies. Only the Cedros Island mule deer can be thought an extinction risk.

It's not clear what things work to create a subspecies. Taxonomists still argue about that. It has been suggested that the mule deer of the Southwest, pretty much undisturbed by glaciers, evolved into several races over the thousands of years the Rockies were buried in ice. The Rocky Mountain mule deer is a newcomer. By the same logic it could eventually form subspecific groups within its vast and varied range.

Distinct in form and habitat from the five main races of mule deer, Columbian and Sitka black-tailed deer are thought by some taxonomists to be a species in the making. The notion that a species produces fertile offspring only by unions within its kind is false. Blacktails imported to Tennessee have crossed with native whitetails and the hybrids have proved fertile. Where their ranges overlap, mule deer and whitetails also interbreed.

How *Odocoileus hemionus* is classified depends on our perception of morphological differences we see and origins we largely deduce. To hunt and manage these deer is to know their habitat.

2

Habitat:
Where The Deer Are

Black-tailed and mule deer occur in all states west of the 100th meridian including Alaska. Canada's three western provinces have them, as do the Baja Peninsula and north-central Mexico. These deer are adaptable, and have inhabited all but two or three of the 60-odd climax vegetation types in the western U.S. They occupy several in Canada and Mexico as well.

Breaking mule deer range into five or six dozen categories isn't practical. Conversely, to talk only of high summer country or low winter range is to ignore important differences in habitat types.

Most biologists are concerned with local deer populations, with habitat in their specific area. They can justify mapping minor habitat features and breaking blocks of habitat with only slight differences into distinct management units. For a larger perspective, though, less detailed criteria work best. Ten vegetation types occur in mule deer and blacktail range:

1) Coastal Rain Forest
2) California Chaparral
3) Mojave/Sonora Desert
4) Semi-desert Shrub
5) Great Plains
6) Colorado Plateau
7) Great Basin
8) Sagebrush Steppe

9) Northern Mountain

10) Canadian Boreal Forest

Each of these vegetation types belongs to one of four major habitat types: desert/chaparral, grassland/plains, mountain/steppe and coniferous forest.

Desert/Chaparral

Deserts are, to many people, hot places where nothing grows. They are places with little to offer, where everything either stings, bites, jabs or otherwise makes life uncomfortable. Like many natural wonders that are seldom understood, deserts don't fit this popular image.

The primary definition of a desert is wilderness. Sand isn't a requisite, nor is heat, and certainly not cacti. The Canadian tundra could be called a desert. Even climax northern forests would qualify. Both are vast areas with few inhabitants. If you aren't comfortable with that, you might further specify low diversity in plant and animal life. Actually, deserts are rich in diversity—more so than many climax forests. Harsh climate? The far north is, too, by our standards.

Deserts are not sterile, not always hot. The deserts that fit our habitat type, though, are otherwise typical. The Sonora Desert straddles the U.S.-Mexican border at the junction of Arizona and California. It extends down both sides of the Gulf of California and, to the north, touches the tip of Nevada. In California it overlaps the southern end of the Mojave Desert. The Mojave reaches east into Nevada and seeps into northwest Arizona.

Its southern end deep in central Mexico, the Chihuahuan Desert broadens to the north. It includes much of west Texas, a bit of south-central New Mexico and a few pockets in Arizona. The Chihuahuan is a hard desert to delineate on the map, and students of deserts point out that its elusive boundaries are that way because it isn't a desert at all. Its semi-arid climate begets variations in plant and animal life other deserts lack.

To the deer, categories and boundaries are of little concern. Theirs is a life of adaptation. In the deserts they find water in little places and survive on the water in forage when standing water is not available. Forage, thermal cover and escape cover are necessary. The deserts provide them.

The critical time for a southern or peninsula mule deer population is fawning. Fawning stresses the does, and the newborn are imperiled by predators and weather. Water becomes crucial.

Black-tailed and mule deer are adaptable animals. They have inhabited all but two or three of the 60-odd climax vegetation types in the western U.S.

Does in Arizona, New Mexico and southwest Texas fawn just before the high rainfall of late summer. Lactation is then supported by available free water and by the nutritious forage springing anew from the moist ground.

Summers are dry in California chaparral. Rainfall peaks in winter and if deer were to fawn when things were wet they'd do it around Christmas. They don't. Instead, parturition occurs in late spring as rains taper off and does are in their best physical condition. They can then give a good start to fawns that have but a few weeks of good foraging before the hot months.

Mule deer in most semi-arid regions depend a great deal on rainfall, somewhat for the open standing water it provides but mainly for its affect on plants. In Texas, fluctuations in forb production are thought to account for 75 percent of the variations in fawn survival. Both the amount of rainfall and its timing are important; each makes wide swings from the norm. In the Chihuahuan Desert during the 1970-1971 season 22 percent of the rainfall occurred in winter. The next season 92 percent fell at that time!

Plants in the desert Southwest are plentiful but, as in climax forests, vegetation by itself does not attract deer. To be useful to the animals, plants must be both palatable and nutritious.

An Arizona study showed 106 forage species in the rumens of 285 mule deer. Obviously the desert is not barren! But forage preferences varied significantly from season to season and year to year. Deer often ate things they didn't like, simply because what they preferred was unavailable. Wide fluctuations in rainfall preclude a steady diet in the desert.

Because deer can't always eat what they want, looking into rumens is not, by itself, an accurate way to determine what deer like. Finding out what deer *prefer* to eat is important to biologists and hunters both. Several studies have been done to this end.

On the Sonora Desert penned deer were fed 168 native plants and the species ranked in order of selection. Mistletoe, especially the broadleaf form, was most palatable. Buckwheat also rated high and emerged as one of the most important local plants because it is widespread and eaten year-round. Other preferred plants included kidney-wood, cat's claw, fairy duster, indigo bush, ceanothus, wild grape, cliff fendlera bush and wait-a-minute. Other studies have pointed to jojoba, mesquite, range ratany, desert honeysuckle, ocotillo, netleaf hackberry, stickweed and shrub live oak.

Not much is known about mule deer forage preferences on the Mojave Desert. Presumably, their preferences are similar to those on the Sonora. Along the Colorado River mule deer congregate in willow and screwbean thickets in dry periods. In winter they seek out paloverde, ironwood, cat's claw and mistletoe. Honey mesquite is important in fall, big galleta in early spring.

Though it accounts for the bulk of deer forage in the desert, browse is rarely chosen when tender forbs are available. Normally, forb use is highest in winter and early spring. It drops dramatically when things warm up in summer and increases only moderately in fall. The summer rains that bring nearly 70 percent of all desert precipitation have little immediate affect on forb growth. That occurs most noticeably after a winter rain.

In early summer desert shrubs set fruit and deer eat as much as they can find. Fruits and forbs in all deer habitats depend on favorable weather; poor production is common on the desert and alternate forage scarce. Deer thrive only where they can be assured of year-round nutrition. Consequently, browse figures heavily in desert diets. On the Sonora and other southwest deserts browse makes up 75 to 90 percent of deer forage, grasses less than three percent. The variable remainder is forbs.

The Chihuahuan Desert, at 3,000 to 6,000 feet in elevation, is slightly higher than the Sonora and thought by some ecologists to be more of a steppe than a desert. It has a climate similar to the Sonora, but fewer plant species. Summer rains account for 75 percent of the 10-inch total most years, and little plant growth occurs in winter. As on the Sonora, good winter rains occasionally produce a fine crop of forbs.

Deer forage preferences on the southern Chihuahuan have not been studied much. Some research has been done in Texas and New Mexico. Preferences recorded on the Sonora hold for the northern Chihuahuan, though many of the top-rated Sonora forages are absent. In 93 Chihuahuan Desert deer, four forage species constituted 54 percent of rumen volume: wavyleaf oak, juniper, yucca and hairy mountain mahogany. The rest of the forage represented 93 plant species, mostly skunkbush and silk tassel.

Other studies show differences not so much in species preference as in plant availability. One Texas study listed evergreen sumac, guayacan, littleleaf sumac and dalea among preferred browse, with lechuguilla and Engelmann prickly pear forming a large part of the summer diet. Another Texas researcher who compiled his list in winter and also noted lechuguilla and prickly pear, but added three species of oak, Ashe juniper, cane cholla, candelilla, sotol and yucca. Still another Texan included acacia, bladderpod and even bluegrass.

In this last study browse constituted only 45 percent of the diet, forbs 42 percent! Rainfall not only affects the growth of plants but the species selected by deer and the relative occurrence of each forage class in their diets as well. This is an important thing to consider when you look for deer, especially in the desert.

Deserts haven't had the human traffic that so drastically changed deer habitat on the Great Plains and continues to claim critical winter ranges from mountain herds. But the desert is a fragile place, easily ruined and slow to recover. Overgrazing by livestock is a danger in the better deer habitat. Off-road vehicles, driven irresponsibly, create erosion and destroy vegetation. Natural water sources used to irrigate crops or serve cattle can't meet that demand and still supply sufficient amounts to plants and wildlife.

Because of climatic restrictions we can do little to improve desert vegetation. What grows there is right for the place. Our attempts to cultivate the desert are usually unsuccessful unless we irrigate. Irrigating deer range is impractical, and there's nothing to be gained by burning or spraying most climax plant communities. The best we can do is tread with a light step, graze only where forage is available and can stand the cropping and curb activities that cause erosion or waste water.

Some good things have been done on deserts, notably the installation of stock watering tanks and wildlife guzzlers. Built properly with an adequate water source, stock tanks serve deer as well as cattle. Guzzlers are special tubs that catch rain and dew and dispense it to birds and animals.

Spot burning, spraying and even seeding have been used in some areas to manipulate plant composition—usually to counter overgrazing. Only semi-arid parts of deserts have responded well to grass seeding. Native shrubs can be established if they are nurtured. But that's costly. More can be done with chaparral habitats than with deserts.

Chaparral is an evergreen oak, but it's also a term commonly used to describe dense oak-brush vegetation or extensive dry-land brush fields comprising a variety of woody shrubs. Chaparral vegetation is deep-rooted, drought-tolerant and quick to recover from fire. Their leathery leaves identify them as sclerophylls. Dense, almost impenetrable stands are characteristic.

In California, chaparral occurs at mid-elevation—from 1,000 to 4,000 feet—west of the Sierra-Nevada summit. There it is year-round range for Columbian black-tailed and southern mule deer, and winter range for the migratory California mule deer that summer in the Sierras. The dominant plants in these chaparral stands are chamise, manzanita, buckbrush ceanothus, photinia, leatheroak, birchleaf mountain mahogany, interior live oak, California buckthorn and canyon live oak. Deer diets, even among resident populations, vary by season. But in large monospecific tracts, dominant shrub species can account for 95 percent of forage eaten.

Deer that inhabit this band of chaparral only part of the year rely heavily on browse. The migratory Jawbone herd was found to eat 89 percent browse, nine percent green grass and two percent forbs. But on the Tehama winter range, which has greater plant diversity, browse, grass and forb percentages in the diet were 54, 26 and 20. That changed to 72, 3 and 25 respectively in summer when the Tehama's grasses dried up. Place, season and weather affect deer diets in chaparral as strongly as they do in deserts.

Arizona's chaparral is also a strip, though at 3,000 to 6,000 feet a little higher than California's. It lies below the pinon/juniper zone and above the desert shrub. Roughly five million acres in size, this part of Arizona is dominated by mountain mahogany, shrub live oak and manzanita. Plant communities are less complex than those in the California chaparral. But as in California, herbaceous understory has a hard time competing for water and sunlight.

Favorite deer forages in Arizona's chaparral include desert ceanothus, hairy and birchleaf mountain mahogany, cliffrose and silk tassel. Shrub live oak, manzanita and juniper are frequently eaten because of their availability. They are not too palatable.

Chaparral gets more water than desert vegetation—from 20 inches annually in Arizona to almost 60 inches in northern California. Arizona's water comes, generally, in two doses: winter and late summer. West of the Sierras a single wet season lasts the winter and into spring.

Early settlers in California didn't like chaparral because it was too dense to let grass grow underneath. Five to 15 feet high, climax chaparral made land worthless for grazing. Deer now have the same problem finding grass and forbs in chaparral, but much of the brush itself is palatable and nutritious. Of 14 major shrub species in Arizona's chaparral all but one have significant value to deer. Security and thermal cover are bonuses.

Chaparral looks like the aftermath of a fire, and it is. Natural fires are expected in dry, dense cover lashed by thunderstorms. Indians set fires periodically to move game, and careless campers do it today. Vigorous sprouters, chaparral species come back quickly after a fire, allowing grasses and forbs only a short time in the sun. Four years after a fire, forbs decline followed quickly by grasses. A climax stand of brush may appear in a dozen years, rarely more than 20. It's been like that for a long time and some ecologists say chaparral communities existed as early as the Miocene Epoch.

The density of chaparral and its lack of species diversity limit its value to deer. But chaparral is still useful. Carrying capacities figured in the 1950s for Arizona chaparral were 10 to 12 deer per square mile. At the same time 25 to 30 deer were often counted in a unit that size.

It's expensive to improve chaparral. Herbicide application, burning and seeding cost about $50 an acre and need repeating every 15 years. In California, chaparral treatments have been successful. Burning five-acre blocks to total 70 percent of south slopes and 35 percent of north slopes creates openings for forbs while leaving ample security cover. Post-burn deer populations in chaparral have reached 120 per square mile—quadruple the figure before treatment. But dominant shrubs recover quickly, and deer use peaks only two years after the burn.

While prescribed burning is costly, especially when done in small blocks, the alternatives are too. Fire suppression allows for the build-up of dry plant material that can burn furiously when ignited. Nature's fires too often jeopardize settled areas, and they don't create the desirable mosaic of cover and opening that block burning does. Spring burning of California chaparral in controlled units seems to be the best way to manage climax stands for deer. It is most effective when treated areas are seeded just before autumn rains with soft chess, ryegrass, fescue, orchardgrass, rose clover or burnet.

In both desert and chaparral, livestock overgrazing often ruins deer range. Though weather governs the habitability of deserts, livestock use can preclude quick recovery of vegetation when rains come. In chaparral, domestic animals compete directly with deer for forage. Livestock properly managed do not harm deer habitat; light grazing even stimulates growth of grasses and forbs. But overstocked or poorly distributed livestock reduces the carrying capacity of arid deer range.

Grasslands/Plains

White-tailed and mule deer were common on the short-grass prairie at the time of Lewis and Clark. That expedition encountered mule deer for the first time in South Dakota's Big Bend country. Lewis observed later that while whitetails sought the cover of river bottoms when disturbed, mule deer headed for open country. The preference of mulies for rough places on the plains kept them away from early settlers who traveled the rivers and roads.

Later in the 19th century deer on the plains were pressured by settlers. Those traveling through shot game for meat; those that stayed cut the timber in draws and destroyed natural prairie vegetation with plow and livestock. By the time of the Homestead Act of 1862 deer were declining. Under the Act more farmers came west to make a home for themselves.

John Wesley Powell's 1879 report on range conditions recommended individual property units of 2,560 acres. Congress dictated 160. It wasn't enough. To increase production homesteaders overstocked their land and turned marginal soil under their plows. Cottonwood trees were skidded great distances to build houses. Junipers were cut for fence posts. Destruction of the prairie was quick. By 1884 deer were scarce on the plains, and bison were all but eliminated. Cattle numbers, meanwhile, were at an all-time high.

Market hunting, originally targeted at bison, affected deer more and more as bison numbers plummeted. Not only the railroad crews but steamboats on the upper Missouri would buy game. While it took longer for mule deer in the shadow of the Rockies to feel pressure from settlers, it eventually came. By 1900, deer were hard to find even in eastern Montana and the Canadian prairies.

From the turn of the century until the 1930s mule deer numbers remained low in accessible places. While the blizzards of 1886 and 1887 had cost cattlemen in the West up to 90 percent of their stock, it was soon replaced and overgrazing remained a problem.

Mule deer rebounded in the 1930s, for several reasons. The dust bowl years had forced many farmers to leave the prairie. South Dakota's population of 680,000, for instance, dropped by more than 50,000 during the Depression. With the people went their cattle and the range had a chance to recover. Stable weather in the late 1930s favored forage growth, and conservation programs aimed at saving soil established tree strips. Stock ponds and tanks were built by ranchers conscious of the need to better manage their land. Game laws were enacted and enforced.

During World War II intensive predator control was practiced on the plains. This no doubt helped deer populations recover. Even so, it wasn't until the late 1950s that deer numbers were near carrying capacity in most plains states. As late as 1955 no mule deer could be found in Kansas.

Prairies, like deserts, are widely misunderstood. More than just grass and far from featureless, they are complex and fragile. Prior to settlement, two types of prairie, the short-grass and long-grass, made up what we call the Great Plains. The tall-grass sector bordered deciduous forest on the east and ran into short-grass prairie at about 98 degrees longitude—somewhere near the middle of Kansas. The short-grass prairie extended west to the foothills of the Rockies. Both reached from central Texas into southern Canada.

The tall-grass prairie, dominated by big bluestem and other robust species, has been largely plowed under. That fertile soil now supports corn, soybeans and milo. The tall-grass prairie probably never had many deer, though it did sustain bison and elk.

The short-grass prairie has shallower, less fertile soil, thinner vegetation dominated by blue grama, buffalograss and other low-growing species. It has been farmed but most is grazed. Native plants have been eliminated in many places by too much grazing, and the short-grass prairie is not as productive as it was before settlement. It does, however, still support a good population of mule deer.

For our purposes, the short-grass prairie is the plains home for mule deer. It comprises several kinds of habitat. The most important are shrubby draws, hardwood draws, badlands and slopes on prairie hills. Flat areas without any of these features likely lack water as well. They hold little attraction for mule deer. Flood plains with shallow cuts fringed by cottonwoods do.

Shrubby ravines are places where many western prairie drainages start. Dominant plants include western snowberry, silvery buffaloberry, chokecherry, common snowberry, golden currant and various wild roses. These are used for both forage and cover by mule deer. Surrounded by open country, shrubby draws often hold concentrations of mulies that retreat there in bad weather or when pressured by hunters.

Hardwood draws are wetter sites and usually at lower elevations. Dominated by trees like American elm, boxelder, green ash, paper birch, quaking aspen, bur oak and hackberry, these draws also have shrubs. Among the most typical are western snowberry, Woods rose, chokecherry, serviceberry, American plum and hawthorn. Silvery buffaloberry, skunkbush sumac, clove currant and other roses are common too.

Deer use hardwood draws quite often, especially where farming or overgrazing makes the surrounding plain unattractive. In settled parts of Kansas and Nebraska mulies will often travel drainages and shelterbelts. Shelterbelts are a kind of artificial hardwood draw, less the ravine. Because it is the only tree cover on much of the plains, the hardwood draw is vital not only for escape and concealment but to cushion the lash of a winter storm. Its shade is important for shelter and to keep forbs and shrubs succulent long into the growing season. Like shrubby ravines, most hardwood draws have some open water.

The badlands of the Dakotas are a unique place, comprising soft shale soils, sandstones or chalkrock, usually with no profile. Erosion is severe. Where there's clay, shrubs like rabbitbrush, saltbush and broom snakeweed grow. These have limited value to deer. The washes in badlands habitat can be reasonably fertile, supporting little bluestem and other good grasses, as well as a variety of forbs. Benches with stable soils are a good location for western wheatgrass, blue grama and buffalograss. Prickly pear, an important deer food, is common in badlands.

The Dakota Badlands are the best-known, but badlands also occur in other states where there are bluffs and buttes.

Slopes mean mountains most of the time, but slopes occur on prairie hills and hummocks as well. Prairie slopes can be as important to deer as the skirts of western mountains. What timber there is on the plains occurs mainly on north slopes, and most is coniferous, typically Douglas fir and Rocky Mountain juniper. At the eastern and southern reaches of the short-grass prairie, Ponderosa pine and eastern red cedar replace Douglas fir. In Texas and New Mexico mountain mahogany, hop tree and Harvard oak grow with juniper.

The understory of north-slope prairie timber comprises chokecherry, skunkbush sumac, common juniper, western snowberry, Woods rose and, in places, poison ivy and silvery buffaloberry. Heavy stands of juniper have few understory shrubs but several grasses, notably western wheatgrass, little bluestem and side oats grama.

On south slopes tree cover is scarce. Ponderosa pine and various junipers are the only species common to the sunny sides of prairie hills. These are scattered; most escape and thermal cover lies on north slopes. South slopes with trees occur mainly in the northern plains. In Texas, woody slope vegetation is chaparral. Shrubs on slopes are scattered, usually over thin stands of native bunch grasses. Shrubs include little soapweed, leadplant amorpha, silver sagebrush, western snowberry, mesquite, dalea and littleleaf sumac. Skunkbush sumac is common. Deer use south slopes only occasionally to bed.

A south suggests a north, which usually has more cover and forage. Deer like south slopes in winter when winds and a pale sun keep snow depth down. After spring and fall rains mulies look for new forbs on south slopes, nibbling at green grasses as well. But in the hot months of summer, prairie draws and north-slope timber hold most of the succulent forage.

Flood plains occur throughout the short-grass prairie. These are simply low, flat areas that abut major streams and rivers. Water channels and erosion cuts mark many flood plains. Soils, generally rich, are piled by wind and water in lees and eddies, sifted by texture in the process. Sandbars are common.

Eastern cottonwood is the dominant tree here, with several kinds of willow. Peachleaf willow thrives from southern Canada into Kansas. In some places green ash, American elm, hackberry and boxelder occur. Salt cedar, an introduced shrub, dominates flood plains along the Arkansas River. Up to 94 percent of the plant cover in southern prairie lowlands is salt cedar.

A variety of understory shrubs grow on flood plains. Besides the sumacs, chokecherries, snowberries and roses of prairie woodlands, several wet-site species occur. Texas panhandle waterways show hackberry, soapberry, forestiera and four-winged saltbush.

Because much of the short-grass prairie is now farmed, deer depend heavily on crops for forage. They choose natural forage when crops are unavailable or too far from cover. In summer the shade of trees is important to deer and they do considerable foraging in wooded draws. Winter winds sweep open hills free of snow. Deer then move out of heavy cover to forage. During hunting seasons and while fawning, the animals find safe places and stay there.

What deer eat is often determined by where they are; the reverse is true less often. While prairie deer move seasonally to take advantage of the best forage, they eat a variety of plants—some because they have to and others because it is the easiest thing to reach.

Mountain/Steppe

The Rocky Mountain deer habitat is the biggest and newest chunk of deer range in the West. It spans over 1,500 miles from central New Mexico to northern British Columbia. One thousand miles broad, it borders the Great Plains on the east and the Cascade summit on the west. There's substantial diversity within the mountain/steppe boundaries, and much of this country isn't mountain or steppe. Except on the fringes, the only deer are Rocky Mountain mule deer.

Mountain weather varies considerably because of extremes in elevation and the seasons. It is a dry climate compared to the Pacific Coast—but certainly not as dry as the deserts on its southern border. Although very little of the precipitation is snow, it affects deer movements a great deal because it buries forage and hinders movement. Many of the deer in the mountains migrate to lower elevations during winter. If there isn't much snow, however, some stay high all winter long. A few low areas have resident deer year-round.

Deer eat at least 788 different plant varieties in the Mountain West. Included are 484 forbs, 202 shrubs and trees, 84 grasses,

The Snake River breaks give mule deer a view, as well as forage, escape cover, terrain and canyons in which to winter.

sedges and rushes, and several lichens and mosses. As in desert and plains habitat, forbs are preferred over woody plants or grasses, but they're used most after spring and autumn rains. In winter, deer eat what they can get. In many areas that's just dry browse. Grasses taste best in spring, when they're most nutritious. Deer eat less grass as it dries up in summer, replacing it with browse.

Deer like leaves, and the greatest variety of browse is eaten in summer when they're in leaf. Some deciduous plants that look good to summering deer are less appetizing come winter when their leaves are gone. Few evergreen browse plants, save juniper, are important to deer in the Rockies.

While hard browse—leafless twigs and the like—keep deer alive in winter, green foliage makes for productive deer range. Plants must not only be nutritious, but those nutrients must be available to deer. Green leaves are both palatable and digestible. They're high in protein and soluble carbohydrates and low in fiber. Dry winter twigs from the same plant are low in digestible nutrients, but high in fiber.

The levels of proteins and carbohydrates in plant cells increase in fall, though leaves become dryer. This is so the plant can move these nutrients into its roots for winter.

There's a substantial difference in what a plant can provide a deer in winter versus summer. Crude protein in a cross-section of mountain browse species averages about 24 percent in June, 12 percent in September, seven percent in November and five percent in February. Digestibility of the browse drops from 60 percent in August to 35 percent in March. Some species, notably big sagebrush, mountain mahogany and bitterbrush, are 50 percent digestible—quite a bit more than other shrubs. Because of this and their availability above snow, such plants are important winter deer forage, though they may be shunned in the warmer months.

Grasses are palatable and more digestible in the spring. In fact, at that time of year they're the most digestible of the forage classes. That's why they're eaten then. Though grasses make up a small part of deer diets they're more important than was once thought. They comprise nearly 25 percent of the forage eaten on one Colorado winter range, nearly 75 percent on another! Some biologists think deer would eat even more grass if it were readily accessible where they hide and bed. Although grasses are more digestible in winter than many browse plants, they are typically harder to find.

What deer eat in fall determines how they weather winter. In deep snow, forage is unavailable and travel saps energy fast.

Snow hinders foraging when foraging is most essential. At temperatures around zero a deer can use 2,000 calories (kcals) a day just to maintain itself—without moving! Walking in deep snow to forage demands considerably more. And only a foot of snow can cover 97 percent of available forage in some areas! A poor winter range limits the health and size of a herd, no matter how nutritious and plentiful the plants on a summer range.

Over 100 million acres of mule deer winter range have sagebrush or juniper of some variety in great abundance. The essential oils in these plants inhibit the digestive action of microbes in deer rumens. Regardless of abundance, sagebrush and juniper make up only 20 to 30 percent of winter diets. Different species within a genus have different oil contents and deer usually select those plants lowest in oils. One-seeded and alligator juniper, for example, are more valuable to deer browse than Utah and Rocky Mountain juniper. Rabbitbrushes, common and available on many winter ranges, also have high oil content and low forage value.

The kinds of plants available on the winter range are more important to deer survival than the amount of forage. Overuse of an area by wildlife or livestock rarely depletes the total vegetation more than a few percentage points. But it can strip the range of desirable and nutritious plants. Deer often die with stomachs full of forage; but it isn't the right kind of forage.

Overuse also changes the species composition of range, eliminating valuable native plants and allowing less valuable kinds to get started. Many intermountain ranges are now choked by Russian knapweed, Scotch thistle and other plants that provide little or no forage to deer. Had grazing been controlled, these plants would not have become established.

The alpine sections of mountain deer habitat haven't been studied much, mainly because deer don't spend much time there in winter and winter range is the critical place. High-elevation deer country is affected very little by human activity, at least compared to winter ranges. That's good too, because alpine plants have a tough time as it is with strong winds, deep snow, cold temperatures and a growing season that barely gets going before it ends. Alpine places are fragile places, easily damaged and slow to recover. They're similar to deserts in that respect.

Deer up high eat well, usually. By the time the peaks are free of snow to expose vegetation it's late May. In the avalanche pockets melting snow generates new forb growth throughout the summer. Grasses are succulent and browse leaves don't dry up as fast as on the hot lowlands. More acres of high country are vertical than horizontal. That makes for more acres of summer pasture.

Not only are most summer ranges bigger on the map than winter ranges where animals congregate, but the rough topography on top multiplies the acres deer can use. It does not necessarily multiply the forage, because snowfields, bluffs and rock walls aren't suitable places for plants to grow.

Deer don't move much on high summer range because, besides an occasional cougar, bear or backpacker, not much is up there to bother them. If a herd of domestic sheep invades, the deer will move to another ridge or basin. For the most part energy requirements in alpine places are low. While the forage may not be as plentiful as in the foothills, digestible nutrients are high. Deer shot on ridges above timberline are likely to be as fat as those taken from grainfields.

High range gives relief from flies, an important consideration if you're a deer. The same knob-top winds that batter the bushes also make flying difficult and cold for insects. Big mule deer bucks like to lie near patches of snow just off ridgeline, letting the breeze fan the flies away and thermal drafts bring news from the lowlands.

Those big mountain meadows that look so lush and green

aren't used extensively by deer. Plant species composition isn't right for one thing. Sedges and rushes dominate wet meadows and grass growth is rank. Besides, foraging in low places makes mountain mule deer nervous. They'd much rather nibble at things on a hillside where they have a commanding view and a choice of going up or down to avoid danger.

It's a blessing for deer that the majority of true alpine habitat in our Mountain West is in designated wilderness areas. Off-road vehicles don't tear up the fragile meadows or leave scars on the hillsides.

About the only thing that has an impact on the forage in alpine habitat—except bands of domestic sheep that in places can destroy a great deal—is the occasional pack train. Horses, if improperly tended, can mow meadow grasses so close as to damage the crown and prevent root storage of essential nutrients for winter. They can also muck up an area quickly, their great weight and shod hooves cutting deep into shallow soils. Conscientious packers include enough grain in their boxes to keep their horses and mules well fed in areas where forage is scarce and the plant communities fragile. They change tethers often and stick to defined pack trails when traveling.

Mule deer winter ranges are less fragile but more vulnerable to human traffic and overgrazing. There are three main types of winter range: sagebrush/steppe, pinon/juniper and mountain mahogany/oak.

The various sagebrushes or native shrubs were not as prevalent in the early days of settlement as they are now. Many dense stands of sagebrush were created by cattle overgrazing.

After World War II it became popular to use 2,4-D and 2,4,5-T to kill sagebrush and give seeded legumes and grasses a chance to establish. By the mid-1960s nearly five million acres had been treated.

Because big sagebrush is an important winter forage, eradication of the plant is not a goal in these spray programs. But with sagebrush on some sites reduced, forbs and grasses more valuable to deer can flourish.

With its high oil content even the most palatable sagebrush makes up no more than 30 percent of a deer's diet, usually much less. A little sagebrush can take care of the needs of a wintering herd nicely. An abundance is not only "too much of a good thing," but also generates a canopy under which succulent forbs and grasses can't grow, and a root system that robs other plants of water.

Wintering mule deer need just over three pounds of forage a day to maintain themselves. That's dry weight. If sagebrush made up 25 percent of the diet of a wintering herd of 200 deer on one square mile—an extremely high density—that section would have to provide only 31 pounds of sagebrush forage per acre. And that for a 120-day wintering period. Heavy sagebrush stands on Colorado winter ranges have yielded 614 pounds of forage per acre. Most sprayed areas retained one-half to two-thirds the sagebrush of untreated sites.

Broadleaf herbicides like 2,4-D did damage other desirable plants, but timing the spray to the most susceptible phenological stage in sagebrush left other species largely intact. Pre-bloom spraying of bitterbrush in conjunction with the mid-May treatment of big sagebrush in eastern Oregon killed 95 percent of the sagebrush and only 10 percent of the bitterbrush. Phenological stage, not date, was the important consideration.

Fire and tractors are more common tools for controlling sagebrush. Both are more predictable in their effects. The biggest increase in grass and forb production is immediately after a fire. In Idaho, forb growth peaked three years behind a sagebrush burn. Grasses and shrubs like rabbitbrush increased for about 10 years. Twelve years after the fire sagebrush began to increase again and in 30 years it had taken over.

The same kind of succession can be expected in areas treated by disk, shredder, root plow or anchor chain. Seeding and fertilizing can boost the growth of herbaceous plants in the wake of sagebrush treatment, but often the increased production is temporary. Changes in species composition are hard to sustain, and the costs of tillage, seeding and fertilizer application are prohibitive on many winter ranges.

Pinon/juniper range, like sagebrush country, is relatively low in elevation. It covers about 89 million acres, mostly in the southern third of mountain/steppe terrain. Arizona and New Mexico have lots of it, as do Colorado, Utah and Nevada. Like sagebrush and chaparral, dense pinon/juniper stands provide little forage but plenty of cover.

Patches of cover scattered through sunny openings that permit growth of preferred deer forage are supposedly better than large blocks of cover. But in some pinon/juniper control programs, deer use after treatment was less than before—even when forage production rose sharply. We really don't know what is the optimum cover for deer.

Reducing security in an area makes it less attractive to deer. Unless the extra forage is worth the risk they won't venture into the open. Deer used to certain cover characteristics won't always accept changes in that cover. What constitutes adequate cover varies by habitat type, and deer habits aren't predicated on what we think is right for them.

Pinon/juniper sites in Utah produced more shrubs and grasses after tree removal, but only for the first few years. That occurred in Nevada too. Grass and forb production was particularly short-lived, peaking two to four years after treatment. Some low shrubs, like sagebrush, snakeweed, bitterbrush, snowberry and rabbitbrush, prospered for up to 40 years. After that pinon pine or juniper again took over, usually in less than 20 years.

Here again, the cost of increased deer forage is the loss of deer cover. And because the best forage is in young plants, succession must periodically be restarted. That's costly.

Mountain mahogany and scrub oaks dominate about 15 million acres of mid-elevation deer range. Found primarily in Colorado and Utah, this brush responds pretty much the same to treatment programs as chaparral. Most of the benefit is derived by elk or livestock; grass yields in treated areas often double immediately. But the gains are short-lived, and five years following a burn or mechanical brush removal grass production can be lower than it was before treatment. Shrub growth did not increase on these sites. In fact, it decreased by as much as 29 percent after spraying! Forbs benefit little.

Forage management in mahogany/oak stands calls for frequent removal of Gambel oak, bigtooth maple, black chokecherry and other woody dominants to let native grasses establish. Because the oak is important deer cover, and because forbs and shrubs do not benefit by tree removal, getting rid of these stands does little good.

Most of the deer in mountain/steppe habitats are migratory. Spread over lots of good summer range, herds congregate in small areas to winter. In some places winter range can be as little as one percent of summer habitat. This creates problems for the deer and the plants they eat. Crowding and competition for limited forage stresses the animals and makes them weaker. Energy used muscling another deer over to get at a twig would be better conserved. All activities are made more difficult by snow. Predators can find deer fast and catch them easily.

Too many deer can strip winter range of available forage. A tough winter then causes many deer to starve.

Winter is also tough from the plant's point of view. Having stored nutrients in its roots for maintenance during dormancy, each bush still has numerous twigs and buds above ground. Unable to find succulent leaves, forbs or grasses, deer chew the twigs farther and farther down. Woody parts not touched in summer are now eaten because there's nothing else. Even big shrubs can be so damaged that they fail to bloom the following year, or more commonly, die in four to six years.

How much browsing is too much varies by plant species and phenological stage. Bitterbrush, a winter deer staple in much of the Mountain West, can live to be more than 100 years old. The oldest plants—rank, coarse and of limited nutritional value—are actually helped by browsing. In Idaho an additional 114 pounds of forage per acre was produced by bitterbrush one year after clipping, and as much as 338 pounds per acre the second year! Increased yields, however, did not continue. In the third and fourth years only about 25 more pounds per acre were produced.

Purposefully destructive clipping doubled forage production

the second year. However, all the plants died the fourth year.

Bitterbrush cropped at a rate of 20 to 40 percent is not harmed and will sprout more vigorously than unused bitterbrush. Cropping 50 to 60 percent of the available growth usually does no lasting damage; 80 percent use kills the plant. Cropping limits are less on young plants and during summer and autumn.

Sagebrush takes heavy use well. It can tolerate 80 percent cropping in winter, and 40 percent in summer. Gambel oak thrives under heavy browsing and grows tall and straight unless cropped about 60 percent each year. Greatest twig yields come from 20 to 60 percent use. Up to 90 percent use is beneficial on some sites.

Mountain mahogany is another hardy dominant. With 100 percent of available forage taken, plants monitored for 11 years produced 15 times more forage at the end of that time than at the beginning. Sustained winter use of 60 to 80 percent is good for the plants and the deer.

Some browse plants, like serviceberry, respond poorly over time no matter how they're managed. Serviceberry can stand heavy use: at least 60 percent of annual growth. But productivity will decline as the shrubs mature. Clipping, fire and animal use will revitalize some plants, but on marginal sites many will die. New serviceberry bushes are needed from time to time. Because they belong to a subclimax stage of succession they do well only if that seral stage is maintained or reintroduced.

Cold temperatures are not the cause of deer migration. It's the deep snow that forces them to low winter ranges. Of the four habitat types, the mountain/steppe gets the most snow. Foothills get less snow than high summer range, so deer migrate to them when deep snow hampers their movement. By early December, and even before, deer move off the ridges and into major drainages, wintering on benches and slopes where wind sweeps the snow off forage.

Wind speed, topography, vegetation and snow conditions are as important to deer as the amount of snow falling. Bushes that stand tall break the wind, forming small drifts to their leeward side. The ground underneath them doesn't catch as much snow as unsheltered areas. Wind crusting is less a problem where shrubs redirect currents and slow them down.

All these things influence deer behavior. Vigorous stands of sagebrush mean loose snow and pockets of available forage beneath the shrubs. Deer usually prefer these areas to sites that are more open. On south slopes when crusting is not a problem, deer

No matter how good the summer range, winter determines the growth and health of a deer herd.

visit treated areas where the wind has swept the hillside bare and the sun has worked the snow. Under these conditions sagebrush stands are less attractive. As with forage, diversity in snow conditions can benefit deer.

North slopes accumulate more snow but are less apt to crust than south slopes that freeze and melt. The heavier thermal cover on north slopes is attractive during storms and periods of high wind that push the chill index down. It provides a hiding place as well. Things are generally cooler on the shady side of ridges, but snow conditions are of greater interest to deer than temperatures. Besides, snow caught on north slope conifers insulates the ground, making the area even warmer than exposed south slopes. Snow underfoot, not that clinging overhead, is the snow that matters. North slopes that haven't thawed can be surprisingly free of snow on the ground.

Snow fences can be used upwind from prime mule deer foraging sites to control drifting snow. Drifts still form in protected areas, but they are of soft snow and not deep enough to impair movement. On unprotected areas the wind blows snow at random into drifts, then crusts their tops. Deer cannot use those sites. Snow fences and barricades have also been used to direct drifting onto new seedings, shielding them from the wind and minimizing deer use during that first critical year.

Coniferous Forest

Coniferous forests are common in the northern Rockies. To the extent that pines are conifers, they're also common in the high places of the desert Southwest. But most coniferous forests are on the Pacific Coast—that strip between the Pacific Ocean and the Cascade Crest, from central California to southeast Alaska. Almost all the timber in this area is coniferous. Deciduous trees are limited to river bottoms, though Alaskan alder reach almost to the mountaintops in places.

Two subspecies of *Odocoileus hemionus* occur here: the Columbian blacktail to the south and the Sitka blacktail in northern British Columbia and Alaska. Some crossbreeding goes on between blacktail and mule deer along the Cascade Range, and California mule deer use some of the range of blacktail in that state. But for the most part, these are different deer, different in appearance and habit from the mulies to the east and south.

The main reason is habitat. In coniferous forests vegetation is lush. Rainfall averages only 20 inches annually in the extreme

South. But the best blacktail range gets much more: more than 130 inches annually, with most of that coming in the winter. Snow comes only occasionally to the southern half of this strip, and winter temperatures at its midpoint usually stay above freezing except at high elevations.

Douglas fir dominates most of the timber in the Pacific Northwest, sharing many locations with Sitka spruce, hemlock and redwood. In climax stands, trees shade the forest floor almost completely, inhibiting forb and shrub growth. Logging opens the forest to the sun and deer benefit immediately from increased forb production. Fire serves the same purpose. Without these factors the dense canopy blocks sunlight until rotting boles and a strong wind combine to topple trees. For this reason, old forests are more attractive to blacktails than healthy climax timber stands.

Blacktail eat many different plants. Of 223 plants recorded on Vancouver Island deer ate 158. Of 92 species noted in Oregon they ate 65. Preference is determined by plant phenology, but generally grasses are used most in winter and early spring, forbs in spring and summer, browse in summer and autumn. In most places there is plenty of good forage to keep resident deer healthy year-round. Climax forests don't provide much forage, but there aren't many deer there to begin with. Openings in the canopy change that, because the mild climate and heavy rains generate forage quickly, leaving the deer population to catch up with carrying capacity. Only when heavy snows bury vegetation is there a forage problem. And that's usually temporary.

Like other deer, blacktail prefer green leaves to other forage in all seasons. Some shrubs—salad and Pacific blackberry, for example—retain their leaves year-round. So do a few forbs, notably cat's-ear. Other forbs like montia and phacelia grow actively in fall and winter, providing green leaves when other plants don't.

Where available, acorns are relished by deer. In parts of California acorns are a major food item, and together with browse (primarily leaves) make up nearly one-half of what deer eat. Young grasses and forbs come next, in roughly equal proportion. Buds and twigs of woody plants are less palatable, and grasses don't get much attention after seed heads form.

Oregon's blacktail ate 59 percent browse in one study. Grasses were especially important in winter, forbs in early summer. In Washington, tame blacktail were recorded eating 65 percent browse, 25 percent forbs and 10 percent grasses.

Logging spurs growth of forbs and young trees deer like to eat.

Vancouver Island blacktails ate differently in two studies. In the first, 71 percent of the stomach contents was browse, 22 percent lichens and mushrooms, five percent ferns and horsetails and two percent grasses. In the second study only 17 percent was identified as browse. Forbs accounted for 59 percent, grasses 15 and lichens seven. One researcher noted that deer ate 92, 64 and 56 percent of available browse, forb and grass, and 73 percent of 26 lichens, mushrooms and water plants.

In most blacktail range woody browse is a small part of the diet. Deer eat the twigs of huckleberry and certain ceanothus plants when leaves are gone, but few others.

Some plants poisonous to livestock are common in the forest and on its fringes, namely tansy ragwort, bracken fern, bleeding heart, red elderberry and horsetail. Deer are unaffected by these.

Bracken is an important forage on Vancouver Island but is seldom used by deer in Oregon, though it is also common there. Starflower, a forb, occurs in both California and Oregon. California deer eat it readily but Oregon deer do not. Red-stem ceanothus is a favorite plant in most places, but it is not plentiful. Pacific blackberry and salal are more important forages. Besides providing green leaves in winter they are widespread in the middle of blacktail range.

Because of these forage preferences, defining a seasonal blacktail diet is difficult.

Deer do their best where plants are in early succession. The most productive areas are those that were recently cut, burned or disturbed.

Burning and cutting to open canopies and generate more deer forage have been overdone in places. In the Rockies, for example, snow gets so deep in openings that deer can't use them in winter. Logged areas provide good summer forage, but summer range does not limit deer numbers. Winter range does.

In most blacktail habitat snow isn't a problem. Except in the northern reaches of coastal forests, openings are accessible to deer year-round. And the quick response of woodland forbs and shrubs to a little light and moisture makes these areas prime foraging spots.

Deer numbers generally increase right after timber is removed and continue to climb for at least 10 years. After that, forage production is no longer up to the demands of an expanding herd. If deer numbers keep increasing, average live weight of the deer will decrease as the forest matures and nutritious forage becomes harder to find.

The classic example of this is Oregon's Tillamook burn of 1933. In 24 hours the Tillamook blaze destroyed more than 250,000 acres of timber, more than any other recorded in this country. By the time it was out it had charred 14 townships—but had killed only one person. It was a terrific economic loss, but a boon to blacktails.

In the years following this burn deer numbers increased to well over 50 per square mile. Potentials were greater; one captive herd on the burn expanded from a density of 56 to 126 deer per square mile in just 21 months!

Forage conditions, however, peaked 10 years after the fire. About 30 blacktails per section were on the burn, and live weights averaged 130 pounds for two-year-olds. Twenty years later deer densities were up to 60 per square mile. But as the population had increased, the available, nutritious forage had decreased. Live weights for yearling Tillamook blacktails in 1964 averaged only 90 pounds, and nearly all the bucks were spikes.

In mature forests more than 99 percent of all plant material is in the trees. The only deer forage, then, is that portion of the available one percent that deer want to eat. When fire or logging opens the canopy, nearly all the plant material produced in the next few years will be available to deer, and most of it will be usable forage. Where cut and uncut timber comprise equal acreage, deer get about 70 percent of their forage from cuts.

The best way to cut timber for sale is not the best way to cut timber for deer. Large cuts make good use of expensive roads and minimize setup time for machines. They also allow fallers and skidders to progress methodically, working a stand or ridge until salable trees run out. But for deer big openings aren't as good as little ones.

To forage in the middle of a large logged area deer must distance themselves from cover. They don't do that very often. Also, big open expanses are windy and susceptible to drifting in winter. In southeast Alaska snow depths in cuts can be twice as deep as snow under a mature forest canopy.

From the deer's perspective, edges are a good thing. An edge is next to escape cover and next to openings. It has sunlight and shade and protection from the wind. It's a secure place, with succulent forage. To get more edges you must open the forest. Small irregular openings are best. Ideally these are scattered within blocks of mature timber and represent several stages of succession.

Because we can't afford to manage timber just for deer,

logging in rotation is useful. Set up for a 120-year period with cutting done every 20 years, one-sixth of the timber would be taken each cut. After one complete period the stand would have six successive stages and always one of salable 120-year-old trees.

This idea of recycling is important. Almost all of the best deer habitat is immature. Climax vegetation is unattractive to deer in most areas. In nearly all habitats deer populations increase with periodic disturbance that sets back succession. In chaparral it might be burning, in sagebrush chaining, in a mature forest logging. In some places the results are immediate; in others deer will respond several years after the disturbance. If treated areas are small they get used quicker and more completely because then deer don't have to risk moving far from cover to forage.

In almost every coniferous forest that supports deer, logging is a good thing. Only in the extreme northern end of the coastal belt does logging, all logging, appear to compound wintering problems. The deep snow keeps deer out of open areas in winter. It matters very little that cuts renew succession, because they are largely inaccessible when deer need them most. The spruce/hemlock forests are unattractive except in the first 12 years following the disturbance. After that the growth is so dense that only a few annuals and low-value shrubs can flourish, and deer have a hard time getting to them. Not until these forests reach an age of 300 years or so, when wind creates openings and the understory has more perennial forbs and shrubs, will blacktails return.

In other areas, like western Oregon, deer immediately look for new growth in cuts and burns. Though total plant production is low to start with, the best years for forbs are the first ones. Lots of water makes the new plants grow fast. As shrubs and young trees sprout, deer switch to them. In dryer climates the heaviest deer use comes two to four years after a disturbance, when new plants have grown big enough to eat.

Logging slash also affects deer use of an area. Too much keeps the animals from moving freely. Too little will make the cut appear a barren, insecure place, especially if it's a big one. Slash determines what plant species will and will not grow in an area. Engelmann spruce seedlings, for example, will not tolerate direct sunlight; slash helps shade them.

Getting rid of slash by burning disturbs the soil and may kill desirable plants. But in the end it benefits deer by promoting forb growth and regenerating shrubs and grasses.

Generally, deer benefit from current management techniques.

Logging is seldom done in large blocks because wildlife use is a consideration in timber management. Usually the size and shape of cuts are compromises. Economics and aesthetics are considered.

This kind of management began in 1960 when Congress passed the Multiple Use-Sustained Yield Act. The Forest and Rangeland Renewable Resources Planning Act of 1974 and its amendment, the National Forest Management Act of 1976, modified the original agreement in favor of timber production. But deer and other wildlife still figure in timber management.

As forest practices affect deer, deer also affect forest practices. Young Douglas-fir seedlings are often heavily browsed by deer. This causes stunting, slows growth and may even kill trees. Continued browsing has a pruning effect, keeping leaders in reach of small rodents that do further damage.

Douglas-fir is only one of several commercial tree species that occasionally gets damaged by deer. Inland, white fir, western larch, lodgepole, Ponderosa pine, Engelmann spruce and blue spruce are eaten. Much of the damage occurs on winter range where good forage plants are scarce. Because winter range in the mountain states has only a little of the region's marketable timber, deer damage to trees is seldom a big problem.

On the Coast Range, though, where winters are mild and forests reach down to the river bottoms, deer can nibble Douglas-fir seedlings all year long. To the deer it's a palatable food; to timber companies it's one of the most valuable things on a stump. Damage estimates, especially for the long term, are difficult to determine. Suffice it to say that in some areas damage is severe.

Several techniques have been tried to keep deer from eating young trees. Not very many work. No chemical systemics have proved practical, and only two topical sprays are effective. They're TMTD (tetramethylthiuram disulfide) and ZAC (zinc dimethyldithiocarbimate cyclohexylamine). Both work for only short periods.

Fences keep deer out of tree plantations but are expensive (roughly $2,500 a mile) to build and require maintenance. They're not feasible in the hills. Little mesh cylinders around each tree are less costly and let the deer browse other plants in the area. Plastic mesh has proven more snow-resistant than chicken wire.

Replanting immediately after cutting or burning can reduce deer damage, because deer don't use disturbed areas as heavily that first year as they do during succeeding years. Early seedling establishment is a particularly good idea on areas where the deer population has room to expand into improved habitat. On the Tillamook burn, for example, planting Douglas-fir seedlings during peak deer production several years after the fire would have been a foolish waste of trees.

Planting big trees can minimize deer damage because deer don't like big trees as well and the damage they do is of less consequence to a vigorous, five-foot-tall conifer. That's expensive, though.

Another ploy would be to substitute relatively unpalatable species like western hemlock for the Douglas-fir in new stands. Provided the hemlock netted timber companies as much money, that might be practical. But no one knows how much hemlock deer will eat if it is the only little tree around. It might be as popular as Douglas-fir.

Overstocking is one way to keep deer from affecting growing timber. Instead of planting the recommended 400 trees per acre in western Oregon, for example, foresters could plant 500. The cost of deer damage would be the extra 100 trees per seeding. Provided resulting stands were acceptable, this approach would work as well in difficult terrain as on lowland plantations.

Leaving slash in cuts protects young trees from damage but makes planting more difficult and keeps deer from using other plants in the opening as well. Establishing other preferred deer forage at planting time can reduce pressure on commercial trees.

Some genetic resistance to deer damage has been found in Douglas fir; production and planting of resistant stock could minimize the effects of deer browsing.

3

What Deer Are

Deer are a lot like us: they comprise an assemblage of bone, muscle, water, fat, protein, blood and teeth. Bones make up a little more than 10 percent of the weight of an adult mule deer, male or female. Half of that weight is in long bones. Muscle accounts for about 50 percent of the body weight of a mature buck, 40 percent of a mature doe. Water, including what's in the muscle cells, ranges from 50 to 85 percent of body weight. It varies inversely with body fat percentage, which in deer can be five to 17 percent, winter to summer. Blood averages nine percent of body weight in bucks, eight percent in does. It amounts to about one ounce for each pound of body weight, so a 180-pound deer has 180 ounces or a bit over 11 pints of blood.

Mature Rocky Mountain mule deer bucks stand between 36 and 40 inches at the shoulder. Does are smaller. Many people think deer are bigger than that, but thinking doesn't make them so. I was astonished when an experienced hunter recently told me he'd seen a deer that was well over five feet at the shoulder. I asked him how big he thought bucks grew and he said most were about five feet, hoof to shoulder. That's elk-size.

Deer are also lighter than most people would have you believe—even the big bucks. In a sample of 142 yearling mule deer shot in Colorado over a four-year period, average bled carcass weight for bucks was 165 pounds, for does 130 pounds. Field

Black-tailed and mule deer are both smaller and lighter than many people suspect. Mature Rocky Mountain mule deer bucks stand between 36 and 40 inches at the shoulder. Average bled carcass weight for yearling mule deer in Colorado is 160 pounds.

dressed they averaged 121 and 98 pounds, skinned after dressing 108 and 84 pounds. A while back I shot an average four-point mule deer and packed it out, boned, on my back. The pack weighed not quite 90 pounds; 70 of that was meat. So, while 250-pound mule deer certainly exist, they're almost always mature bucks—and unusually heavy ones at that. I've seen them and shot them and you may have too. Someday you might see one that would scale 300 pounds. They exist, but they're not common. Mule deer does weigh about 20 percent less than bucks.

Rocky Mountain mule deer bucks vary in weight more than

does and commonly lose 20 percent of their weight during winter. Yearling growth rates among mule deer subspecies vary, with Sitka blacktails, the smallest of the lot, showing one of the highest rates. Studies to determine the ages at which deer stop gaining weight (growing) are inconclusive; estimates range from 30 months to eight years.

Vital Parts

Adult mule deer have 32 teeth. The permanent dental formula is:

incisors	canines	premolars	molars
$0=0=0$	0	$0=2=3=4$	$1=2=3$
$1=2=3$	1	$0=2=3=4$	$1=2=3$

This means that, as in all our ruminants, the front upper incisors are missing and the lower six incisors meet a hard upper palate when they nip browse or grass. Each side of the mouth has one lower canine, upper and lower sets of three premolars and three molars. The first premolar and the upper canine are absent.

Deer are generally aged by their teeth, but there are several ways to do this. The first, recorded by Robinette and co-workers in 1957, involves a molar tooth ratio. The ratio is the sum of the buccal widths of one mandibular tooth row divided by the sum of the lingual heights of the same row. The rear crown of the last molar is included in these measurements, so there are seven values to be added in each sum.

Another method, often used by biologists in the field, is to simply compare the teeth of the deer with teeth on a jaw board—a collection of jaws from deer of known ages with representative tooth wear. Biologists who look at a lot of teeth get a feel for aging. Jaw boards are just a check.

Lengths of rows of cheek teeth, both mandibular and maxillary, increase with age up to two years. That's because the teeth are growing bigger at the crown, pushing to back and front and extending the length of the row. Deciduous teeth are being replaced by bigger permanent teeth. After 2½ years, though, tooth wear reduces crown size and cheek rows may shrink in length.

The problem with any aging technique that uses tooth dimensions as a gauge is that teeth wear differently from one deer to another. Abrasive forage can accelerate tooth wear. The teeth of blacktail bucks have been found to wear more rapidly, in some areas, than those of blacktail does.

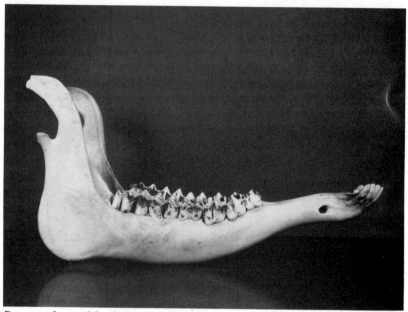

Deer can be aged by their cemetum annuli—deposits between molar roots. Adult deer have 32 teeth, with no upper incisors.

In 1977 Robinette and his associates developed a regression equation for aging by molar tooth ratios. Of the 109 deer of known age used in that project only 55 percent would have been aged correctly using the equation! So, while tooth wear is useful in aging mule deer it is not a definitive method.

The best way to age deer by their teeth is examination of cementum annuali—deposits between molar roots that can be counted on a sectioned tooth under a microscope. More accurate than any tooth-wear method, this technique takes a considerable amount of time and can't easily be done in the field. It's a subjective thing, too, not as simple as counting tree rings and best done by people with experience on known-age deer.

Deer have both deciduous and permanent teeth. Shortly after birth, deciduous incisors and canines appear. They're fully erupted at the age of 10 days. By the third month of life the fawn has a lower set of deciduous premolars. Three months later the upper set is complete. At this time the first permanent molar appears, followed by a second at the age of one year. There are no deciduous molars. During its first hunting season the deer will have one or two of its permanent incisors. By the following spring all incisors and canines will be permanent. Permanent premolars and the last molar erupt at 2½ years.

Without a sensitive nose, good eyes and alert ears a deer wouldn't live long. That nose is useful even in open country where distances are long and danger rarely threatens close. Thermal and prevailing winds keep the deer apprised of hunters and other predators well in advance so an easy retreat is possible. That is why hunters in open country don't see the bucks that are there—they don't realize just how good a deer's nose is and how much the deer relies upon it.

Mule deer ears probably looked funny to American pioneers. But if they laughed, it wasn't for long. Those ears are among the best of any big game animal, and deer use them constantly, funneling them front, back and to the side individually to monitor all sounds. Because mule deer and blacktails are pretty quiet themselves, it isn't easy to sneak up on them; they know that almost every noise is a foreign noise. A mule deer's big ears may be its most underrated defense.

People are still arguing whether deer are color-blind. The deer aren't telling. It doesn't much matter though, because a mule deer's eyes are among the best for spotting movement and odd objects. Numerous and well-developed rod cells help it see in the dark, too—long after the details are lost in your binoculars or rifle scope. Few animals have such a complete defense system as a mule deer, its nose, ears and eyes keen and constantly on alert!

Body temperature in mule deer varies from 96 to 104 degrees Fahrenheit, close to ours. But humans succumb more easily to a drop in body temperature. While few people would survive if they cooled to below 77 degrees, lethal temperatures for deer are closer to 65. One buck rescued from freezing water recovered quickly after his core temperature had slipped to 79.5 degrees.

The heart of a mule deer is about .8 percent of body weight—twice as big, relatively, as one of ours. Heart weights vary with metabolic rates, the minimums coming in January for bucks, April for does.

Heart rates of mule deer were first obtained by Aldo Leopold in 1951. Pulse in summer fawns ranged from 189 to 250 beats per minute, in winter fawns 109 to 250 and in yearling deer 105 to 121. Because these were wild animals, captured for the data, heart rates were no doubt elevated. The latest telemetry has allowed heart rates to be monitored without stressing the deer, by use of a transmitter implanted at the base of the animal's neck. Resting pulse in adult deer is as low as 50 beats per minute.

Lungs in mule deer equal about 1.7 percent of body weight and vary, as does the heart, by season. When deer are fat and heavy in early autumn lungs are too. In January when bucks are leanest (in March for pregnant does) lungs shrink. In fact, except for eye, brain and spleen, all major organs vary in size with the condition of the animal.

At two percent of body weight, the liver is a deer's heaviest organ. Buck livers are quite a bit bigger than those from does. As versatile as it is essential, the liver synthesizes protein and hemoglobin, detoxifies foreign substances, metabolizes fat and produces vitamins. Deer liver can regenerate itself too, repairing damaged tissue to 30 percent of its total weight.

A deer's brain and spleen scale about the same: just under .3 percent of body weight. But the spleen, while it filters and stores blood, is not necessary for life. Kidneys, as a pair, weigh a few ounces more than the spleen and are larger in bucks than in does. Mainly they filter the blood and store fluid waste until it can be shunted.

The biggest part of a deer's body cavity is filled with digestive organs. A ruminant stomach comprises four chambers: from front to back the rumen, reticulum, omasum and abomasum. The abomasum is small but closest in function to the human stomach. In fawns, milk goes directly to the abomasum for digestion, by-passing through an esophageal groove the undeveloped rumen and reticulum. As a young deer eats more roughage its rumen grows and becomes by far the largest stomach section. Still, it is small compared to the rumens of domestic livestock. The gastrointestinal tract of a black-tailed deer has a capacity of just over eight quarts. The gut from a domestic sheep of the same weight has nearly twice that volume.

Stomach tissue comprises just over one percent of body weight in mule deer, with contents about 10 percent. The alimentary canal has a total length of nearly 80 feet; rumen-reticulum volume averages 6½ quarts.

There are four endocrine glands secreting hormones inside a mule deer and controlling life functions. The pituitary at the base of the brain has a glandular lobe and a neural lobe and secretes 12 hormones, including those needed for reproduction. Adrenal glands lie next to the kidneys and control the body's water and electrolyte balance as well as the "fight or flight" hormone epinephrine. The two-lobed thyroid, near the larynx, has a gelatin colloid to store secretions like thyroxine. Thyroxine helps maintain body temperature, metabolize protein and regulate fat use. Close to the heart, the thymus gland also has two lobes. Its function is mainly to control the lymphatic and immune systems. All endocrine glands vary seasonally in size and all comprise a very small part of the mule deer's body weight. The thymus is often so obscure that it cannot be found.

Outside, deer have four major glands: the preorbital, interdigital, tarsal and metatarsal. Each secretes a different pheromone; each pheromone has a unique smell and purpose. All external glands are thought to function as communication devices, identifying individual deer. The preorbital gland in front of the eye is used to mark trees and bushes. Interdigital glands in the split of the hooves mark trails.

Besides emitting their own scent, tarsal glands inside the hocks are used as pads to catch urine. Fawns urinate on their tarsals and rub them together when frightened; big bucks do the same to show aggression. The metatarsals on the outside of the lower hind legs secrete an alarm scent in blacktails—though in white-tailed deer the metatarsals are not used this way. The metatarsal glands in black-tailed and mule deer are distinctly longer than in whitetails.

The skin that keeps deer organs together and protects the inside of the animal from the outside is elastic and tough, but not very thick.

Deer depend mostly on hair to insulate them from heat and cold. There are six types of deer hair and most deer go through two molts each year.

Natal hair is fine and short, replaced by juvenile hair beginning in late summer. By October this molt is complete. At 85 days the fawn's white spots are gone and at 95 its coat is decidedly gray. Adult deer have four types of hair, including large guard, intermediate guard, mane and wooly.

Most deer retain their summer coats for five months and winter coats for seven. Molts occur from April to June and from August to October. All follicles shed hair in autumn, but during spring only the guard hairs are shed; the wooly winter undercoat gradually breaks up. Molting progresses from the ears down the head, then back to the neck, shoulders, loins and flanks. Next the rump, abdomen and legs get new pelage. The tail sheds all summer. Barren does molt earlier than pregnant does, and deer in poor health molt slowly.

Northern deer like the Sitka blacktail have longer, stouter

Albinism is rare in deer. This partial albino buck was otherwise normal.

guard hairs than southern deer. These coarse, hollow hairs are their primary insulation in winter, and are so effective that snow accumulates on their backs without melting.

The color of deer hair varies quite a bit. Each winter hair has four color zones from tip to base: black, yellow, gray or russet and unpigmented. Natal hairs and summer adult hairs have only three color zones. The appearance of a deer depends as much on the amount of wooly underhair as it does on the color of the outer guard hair. Regional variations in color occur and sun bleaching can alter pigments. Generally, winter coats appear dark brown to gray while summer coats are more red and certainly much shorter. There are some differences in coat color and markings between species as well. But whether the dark chestnut of the blacktail or the pale dun of the desert muley would prevail in foreign habitats is speculation.

The tail of a mule deer is short, rounded in appearance, with white hair on the front two thirds and black hair on the tip. In contrast the tail of a black-tailed deer appears slightly flattened—though not nearly so much as the flag of a whitetail—and the top side has black hair down its entire length. The underside is white except for the black tip, just like a mule deer. White-tailed deer have much longer hair on their tails than black-tailed or mule deer, and no black tip. The top side is the color of the deer's back, the underside white. Whitetails erect their tails when bounding away from danger, probably as a warning device.

Where the Food Goes

To know deer is first to know what they like to eat and how they eat it, when they eat and what happens if they don't. The next step is to understand the relationship of habitat type and condition to herd productivity.

Compared to domestic ruminants deer are small, fragile creatures. While they can digest forage high in cellulose like other ruminants, they can't handle the rough material a Holstein could grind up and put to work. Deer were designed to feast when the forage is tender and high in protein, and simply maintain themselves during the rest of the year. This schedule works pretty well in most places. But occasionally, maintenance gets hard and the deer die.

During the warm summer months when forage is plentiful and green, deer are selective feeders. They're able to eat far more than they need, even to store fat, and they can afford to choose plants they like. Almost always these plants are nutritious as well as palatable. Range people call them ice cream plants.

A deer's pointed face allows it to get into tight places to pick at tender forbs, grass shoots and twigs. Unlike a Holstein, the deer is not a grazer concerned with mowing wide swaths of grass. If it were it might have a wide mouth and nose like the cow. Instead, deer look for specific plants and parts of plants. Depending on the habitat, that can include a lot of hard-to-reach browse and small forbs. Pointed noses work better.

When a deer finds something it wants, it grabs the plant with its mouth. Lacking upper incisors a deer has to crush the stem or leaf against a hard upper palate with its lower incisors. The severing action is sufficient, but not clean—which is why you can tell the difference between a plant used by a deer and one nipped surgically by a rabbit.

When a deer bites—or, more properly, tears—off a piece of forage its tongue pushes the material back against the premolars and molars lining the cheeks. All rear teeth have ridges of hard enamel alternating with soft dentine. These irregular and abrasive surfaces grind the forage to bits as the deer chews with a swinging lateral movement of its jaw. At the same time saliva from under the tongue, in the cheeks and behind the teeth coat the forage, breaking it down chemically and forming a mucus-coated bolus. Easily swallowed, the bolus carries with it salts from the saliva that help maintain the acid of the rumen at levels supporting microorganisms necessary for digestion.

Deer eat quickly. Chewing takes only three to 10 seconds, and as one bite is swallowed the deer is reaching for another. This allows the deer to gather forage in a short time, filling its rumen for regurgitation later in a safe spot. Deer are vulnerable when feeding, and the less time they spend at it the safer they are.

Often hunters think only young deer or does are about, or they wonder, after spotting a big buck, how it could have survived in a heavily-shot area. Part of the reason is that mule deer don't have to spend much time away from secure bedding cover. Young bucks and does are less cautious and more likely to wander in search of forage even if they could survive without moving. The mature bucks, if they suspect danger at all, stay hidden for all but a few twilight minutes each day. And they grow fat doing it!

Plant parts with lots of sugar or fat can be digested by just about any mammal. We eat apples and peanuts and our bodies make good use of them. But the leaves and stems of most plants are high in cellulose, something our monogastric stomachs can't handle. It doesn't hurt us, but we can't digest it so it doesn't do us any good. Deer, like other herbivores, have special bacteria and protozoa in their gut. These break down cellulose by fermentation, rendering it useful.

Carnivores have small stomachs and short gastrointestinal tracts; an herbivore's gut is much larger. The intestine of a dog, for example, is only about six times its body length. But a deer's intestine is 15 times its body length. This extra tubing, and the bigger stomach, help absorb nutrients that are hard to extract from a high-cellulose diet.

Not all plant-eaters are ruminants like the mule deer. A horse has an intestine almost as long as a deer's, but its single stomach has no mechanism for digesting fiber and comprises only about 10 percent of the volume of the entire gut. To make use of hay and other roughage a horse's cecum and large intestine have been modified to promote fermentation. Together they are 60 percent of gastrointestinal volume, and they wring from the forage the vitamins and proteins released in the rumens of deer. Still, the ruminant is a more efficient animal, and because a horse's nutrient synthesis is limited it must have a diet higher in protein and vitamins.

A deer's thick-walled rumen comprises 60 percent of the gut volume and when full can be 75 percent of its weight. The inner lining is covered with papillae about one-half inch long and as wide as a match. Their function is to increase surface area so more nutrients can be absorbed. Rumen bacteria, at least 13 kinds of them, number from 11 to 12 billion per milliliter of fluid in a mature deer! These bacteria increase as the quality of forage declines in late fall and winter because their main function is to digest the cellulose in roughage. Succulent spring plants don't require the number or diversity of rumen microbes for digestion.

Rumen protozoa vary from 160,000 per milliliter in winter to 730,000 in summer. They increase as forage improves because, while they help digest cellulose, they also work on plant sugars and proteins. These are highest in young, succulent plants. The proteins in protozoa that pass from the rumen are digestible and useful to the deer.

The rumen environment is a messy one. But there's a delicate balance in place, one that enables the deer to make the most of forage other animals can't use. Rumen contents are about 85 percent fluid. This stuff is warm (102 degrees Fahrenheit) and acidic (pH 6 to 6.5). Changes in rumen environment can cause the microorganisms to die. And then the deer may die.

When a deer swallows a bolus it is added to this vat of fermenting soup. At 75 percent capacity rumen material begins to spill over into the smaller, thin-walled reticulum. Big, solid pieces of forage are regurgitated from here to be chewed again. Cud chewing further breaks down plant tissue chemically and physically so it can be more easily digested the next time down.

The omasum is a rigid pouch with folds up to four inches long and two wide. These run almost the length of the pouch and are covered with papillae. Many of the soluble nutrients passed from the reticulum are absorbed here. Solid particles continue on, to the true stomach or abomasum. Here, as in the stomachs of monogastrics, highly acidic juices work on the material. Then it is shunted to the small intestine.

Roughly 49 feet long and one-half inch wide, a deer's small intestine comprises about 25 percent of gut volume. Still, it is only half the length of a domestic sheep's! Pancreatic secretions, basic in pH, convert plant and microbial proteins into peptides and amino acids. They also change starches to glucose. Bile from the liver helps absorption of long-chain fatty acids and fat-soluble vitamins. What is digested in the small intestine is taken into the lymph capillaries of villi in the intestine walls. Most nutrients needed for a deer's metabolism are absorbed in its small intestine.

Behind the small intestine the muscular cecum (about eight inches long and 1½ inches wide) absorbs volatile fatty acids. From the cecum, material is passed into the large intestine, a tube roughly 16 feet long and one inch wide. Full, it may be 10 percent of total gut volume. The large intestine is where water is absorbed from food residue, and feces are formed as pellets.

The first milk from a lactating doe is colostrum, rich in ash, fats, proteins and antibodies. With the esophageal groove piping milk directly to the abomasum, fawns use colostrum efficiently, and feeding intervals can be long. That helps the fawn stay hidden. While its rumen develops quickly and the fawn starts foraging after two weeks, it relies heavily on its mother for five weeks. If abandoned during that time it will likely die. After five weeks, when the fawn weighs about 22 pounds, the volume of the rumen-reticulum equals that of the omasum-abomasum. Weaning is then possible. Normally, weaning is gradual and is completed at four months.

What a deer eats determines not only its health but its activities. Deer with good forage don't spend much time eating. Deer that have to scratch for a living are out foraging, visible and vulnerable much of the time. Mortality in deer herds is more closely associated with food supply than with any other factor. Deer don't have to starve to have been victims of poor range conditions. Deer in good health are never eating poor forage.

Unlike people, deer like best what is most nutritious. They eat what they need, what will improve their condition. Taste is linked to requirements; that's why deer survive. They must not only make good use of summer forage but must store nutrients for the harsh winter. Even in their prime they have little body fat, and in the best range they have limited opportunity to build their reserves for the cold season. Pregnancy and nursing drain those reserves in does; the rut and hunting season sap energy in bucks. All deer must stay alert, run frantically on occasion to escape predators and man, weather storms, paw through snow for forage, negotiate migration routes and metabolize fat to keep warm. No matter what they eat, deer have plenty of demands on their energy!

Most dietary problems in deer herds have to do with too little energy. Herd losses to starvation are easy to trace; more obscure are deaths to fetuses and fawn losses during lactation. Well-nourished does in one study lost five percent of their fawns after birth. Does underfed during the last term of their pregnancy lost 33 percent. Does malnourished during the length of their term lost 90 percent. Some of these deaths were stillborn fawns, others came after live births, the young deer being too weak to recover.

Energy requirements of lactating does are greater than for any other sustained activity and any other deer—2.3 times the demands for normal body maintenance. The fawn drains the extra energy as it sucks. Mule deer milk contains about 25 percent total solids, including 1.4 percent ash (calcium and phosphorus), 5.4 percent lactose (milk sugar) and 10.9 percent fat. Energy values average 227.4 kcals per ounce! But the high metabolism of fawns demands a rich diet. A constant one, too.

One study showed that while most mature does recovered quickly from a 30 percent loss of body weight due to poor diet, one-third of the fawns housed under similar conditions died.

The energy in forage is only partly accessible to the deer. Digestibility of plant material varies by species, season and plant part. Digestibility also determines how much the deer will benefit from eating. The cell contents of living plant tissue (sugars, starches, fructose, organic acids, lipids and nitrogen) are about 98 percent digestible. But the lignin, hemicellulose and cellulose in cell walls are very hard to digest, even for ruminants. Mature woody plants can be over 60 percent fibrous cell-wall material and are less digestible than young plants. Mushrooms are more digestible than grasses, buds more so than stems.

Digested plant cellulose is useful as an energy source, but not nearly as useful as starches and other carbohydrates. Acetic acid comprises as much as 70 percent of the volatile fatty acids produced by fermenting cellulose. Starch fermentation produces comparatively more propionic and butyric acids. Acetic acid has a heat of combustion only 59 percent that of propionic acid and 42 percent that of butyric acid. That means it's only worth half as much to the deer.

Another factor that determines forage value is the microbial content of the rumen, not only numbers but kinds. Bacteria "bloom" following a feeding, and the kind most prevalent at any time are those best adapted for digesting the forage in the rumen. That forage can stay there for days. If high-carbohydrate forage like acorns and young alfalfa dominate the diet, rumen microbes

Even in their prime, mule deer have little body fat. Come winter, the deer have plenty of demands on their energy.

specific to these forages will multiply. A change to dry range plants high in cellulose means that for a while the new forage won't be used as efficiently as it could be.

Deer normally don't deposit fat until late summer, no doubt because winter's deficit must be overcome before the body can rebuild itself. The kind of fat in the diet has little to do with what is deposited on muscles and around organs. Fat on deer is highly saturated, mostly with stearic and palmitic acids. Other fatty acids are synthesized in the rumen from plant lipids and carbohydrates. Digestible fat in forage is useful to deer because it contains twice the caloric value of carbohydrates. Forage fat content can range from one percent in dry high-country grasses to 19 percent in lowland shrubs like juniper.

Plant protein varies by season and species. Deer need roughly 16 percent protein in their forage during pregnancy, lactation and periods of fast growth, but can maintain themselves on a diet with only 10 percent protein. Protein quality is important, but not so much as protein quantity. Monogastric creatures like us absorb proteins as peptides and amino acids. We can't manufacture protein, only convert it, and protein of low quality will not benefit us as much as high-quality protein. But ruminants like deer use the nitrogen in plant protein to synthesize amino acids and microbial proteins to be digested later in the abomasum and small intestine. The quality of these proteins, and their value to deer, is pretty constant.

Mineral deficiencies in mule deer are rare. Most western range provides enough minerals for maintenance and growth. But mineral balances are as important as levels, and sometimes there are problems. For example: A .40 percent calcium requirement is easily met, but phosphorus levels are low in many mule deer ranges. That pushes calcium levels to more than five times that of phosphorus, creating an imbalance. Recommended phosphorus levels for maintenance are .25 percent, with .54 the ideal for best antler growth. For either mineral to benefit deer they must be available in proper proportions: between 1:1 and 2:1, calcium to phosphorus.

Calcium is the bone mineral and helps maintain healthy teeth. But it also has to do with muscle control, blood clotting and the body pH. Phosphorus is important for skeletal growth too, and for the transport of nutrients in the deer's body. It's a main constituent of red blood cells.

Most deer get enough sodium and potassium, the potassium

from forage, the sodium from natural licks and livestock blocks. While sodium is low in typical deer forage, potassium levels are generally well above the .5 percent needed.

Iron, sometimes deficient in grasses, is vital to oxygen transport in deer and a primary constituent of blood. Because deer eat a variety of plants iron problems are rare. Iodine, necessary for thyroid function, is most in demand during the warm months when forage is best. Deficiencies in deer are not common but could be remedied by the use of iodized salt blocks.

Magnesium levels of .15 percent are easy to find in most western forage. Chlorine, sulfur and nearly all trace elements occur in levels appropriate for deer in most plants they eat. Copper and molybdenum, like calcium and phosphorus, must be in proper balance and usually are. Toxic conditions can result from high or low levels of either element.

Deer apparently have no problem getting the right kinds and amounts of vitamins. As ruminants they have no need for vitamin C, and they get plenty of carotene (vitamin A) and vitamins D and E from green forage. Thiamine, riboflavin, nicotinamide, biotin, folic acid, pantothenic acid and vitamins K, B6 and B12 are all synthesized in the rumen.

The only other thing a deer needs from its diet is water. That's an important item, and one that has a lot to do with deer activity. Lubricant, solvent, cleanser, thermostat, transport medium, buffer—all these are what water is. A deer's cells are 50 percent water and most of what it eats is water. Mushrooms are 95 percent water, fruits, berries and succulent twigs 80 percent, mature leaves and twigs 50 percent. Dried grasses are low in water.

What a deer eats determines how dependent it will be on free water. Dry diets in fall make free water more important than in spring. Captive deer fed dry pellets drank nearly three times the weight of those pellets, while on a diet of fresh browse they drank only one-half the weight of the browse. Fawns need lots of water, as do pregnant and lactating does.

The Bone On The Top Of The Head

Deer antlers are, oddly enough, the part of the deer most prized by deer hunters. They aren't edible; they aren't permanent. They have nothing to do with the prowess of the hunter. They vary in size and shape between populations and individuals. Their conformation is affected by diet, genetics and injuries. Antlers are simply sharp bones on a deer's head.

Antler growth begins in male deer at age three months. Four to six years later the buck has his biggest antlers. This superb typical mule deer was shot in Teton County, Wyoming.

Still, we measure them to the one-eighth inch, photograph them, mount them, rank them, write books about them, all but enshrine them.

It's appropriate to describe them. Only male black-tailed and mule deer have antlers. Occasionally hormone imbalances in a doe will result in antlers. These imbalances may affect fertility but not necessarily. I watched an antlered doe raise healthy twin fawns during a summer in Oregon's Ochoco Mountains.

Antler growth in male deer begins at about three months with the formation of pedicels on the frontal plate of the skull. Pedicel growth may be initiated by testosterone, though some biologists doubt the activity of this hormone at such a young age. Photoperiod influences but does not completely control antler cycles. Sitka blacktails produced four sets of antlers a year when photoperiods were manipulated by experimenters to complete a seasonal cycle every three months.

As the pedicels enlarge they expand outward and upward. The first year they are the longest they'll ever be, but small in diameter. In subsequent years they are shorter but larger in cross-section, showing rings similar to a tree. These rings are not reliable indicators of time. Special cells called osteoblasts on top of the growing pedicel deposit cartilage as blood from the supraorbital artery feeds them. The arterioles grow upward from the head through the pedicel, alongside the budding antler. Then they corkscrew into it. The antler is thus fed from the outside, with arterioles branching to form a fine network of capillaries. Venules carry the blood back to the surface.

As the antler develops the osteoblasts secrete bone-like osteoid tissue that becomes mineralized and forms hard bone where once there was only cartilage. While little data is available on the composition of mule deer antlers, elk antler bone is a tricalcium phosphate with a calcium-phosphorous ratio of 1.667 to 1.

A mule deer buck will show only "buttons" his first fall. These are visible, palpable bumps on the head, and quite hard. They don't grow or change during the winter. His second summer the buck's pedicel will again become active, this time completing the antler it threatened to start the year before.

The antler grows fast, starting in March. As it rises from the pedicel it's covered by fuzzy skin called velvet. In the velvet, arteries supply nutrients to the hardening antler. Sensitive nerves are there too, and summering bucks avoid touching things with their antlers.

By the end of August the velvet starts to split and peel from the now-hardened antler core. As the velvet wrinkles it exposes the antler, which may show blood stains from the remains of ruptured vessels. Once the splitting begins the velvet dries quickly from inside and out. It is then easily stripped when the buck rubs his antlers on trees. By the end of September most bucks have polished their antlers. This rubbing is not a rutting activity and is probably not in response to an itch, because the velvet and the antler itself are, by fall, dead to feeling. Rubbing is apparently just something bucks do. Perhaps it is a first show of aggressiveness for the rut later on; maybe the dangling velvet prompts it.

Bucks in velvet are reclusive, living alone or in small bachelor groups. Pre-rut activity breaks up these groups.

Antlered does and bucks with injuries affecting hormone balance may not lose their velvet or their antlers. While nobody has yet named the hormones responsible for all phases of antler development, testosterone levels correlate strongly with antler growth and shedding in mature bucks. Testosterone must not only be available but secreted in the right amounts and at the right times for normal antlers to grow, harden and drop.

Fresh antler bone is firmly attached to the skull through the dormant pedicel—so firmly, that under severe stress to the antler, the skull is as apt to crack as the antler is to separate at the pedicel! Usually, though, a fight or a fall or some other sudden impact will cause an antler to break before the skull is injured.

Hard, fresh antlers are about 45 percent water and still quite elastic. They're elastic enough that once in a while two sparring bucks will collide at just the right angle to spring their tines into a deadlock. It happens rarely but is usually fatal to both deer. Locked antlers can be hard to separate even by determined biologists working with the skull plates.

Antlers are a sign of masculinity and are used by bucks to prove and show dominance during the rut. Fights are seldom serious, because subordinate deer find out that they're subordinate soon enough. Besides, breeding bucks would rather chase does than rivals. Still, antlers can be used to kill.

Coyote know that as well as deer, and hunters who have rushed up to stunned bucks have sometimes been badly injured when the deer got up. Not that does are helpless; their lashing hooves are quicker and just as dangerous as a buck's antlers.

By mid-winter each pedicel's surface begins to prepare for its next antler, and a line of dehiscence forms. This can occur as early as November, but most black-tailed and mule deer carry their antlers through December. As the separation becomes more pronounced the buck may strike at his antlers with his rear hooves, knocking them off. If he does this too soon the pedicel will bleed. Usually it won't bleed much. A buck that has just shed his antlers will avoid contact with other deer; those I've observed acted as though the newly-exposed pedicels were very tender.

Some bucks allow their antlers to drop naturally, and this happens most often in January. On western winter ranges at this time many deer have only one antler. Several years ago I was out photographing—actually skidding down a snow-covered mountain trying to keep my balance—when I jumped a small group of mule deer bucks. They bounced through the opening in front of me and as one big deer hit the ground at the end of a leap an antler fell off. I retrieved it. There was the tiniest spot of blood in the middle of the base.

That antler was very loose, no surprise in late January. But any sudden strain on antlers that have begun to loosen can knock them off long before they're ready to fall. Late-season hunters have occasionally shot deer that have tumbled down a hill and lost their antlers before they came to rest.

Black-tailed and mule deer antlers are dichotomous or bifurcated, meaning the normal adult deer has antlers that branch from each tine that emerges. There is really no main antler beam as with white-tailed deer or elk, where several subordinate points rise from a common, heavier piece of bone. The typical black-tailed or mule deer buck has four points or tines on each side. There may be brow tines on mule deer, but these are rarely as developed as the brow tines on whitetails. Columbian blacktail bucks usually lack

To manage deer well biologists must know not only herd size, but sex and age ratios. Managing for bucks like this means restricting the harvest of young bucks.

brow tines, but Sitka blacktails have long ones. In a Colorado study brow tines occurred on six percent of yearling mule deer bucks, 43 percent of 2½-year-old bucks and 77 percent of bucks 40 months and older.

Antler size is determined by diet, genetics and age. Healthy deer grow big antlers, but nutrients necessary for survival can hardly be shunted to bone on top of the head. Deer from different gene pools show different antler characteristics, not only with respect to size, but shape and color as well. In fact, some biologists contend that size is a function of nutrition, while shape and conformation is genetic. Habitat, through natural selection and genetics, may also influence antler growth.

Although big antlers are usually carried by older bucks, it's difficult to tell a deer's age by the antlers. Normally, a yearling mule deer will have forked antlers, but some will have three points on a side, a few four. During its second year a buck should have four points, though many have just three. The third and succeeding years a typical four-point antler will get bigger, longer and fatter without developing more tines.

Spike antlers are more common than they should be and usually indicate poor nutrition. After a stressful summer on the Kaibab Plateau in Arizona, 52 percent of yearling bucks were spikes. Normally in that area only 12 percent of yearlings had spike antlers. Small antlers can result from individual problems too—like sharing milk with siblings those first crucial weeks or being orphaned.

A mule deer buck can live a long time in captivity—up to 15 years or more. But usually he dies or is killed before age 10 in the wild. Hunted populations of bucks have relatively few deer older than age five, and some heavily-shot herds comprise almost 80 percent yearlings. Big antlers then, even in areas of abundant, nutritious forage and impeccable genetics, are often hard to find. Only mature deer grow big antlers, and if the mortality of bucks age three and younger equals production there won't be many big antlers available.

Antlers reach a peak size and weight about the same time the buck reaches his physical plateau. If in succeeding years the deer loses vitality or cannot eat as well as he once did, his antlers will change. Sometimes they'll just become smaller. Often, though, they'll retain their mass—or even get thicker—while points get shorter or are deleted. Among the finest deer I've seen was a buck with four points on one side and only two on the other. But his antlers were exceedingly heavy and nearly three feet wide. The normal four-point buck next to him looked small indeed.

Some deer get more short points as they age beyond five or six years. Non-typical antlers result. Some are thick and gnarled, without any standard form. Others add points in a more or less logical way, branching like they're supposed to, only more often. A buck I shot several years ago looks normal enough until you count points. With seven on one side and eight on the other, he has lots of non-typical bone. But the tines are well-proportioned, the branches where you expect them to be and the original four points clearly evident.

Some hunters today look at deer with numbers in mind, sizing each animal up like they might read a sticker on the window of a new car. While scores are useful and provide the easiest way to compare one deer with another, antlers are interesting even if they don't score well. Looking at antlers should be done in a reasonable way. If you get excited it should be for the character of the antler, not the score. They are, after all, only bones on top of a deer's head.

4

Behavior: What Deer Do

There's a difference between what deer do and what we see deer doing. What we see is an activity; what they do is a function. For example, you might observe a buck running behind a doe. That's all you can say for sure, unless you watch him do other things and unless you know something about deer behavior and can use reason to form hypotheses. That buck may be in the mood for mating, but you can't say that just by watching him walk or run behind a doe. And maybe there's no chase involved at all; it could be the doe is just moving along the easiest path and the buck wants to use that same path.

We like to conclude things on the basis of what we see. And that makes for false information. When a little buck precedes a big buck on the trail does that mean the big buck is using the little one as a scout? Maybe. Maybe not. We're pretty good at picking up the fundamental habits of deer. We can say that when a deer opens its mouth and grabs a shoot of ceanothus it intends to eat the ceanothus. Normally deer don't mouth things they don't intend to eat. But even here we're assuming that deer don't play with plants like a dog will play with a ball. It's an assumption borne out by lots of qualified people observing lots of deer.

Examining the rumen contents of deer might show an overwhelming percentage of ceanothus from animals shot in a certain area. You might conclude that deer like ceanothus and that, the next time you saw a deer in a patch of ceanothus, it was there because it wanted to eat ceanothus. Well, you might be right. In most places deer will select ceanothus. But deer like other plants too, and they go places for reasons other than to eat. Maybe the deer you saw had been bedded in a clump of whitebark pine well above the ceanothus and had been spooked downhill by a hunter. Knowing that doesn't prove that deer like to eat whitebark pine, but neither does it mean they prefer ceanothus.

Many things written about deer are untrue or only partly true because *observations* have been mixed up with *conclusions*. Repeating observations will strengthen the case for a conclusion, but doesn't necessarily justify one. You might find, for example, that deer on a desert winter range appear to eat a lot of sagebrush. Over the course of several years you watch deer eating sagebrush, and you even open the rumens of shot deer to check your observations. Sagebrush, you conclude, is an important deer forage on this winter range. You're right. But you cannot say that sagebrush is important deer forage in every location because sagebrush doesn't exist everywhere. Nor can you say that sagebrush is a favorite deer forage or even a good one. If sagebrush is the only food available deer will eat it whether they like it or not.

Besides, there are many kinds of sagebrush.

It's foolish to conclude too quickly that what we are seeing is what the deer are doing. And it's even more presumptuous to ascribe motive to their actions.

Understanding deer behavior and being able to predict what deer will do can certainly help you hunt deer more successfully. Studying deer, therefore, is one of the most worthwhile things you can do. But observations must be recognized for what they are. Conclusions must, like fine wine, be reserved for special occasions.

One problem with getting at the truth in wild animal behavior is that to observe behavior you must be close to the animal. Usually, that means it will know you're around. By interpreting your presence as a threat, the animal's behavior may change. We must acknowledge this possibility. Wild animals in sanctuaries can become so accustomed to people that they seem to pay them no attention at all. But any observations made of these animals must be qualified; we can't assume that humans are ignored.

Some animals get accustomed to people rather quickly. Range cattle have little contact with man but come winter are easily rounded up and confined. Cougar, on the other hand, don't like to

This researcher is ear-tagging a Columbian black-tailed deer. The results of his work should be published. Reading condenses for you the experiences of many people, and makes you a more knowledgeable hunter.

be around man and are hard to approach even in sanctuaries. Deer are somewhere between these extremes, and mule deer drop their defenses more readily than whitetail. Both adapt well to living near people, but there's a difference between adapting and accepting. Valid observations of natural behavior are possible only when the deer acts as if no one was around.

What this means is that you should evaluate carefully my observations and research on deer behavior. Some of what I've seen in the field I've seen often enough that I'd plan a hunt assuming deer would repeat those same actions. Occasionally I'd be wrong; but most of the time I'd be right. Still, there are a few things I can predict with that much confidence.

Part of the excitement of studying or hunting deer has to do with the wildness of the animal. If you always knew what deer were going to do there'd be little to wonder about. Predictability precedes boredom.

To try to figure out everything about deer is a monstrous job with little chance for success. You'd probably succumb to making conclusions from observations and in the process, destroy your own incentive to study deer further. There must be other reasons to reject so preposterous an undertaking, but these are enough.

One basic reason to read about deer is to broaden your base of experience. Taking the observations of others whenever you can, sifting them and filing those that appear reasonable are helpful. Most of what you read in this book you'll want to check with other references and with what you experience afield. None of us can rely solely on our own observations. We don't spend enough time with deer. Even veteran biologists constantly review literature to compare their findings with those of others and to strengthen their background.

To learn anything is first to approach the subject with a critical but open mind.

Behavior That Works

Deer do what helps them survive. Sometimes they make mistakes, but often what we think are mistakes are just actions that most of the time would be helpful but this time are not. A deer running toward the sound of a shot might seem stupid. But perhaps the echo of the shot confused it, or the bullet smacked loudly and closer on the opposite side. Besides, a deer doesn't understand distant concussion; what is near and physical is far more alarming. If deer weren't right most of the time they would not survive.

Doing the right thing can be as simple as selecting a forb with high protein over a grass stem with low protein, or as sophisticated as deliberately crossing or overprinting the tracks of other deer to confuse a trailing predator. Deer probably don't think in terms of right and wrong; they just do what other deer have done successfully. Beneficial traits are passed on genetically or taught to the young. Deleterious traits are eliminated by natural selection.

Eating is one of the most important things deer do. They do it selectively, bite by bite, from ground level to about five feet up. Rarely will they stand on their hind legs to reach forage. When they do they are either desperate for forage or reaching for something they prefer very much. Their diet varies by season and location. While mule deer are commonly called browsers, meaning they eat a lot of twigs, the fact is they readily adapt to other forage.

In some places browse comprises the biggest part of deer diets; in other places grass does. Farmland deer eat a considerable amount of grain and alfalfa.

In spring, grasses are lush, easily digested and high in protein. They're taken more readily than in late summer when they're brown and tough and not nearly as nutritious. Deer eat small forbs when they're available, mostly in summer. Browse is a year-round staple but a second choice if tender grasses and forbs are available. When deep snow covers the ground, browse becomes more important. Dry grasses that weren't touched in autumn become more desirable.

Deer forage preferences are hard to rank, even within one area. Watching a deer eat is easy; determining what it eats is not. Finding a pattern in its selection of forage is very hard to do. While they're normally very selective, deer may sometimes just eat to fill. Mountain goats do this, nibbling more selectively after they've eaten enough to satisfy their needs. If a deer crops a gentian after chewing a Saskatoon berry and reaching for a dogwood shoot, did it select the gentian or eat it because it was easy to get? Is it a preferred plant or simply acceptable?

The palatability and nutritive value of all forage changes with each season, and the ranking of forage preferences must too. Some plants are almost never eaten. Others are all-time favorites. But many are standard deer forage, differing in appeal relative to one another as seasons change.

Like children, deer eat the best of what's available at the time, but they can't gorge. Deer don't store food like squirrels or pikas. Neither can they convert it to huge fat reserves like a bear. A deer has to eat well and often. What it eats is dictated by its habitat.

In northern habitats, natural silage is an important deer food. Silage results when frost-killed forbs drop to the ground and are attacked by fungi. They rot and ferment, becoming like corn silage in a silo. False hellebore and cow parsnip, toxic when green, make a favorite silage. There is no silage in southern mule deer range. Where it does occur its importance depends on the weather. Early snows may cover the forage before the deer have a chance to use it. By Thanksgiving deer may chew on Douglas-fir rather than eating fermented false hellebore. This doesn't mean they prefer the Douglas-fir over all other plants. It simply means that based on what is available deer selected Douglas-fir.

Deer will travel long distances in the open to get to good forage. Generally they travel at night. Expansive wheat fields in the West have deer tracks in their centers as well as along their borders. At times, nutritious food is a higher priority than safety.

But stressed deer won't travel far if they'll lose more in energy or body condition than they might gain from the forage. Mule deer, like whitetails, will winter in large groups, generally on south faces of ridges where wind and sun clear the snow off the forage. When forage is scarce and snow deep, energy conservation is critical. Winter fat reserves in mulies routinely dip below five percent. Energy spent foraging must be used efficiently to survive.

To get at forage beneath snow deer move it with their muzzles and paw it back with their front feet. Each piece of coarse forage is chewed and swallowed separately. When eating tender shoots and grasses, though, deer nibble and chew almost continually. If they take this soft forage in bites they are small ones, roughly 10 to the mouthful before swallowing.

Deer that aren't eating are likely resting. They generally lie on their bellies, legs tucked underneath. Sometimes deer extend their forelegs. This may be a way to radiate heat, keeping the deer cool in warm weather. Now and then a deer stretches its neck out, resting its head on the ground and closing its eyes. Asleep in this position, it is still alert.

Deer ruminate most when they rest, and it's easy to see a bolus moving up and down in a deer's throat.

Like dogs, deer scratch themselves with their hind legs. Bucks will rub growing antlers against the insides of their haunches. When they get up deer often stretch, again like a dog. Sometimes you can tell a buck's bed by the urine stain in the middle of it. But usually deer urinate and defecate before and after bedding, so absence of a stain in the hollow simply means you can't tell the sex of the bedded deer.

Neither can you tell the sex of a mule deer by watching it void. Urinating mule deer of both sexes act like the females of other deer, assuming a low crouch. Often the buck will move his tail up and down, but not all the time. Only when mule deer rub-urinates do they behave differently than other deer.

Rub-urination is voiding from a squat; but here the animal brings its rear legs forward and pinches them together underneath the stream of urine. Bucks move their legs farther to the front than does. As the urine trickles down the legs it reaches the tarsal glands inside the hocks. The deer then rubs its hocks together by rocking from side to side. Afterward does and fawns may lick the urine off. Bucks do not.

Bucks rub-urinate primarily during the rut, and dominant bucks do it frequently—even when little urine is voided. Subordinate bucks urinate in female fashion when a dominant buck is near. When a dominant buck stops rub-urinating the rut is, for him, over. Does seldom rub-urinate during rut but do it quite often in winter.

Tarsal glands apparently figure heavily in the recognition of deer by other deer. During the rut does and small bucks sniff the hocks of larger bucks, perhaps because dominance can be determined by the scent of the tarsals. Black-tailed deer rub-urinate and sniff tarsals more than mule deer. At night deer nose each others' tarsals five times as much as in the daytime.

When feeding or bedding, mule deer rarely face each other. Combined with submissive behavior like tucking tails and crouching, this may be a courtesy. It's a good way to survive, too. When every deer faces a different direction it's hard for a predator to approach. Generally the dominant deer of a group orients its body and looks the way it wants to; the rest arrange themselves accordingly. Eye contact is rare among adults.

As survivors, mule deer have three main jobs: eating, resting and avoiding danger. Danger means predators, including man, and deer avoid danger by several means. The first is to stay out of areas where there are predators. This may seem too obvious to mention, but many hunters repeatedly scour areas with such heavy pressure that the deer move elsewhere. This isn't to say a deer can't or won't hide in a pocket in the middle of a pressured area. But what it wants is peace and safety.

Another way deer avoid danger is to stay where there's thick cover or rough terrain, where predators have a hard time moving or at least chasing. Sometimes the best defense is a place in the open where approaching danger is easily spotted. Depending on the season, terrain and type of predator they want to avoid, deer restrict their movements to areas that give them the best chance of detection and escape.

Timing is another thing deer use to their advantage. In hunted areas they move almost exclusively after dark, foiling hunters. And when danger is close they time their burst from cover so the predator is not only surprised but has a poor chance for a shot.

Knowing when to break cover and when to stay motionless is vital if a deer is to survive. Old bucks cultivate the ability to stay still when hunters are near. The more often this ploy is successful, the more often it will be used.

Deer break cover in a variety of ways. An experienced buck, jumped by a hunter he has watched approach, usually rockets away at a gallop, dodging brush with head held low and antlers back. His movements are strong, purposeful and surprisingly quick. Like a flushed grouse, he artfully puts rocks, brush and trees behind him in his escape. This makes chase difficult and shots impossible.

Young bucks and does especially, but older bucks on occasion, will move from danger in a stotting gait—that peculiar bound that puts all four feet on the ground at the same time. Columbia blacktails as well as all mule deer do this, but it's a rare thing for Sitka blacktails. Stotting is not only an easy way to negotiate broken, semi-open terrain, but it makes an audible thumping noise that warns other deer nearby. It also allows the deer to see well from the top of each bound and to change directions instantly. The up-and-down movement helps the deer clear blow-downs and other obstructions while making it an elusive target for predators. Though it doesn't appear as fast as the frantic gallop of a buck in heavy cover, stotting may be faster in some terrain. It's used most often when a deer is surprised but has room to move.

Deer sneak away more often than many hunters think. Sneaking requires less energy than a rush and a deer doesn't always have to leave cover. After the danger is past the animal can carry on comfortably without checking out a new environment or worrying that its escape has attracted the attention of another predator. Big bucks sneak more than little bucks and does, and blacktails sneak and hide to avoid danger more than mule deer.

Grouping can be a form of protection because animals in large groups are less likely to become a victim than if each had to evade a predator alone. Groups have more eyes, ears and noses, and it's very hard to approach an alert group of deer. Finally, groups confuse predators. The short time it takes to single out a target—or change targets in a moving, mixing herd—may be just the time the deer need to escape.

Like whitetails, black-tailed and mule deer are good swimmers. Mulies seldom swim to escape, no doubt because there's almost always a better way. But blacktails in the river bottoms of the Pacific Northwest swim even in normal travel. They're accustomed to heavy rain, flooding and living where water can inundate bedding and foraging areas. General blacktail habitat is similar to the cedar swamps of northern whitetail country.

Like whitetails, mule deer normally live in small places. A home range of one square mile is typical, though migrating deer cover several miles between seasonal ranges. It's pretty easy to find spots within a home range that deer like to visit. But mule deer are not as predictable in their patterns as whitetails, and the country they live in is much bigger. Though a predator checks likely spots when looking for deer, there's only a fair chance the deer will be in any one spot at a given time. Because a muley's home range has weakly-defined boundaries the deer will readily leave if it discovers a predator. Maybe it will change drainages. It could move far or stay close. The predator doesn't know, and that helps the deer survive.

Sometimes deer will face the danger rather than run from it. This is most likely when does are protecting fawns or when a buck feels cornered. In heavy cover blacktail bucks will occasionally turn on pursuing dogs, and hunters approaching wounded deer have been gored or kicked.

Mule deer are less excitable than whitetails, and more inclined to investigate danger than bolt immediately. They're noisier in movement, more vocal and smellier. Alarmed mule deer often erect tarsal hairs and emit from the metatarsal glands an alarm scent. In running from danger they do not use trails as much as whitetails. While a black-tailed or mule deer typically stops for at least one look at what disturbed it, mature bucks rarely skyline themselves for a shot. That habit, often fatal, is absent in most populations. The backward glance, if it does come, will likely be from behind a rock or tree.

Reproduction

To survive is to eat, rest and avoid danger. But to survive as a species mule deer must procreate. Fawning time for Rocky Mountain mulies is late spring, with most does giving birth the first part of June. In the desert, deer fawn later, perhaps so the young won't have to endure the normal spring drought and can take advantage of August rains that increase available forage, sustaining adequate milk production in the does. Sitka and Columbia blacktail fawns drop in May. Their first months are the driest of the year, but vegetation is still lush in the Pacific Northwest and those warm summer days make for easy living and fast growth before the cold rains of fall.

The gestation period of black-tailed and mule deer averages 103 days but may vary up to 30 days. Fawns weigh about seven pounds at birth. Blacktails average a few ounces less than mule deer, and individual birth weights for both species range from 4½

Fawns, camouflaged with spots and for a time almost odorless, lie low to avoid danger. Their dams leave them alone except at feeding time so as not to attract attention.

to 10 pounds. Twin fawns are standard for a healthy mature doe; triplets occur less than five percent of the time. Deer less than a year old will breed, but the number of pregnant fawns varies significantly between herds and from year to year. Usually less than half the female fawns will bear young, with most being singles. Pregnancy rates in yearling does (two years at parturition) are much greater, approaching that of adults. But many yearlings have single fawns. Data on healthy does three to nine years old show little difference in productivity between ages. There's not enough data on does older than nine to draw conclusions for them.

Deer are hiders by nature, secretive most of the time and timid. Fawns show this hiding trait more than adults; the young deer are most vulnerable to predators. Hiding starts even before birth, as the doe seeks cover far from other deer. Fawning areas are usually thick with concealing brush and offer more than one escape route.

A fawn is born with a faint body scent, cryptic coloration and an instinct to lie still. These things make it hard for predators to find. The doe helps by licking the placenta free and eating it immediately. She also eats the fawn's urine and feces for a time; the fawn obliges by voiding only when she is nearby.

Because the young deer needs a lot of energy right away it guzzles itself full of rich milk at each feeding. Feeding intervals are widely spaced, though, and the doe keeps away from her fawn between nursings lest she attract predators. This behavior causes many fawns to be picked up by ignorant people each summer. Thinking they have found an orphan, they truck the fawn to their nearest game agency office and expect everything to turn out fine. Almost without exception the fawn dies or is mercifully shot.

While a fawn is able to stand during its first day, it will not move about freely for six to eight weeks. During this time the doe must eat very well to keep up her strength and provide milk for her young. She does this by becoming territorial, defending not so much the area around her fawn as her favorite foraging places. Having been alone for several weeks, she'll chase off even familiar deer. This trait is more pronounced in blacktails than in mule deer, possibly because mule deer in their open environments aren't as crowded by other deer.

After the fawn is strong enough to follow her, the doe will join other does with young. In most places this happens in late summer. Migration to summer range in mountain habitat is thus later for does than for mature bucks. Fawning occurs at low to middle elevations, and the does usually move high in August. Banded does stay together throughout the fall and winter, separating about a month before fawning the following spring.

Fawns don't take life as seriously as adult deer and play more often. This not only exercises the body but helps the fawn find out about other deer and how to act as a deer. Adults will play with the fawns occasionally, frequently when forage is good.

In the group, which often includes yearlings from the same dams, there's the chance of deer getting mixed up and trying to get together with the wrong partner. It doesn't happen very often in small groups or large ones loosely associated and widely spread. Scent or vision may tell the fawn which is its mother. In one experiment a fawn was imprinted with the scent of a pronghorn and thereafter stayed closer to resident pronghorns than to its own kind. Different facial markings may help mule deer fawns distinguish between their group and a group of whitetails in the same area. Does and their fawns routinely groom each other; this may also help establish family bonds.

Fawns wander during the rut, the males more than the females.

Fawns can stand their first day but move about freely only after six or eight weeks. For this reason does and their young move to summer range later than bucks.

Both can be sexually active, but fawns are responsible for a small part of the production in black-tailed and mule deer herds.

Much of the adult deer's social behavior has to do with reproduction. Identifying other deer, marking territories, sparring, chasing and courtship during rut are all factors that contribute to the population. There isn't much idle chatter among deer, no empty party talk and little wasted activity. Except for eating, drinking, resting and escaping a deer's activities are linked to reproducing its own kind. Species survival is the result.

One could say that behavior basic to survival is geared to reproduction, because if deer don't survive they don't breed. That's stretching the point, but it's true. Surely the conflict between deer, their social interaction, establishes an order of dominance and determines which deer have the advantage during the rut. A gene pool fed by natural selection ensures fawn crops that can cope with their environment.

After a fawn's second summer its association with the group has changed. The doe has new offspring and while concerned with birth and nursing she does not allow her one-year-old fawn near. So the fawn has become independent, foraging for itself and consolidating its place in the social structure of the group.

Deer Dominance

Deer don't fight very often, but dominance is an issue even in groups of does and fawns. In fact, fights among adult does are more common than fights among bucks. Fights don't last long; a typical confrontation goes something like this:

The opponents circle each other, body hairs erect and tails up. Tail hair and that around the tarsal glands is usually flared. Sometimes the deer snort at each other. If one is dominant it will likely keep its head high, and the hair on its body will be relaxed. Its movements, compared to those of the other deer, will seem assured, purposeful, not as stiff. A fight is unlikely if one deer is decidedly dominant. Often just a glance from the dominant animal and a dropping of the ears will send the other deer packing.

This posturing is a sort of bluff, a way to assert without getting violent. If neither deer backs down, a more threatening show occurs. The head stays up and the chin points toward the opponent. Preorbital glands and eyes are wide open. The deer lowers its rear slightly, almost crouching. If it attacks it rises on its hind legs and uses sharp front hooves to rake or jab the other deer. A little of this treatment goes a long a way, and the subordinate deer almost always turns and runs. Serious injuries are rare. The hooves, though, can be dangerous; a deer's legs are very strong and quick.

I've helped subdue healthy mule deer—it's all two strong men can do to restrain a 150-pound doe! I know that's hard to believe, and I care not if you think me weak at six feet four inches and 185 pounds. The strength in a deer's frail-looking legs is amazing!

Unlike moose, mule deer don't kick with their hind legs. They don't bite either; blacktails rarely do. Vestigial canines occur in quite a few white-tailed deer. They use these to grasp branches in rut rituals and occasionally when fighting.

Fights among female and juvenile deer are usually preceded by some posturing. But a quick face-off with heads up, haunches down and poised to rear may be the only visible sign something is amiss. This no-nonsense approach conserves calories and allows the deer to spend time and energy constructively. No doubt the rarity and brevity of fights among deer also contributes to their well-being.

Deer that win fights often stamp the ground a couple of times and snort repeatedly.

At 1½ years old, young buck mule deer have their first set of hardened antlers. These are usually thin forks, big enough to engage other yearling deer but hardly what's needed to establish herd dominance. Young bucks will spar, meshing antlers and shoving each other around, but little comes of it. Even among adults, sparring seldom has anything to do with fighting or determining dominance in mule deer or whitetails.

Dominance, or the social status of a buck relative to other bucks, figures in almost all buck behavior. There's no way to predict before maturity how bucks will rank in dominance. As with people, a complex mix of physical and psychological factors determines how a deer will react to others and to itself. Deer determine dominance by pitting themselves against others in a dominance display. If this fails to establish an order, fighting may occur.

A dominance display begins when one mature buck approaches another in the prerut of autumn. If the approaching buck is unfamiliar with the other deer he will stare at it intently from a distance, then, as it comes nearer, avert his eyes. Direct looks up close are a sign of submission.

The approaching buck walks stiffly as he comes, head low, neck extended, ears back and out. Body hair is erect, back arched. His tail, held out, flips up and down with each step. Periodically,

A dominance display begins when one mature buck approaches another in the prerut of autumn. If the approaching buck is unfamiliar with the other deer he will stare at it intently.

the approaching buck will lick his nose.

At 30 yards or less the approaching buck will change from a direct path to a tangent. Still the eyes are averted. If the other deer acknowledges the first as dominant he will be standing still at this point, splay-footed, with back caved and tail tucked. When the dominant buck begins walking at a tangent the subordinate may circle downwind or approach the dominant from behind, sniffing at his tarsal glands. All the while he'll be looking directly at the advancing deer.

Close to the subordinate the dominant buck may snort, inhaling in a pig-like way, then exhaling through appressed nostrils for a long terminal hiss. This rut-snort is different from the blowing of deer on alarm or incidental snorting when foraging. When rut-snorting a buck first lowers his head to inhale, and points his nose upward. On the exhale he stiffens his legs, arches his back and seems to strain. His flanks compress and his tail quivers. Blacktails rut-snort like mule deer, only louder. They also add grunts at the end.

A subordinate buck generally runs off when a dominant buck rut-snorts. If not, he'll watch the dominant closely, always in a submissive posture. If the dominant stops to horn brush—an aggressive action—the subordinate will horn brush too, until the other deer stops.

Sometimes dominance is not so quickly acknowledged, and both bucks display aggressively. Finally one will rut-snort. This often causes the other buck to bolt. If he doesn't run the displays continue, each deer crouching lower and lower in the event of combat. Usually during these displays one deer will tilt its antlers toward the other or glance at the other more frequently. These are signs of submission, and both bucks soon know who is dominant and who is subordinate. The dominant buck will then escort his opponent out of the area, as far as a mile. A dominant buck will not tolerate subordinate rivals in his breeding area when does are in estrus.

The defeated buck, abandoned and alone, often starts horning brush. He's timid about it at first but soon gets enthusiastic. Afraid to challenge the dominant deer, he takes out his wrath on the willows, no doubt imagining the damage he's doing to the dominant's hide!

While antlers are effective and at times deadly fighting tools, they're seldom used that way. Fighting is counterproductive, not only wasting energy but risking injury. Dominance is usually acknowledged and accepted in confrontations long before antlers are brought to bear. Horning is harmless and bucks of all ages do it. It is to mule deer what bugling is to elk. Thrashing young trees and brush vents frustration and demonstrates masculinity. It's an audible thing, and horning bucks stop every so often to listen for the activity or approach of other bucks. They'll also investigate horning sounds—much as whitetails do the clashing of antlers. Horning is prerut behavior.

Sparring is another use of antlers among mature bucks. It happens like this:

Sparring partners are obviously mismatched in dominance. The only even matches are among juvenile deer. Body size probably has more to do with dominance than antler size, and most of the time it's easy to tell which of a sparring pair of bucks is dominant:

he's bigger. In sparring matches there are no winners or losers, so a small buck is at no disadvantage. In fact, the subordinate deer initiates and terminates the match!

However, sparring is solicited by the dominant buck. After recognizing the subordinate deer and displaying his dominance he acts as if the subordinate were not there at all. If the subordinate moves off, though, the dominant will follow, appearing nonchalant but keeping close. At length the subordinate will approach from the rear, cautiously, sniffing at the dominant's tail and hocks. These antics may be repeated over a long period—perhaps a couple of days—in bucks of nearly equal size, but can take only a few minutes if one deer is very much the superior.

During preliminaries the dominant buck takes care not to scare the subordinate, sometimes behaving in a weak or appeasing manner. He might crouch when foraging close to the subordinate, or slowly move in short semicircles to block his path. Finally, with his body at right angles to the subordinate he turns his head and antlers directly to the deer. He won't eat then but may lift his head expectantly, waiting for the subordinate deer to respond. The dominant may challenge this way several times before his partner responds. Accepting the challenge, a subordinate mule deer buck almost always engages antlers with the dominant buck.

Whitetail behavior is different: the subordinate first displays appeasement and may even lick the dominant's face.

If the dominant mule deer is considerably bigger than his sparring partner he often uses just one antler in the tussle, engaging both smaller antlers of the subordinate. Bucks more equal in size use both antlers.

The first movements in a sparring match are cautious ones and the deer are likely to disengage within a few seconds. The subordinate usually jumps back, then both deer raise their heads and avert their eyes. After a few seconds the subordinate buck steps forward, the dominant offers his antlers and the subordinate reengages.

There isn't much forward shoving in a sparring match; mostly it's a lot of neck twisting. The deer circle around their meshed antlers, getting more vigorous with each bout. The bouts last longer as the bucks become more used to each other. Eventually the dominant will initiate a bout. Still, during pauses, the dominant will rub-urinate while the subordinate urinates like a female in deference. Sparring matches end when the subordinate refuses to continue. He may start foraging or move away, ignoring the dominant. The dominant follows, eyes averted. If he fails to get a response, the bucks likely will forage and rest together, perhaps to spar later. They may stay together a couple of days.

Sparring matches can last for more than an hour, and during that time a bond is formed between dominant and subordinate. Afterward, the dominant will support the subordinate buck in conflicts with other bucks. Indeed, the subordinate may, in view of the dominant, display dominance to other bucks bigger than himself, provided they are smaller than the dominant buck. This is parasitic social behavior, rare in mammals. Even during the rut, dominant bucks are less aggressive with their sparring partners than with other deer of the same size.

Old bucks spar less frequently than young ones.

Fighting for dominance differs markedly from sparring in that fighting occurs almost always between mature, evenly-matched bucks. Even at the peak of the rut, fights are rare and usually very short. But injuries occur and hostility apparently remains after the fight. Unlike sparring, which forms bonds, fighting reinforces differences in social status between bucks. Fighting also attracts and sometimes engages other bucks. The dominant buck may interfere to end a fight.

Before a fight the opponents crouch low, their hind legs spread and crooked. They display aggression and dominance, each alert to an attack by the other. The attack comes quickly, from the crouch position and at a distance of about six feet. With antlers tilted forward, the aggressor lunges quickly toward the other. On impact one or both may be thrown to the ground. The antlers clash loudly on contact and as the bucks twist their heads, pushing and pulling to throw the opponent off balance, their breathing comes in audible grunts. Movements are quick and powerful, and if a tine slips past the protection of antler bone it can easily puncture the body. One five year old mule deer buck had its skin torn in 47 places, presumably from fights.

Because their skin is easily punctured mule deer thrust and parry as swordsmen when they fight. There's nothing to be gained by trying to jab a vital spot if in the process one's own vitals are exposed. The low crouch preceding a charge braces both deer for the impact, and the rearward angling of the legs prevents one buck from easily pulling the other off balance. Still, in observed combat one blacktail buck tossed his opponent over his back; another was stood on his head by a larger, stronger deer!

The Rut

All this posturing, bluffing, horning, sparring and fighting have as their motive the prerequisites of the rut. Courtship is the culmination of prerut behavior. With mule deer, courtship is necessary because bucks do not advertise or collect harems like elk. A mule deer buck stays with a single doe until she's bred, then moves to another. This is serial polygyny. Bull elk don't have to worry about courting because the cows in their harem are always available. Once a bull has established himself as herdsmaster he need only confirm that status once in a while and keep reasonable control of his cows. A mule deer buck must tend to individual females; they'll not follow him.

To ensure the best genetic possibilities for her offspring a doe must be bred by a dominant buck. To be sure a dominant buck notices her when she's receptive she must advertise her estrus, attracting many bucks. The dominant buck then chases off the others and stays with the doe until he has bred her.

Mule deer does in estrus travel a great deal more than at other times. Their estrus is conspicuous too. Because a buck cannot afford to spend time with a doe that isn't going to be receptive soon, his main purpose of courtship is to find out if a doe is or will immediately be in estrus. The buck checks a doe by stimulating her to urinate. Then he licks the urine and he knows.

Bucks prompt urination with either a coax or a rush. Coaxing begins when a buck approaches a doe from the rear and bleats softly like a fawn. His head is low as he comes, his tongue flicking in and out. After he bleats he makes a weak buzzing sound and when he reaches the doe pushes his nose at her, licks her, bobs his head and finally averts his eyes. Most does accept this behavior quietly, foraging in the presence of the buck but keeping close watch on him. She may circle him as he continues to buzz, flick his tongue and occasionally reach out to lick her.

After some time the doe will urinate—perhaps not much, as she will likely be courted by several bucks and cannot urinate for all of them if she does not conserve. The buck may wait during urination or come forward to lick the urine from the doe. After he gets it on his tongue, from the ground or from the doe, he raises his head, draws his upper lip back and opens his mouth. Saliva drips as he waves his head from side to side. This lip-curling behavior is thought to expose urine to the Jacobsen's organ in the buck's palate, telling him whether or not the doe is ready. After lip-curling the buck relaxes, licking his nose repeatedly.

Bucks court does in two ways: in a coaxing manner like this, or with a rush. The purpose is to get the doe to urinate so the buck can check her readiness.

Rush courtship is a more direct approach. Here a buck tenses in the presence of the female, looking intently at her as his lips twitch. He may bleat. Suddenly he leaps forward with a loud cough, charging at the doe with head lowered. With each lunge he roars. As the doe runs at high speed to escape, the buck follows. In a short while, the buck stops and assumes the low-stretch posture he might use in the coax. The doe then stops as well, poised and alert. Directly she urinates, then hops off a few steps. The buck approaches, samples the urine and lip-curls.

Blacktail courtships are like those of mule deer. White-tailed deer use only a rush courtship. Whitetails are less vocal, and the rush posture is a more exaggerated crouch—often a buck's belly will almost touch the ground.

Unlike harem-gathering elk, mule deer bucks try to make themselves obscure when they've found a female in estrus. Tending a doe is staying with her, hiding with her, shadowing her—but not scaring her away. He may circle her to head her off if she strays, perhaps cough and pounce to show his displeasure. Rarely will he use his antlers to herd her.

A tending buck will chase subordinate bucks that come close and may even leave a doe nearing estrus to run another buck off another doe. Subordinate bucks risk injury by persisting, but they do persist. In a group of does a dominant buck can effectively guard only one from advances by bucks on the fringe.

Often does make it easier on everybody by clustering around a large buck, but this is not a harem. The does save energy by not having to wander far to attract a dominant deer, and the buck conserves his by not having to tend one doe at the expense of others with concurrent estrus. The losers are the little bucks that, in a loose grouping, would have a chance to breed. But even they are better off in the final sift, because clustered does give them little opportunity for mating and save them the trouble and risk of chasing near a dominant male.

Interaction between large bucks during rut is apparently random. Bucks, without a doe to tend, roam great distances looking for one. As they travel they may meet other bucks and engage in dominance fights. Frequently they horn brush; once in a while they bleat or grunt. Blacktail bucks in chaparral have been noted to stop at the tops of hills, scanning the country below, presumably for does. Mule deer don't do this. A buck's response to the activities of other bucks is unpredictable. Sometimes he moves quickly toward the disturbance; sometimes he ignores it.

Dominant bucks tending does guard them jealously. But occasionally a group of bucks will form near a tended doe. What can follow is confusing, but unique to mule deer. One of the spectator bucks suddenly blows an alarm and bounds directly toward the pair. His tail is up, rump patch flared. He blows at every bound. The doe bolts and all the bucks dash after her, the intruder first. Sometimes the dominant tending buck is close behind; if he's tired he trails in the rear of the group. Eventually the doe circles back to him. Then big bucks chase little bucks in order of dominance as the original pair gets back together. If individual spectator bucks advance toward the tending dominant he wards them off. Soon all is quiet.

Roving mule deer and blacktail bucks will spend time checking those areas most likely to have does. While they do not make scrapes like whitetail bucks, it might be said that they run circuits.

They visit the same areas but do not necessarily breed the same does.

Three days before a doe reaches estrus the tending buck apparently knows what's coming. He stays closer to her and as estrus nears, approaches her repeatedly in the same way he coaxed urination. The doe's tail is angled away from her body and her vulva is swollen and pink. As soon as she permits the buck to lick her vulva breeding is imminent. Next the buck may rest his chin on her croup, then perhaps mount her. She breaks the contact each time, only to jump ahead a few feet. When she does the buck stands stiffly, averting his eyes. His next approach is low, swift. Each precopulatory mount can be as long as 15 seconds, and either the buck or doe can break contact. As they separate, the doe bounds forward then circles the buck. While the number of precopulatory mounts varies, there are usually more than five. One mule deer buck was seen to make 43.

Finally, copulation occurs. The buck covers the doe in a sudden upward bound, his hind feet leaving the ground. At the same time he arches his back and throws his head up and back. The doe jumps forward, contracts her belly upward, straining hard with head and tail extended. Sometimes blood drips from her vulva. Contractions may continue for an hour after copulation.

Immediately after copulation the doe often urinates. The buck will sometimes just lie down. If other bucks are nearby it may behave aggressively. The breeding partners will stay close to each other for about three hours; then another copulation occurs. In about a day and a half of active estrus a doe is normally bred four to six times.

Occasionally a buck will fail to mount a receptive doe because he's tired or for some other reason. Then the doe may court the buck, circling him repeatedly, bolting suddenly, trying to excite him. She may brush a foreleg against his side or lay her head on his croup. Rarely will she mount. Does not bred during estrus will cycle again and again, each period lasting three to four weeks. In a Colorado study about 70 percent of wild deer were bred in the first estrus during a period of 20 days.

Near the end of the breeding season bucks become less aggressive. They've eaten during rut, but not enough to balance the energy lost in fighting, chasing, roving, tending and mating. They carry battle scars, some of them serious. From the hocks down their legs are streaked from urination. When a buck stops rub-urinating and starts squatting like a doe the rut is over for him.

5

Ammunition For Hunting Deer

One autumn afternoon in 1954 Colorado rancher Steve Herndon drove into the nearby hills to pick up some friends who were hunting deer. Before he got to the rendezvous, Steve spied a big buck coming out of a patch of oakbrush. He shot it dead with his .30-30 Win. A non-typical mule deer, that buck had the biggest antlers ever recorded in Colorado. Scoring more than 306 points, they're still the biggest.

Cartridges That Work
    The best cartridge for shooting mule deer is probably the one you have in the chamber when you see the deer you want to shoot. Most deer are shot close, where cartridge choice is academic. Most of the time it's not what you shoot but how well you shoot. By all odds you'll hunt the rest of your life without seeing a deer that scores 306, but if you do see one that big it's as likely to be within talking distance as the next forkhorn you come across. It will be just as easy to kill if you shoot well.
    The .30-30 Win. cartridge has probably killed more deer than any other. Someday, that will not be true. Much better cartridges are available and hunters are using them. The reason is that most hunters want to be efficient killers; they want to seize every advantage they can, every prerogative. Therefore, a cartridge that extends their effective range is one that enables them to take shots

they would have to decline with a lesser cartridge.

In most areas seasons are short and competition is heavy. If you've chambered a superior cartridge you'll have more chances to shoot and can pass on some shots, with the reasonable expectation that there'll be another opportunity for a bigger deer later. Selective hunting like this, however, is hard if your cartridge limits you to short shots.

When you see a deer that you want to shoot, it's best to have a bullet that can kill farther out than you can accurately shoot. In other words, you want a cartridge that does not limit you. There are plenty that fit your needs.

It's no disgrace to use a cartridge with more potential than you have for long-range hits. Consider the potential of a .30-30 Win. bullet to hit a buck bounding through brush 100 yards away. That you misplace your shot most or all of the time is no fault of the cartridge. The situation is simply beyond you. You aren't up to the job. But neither is anyone else.

Quite a few hunters enjoy shooting obsolete black-powder cartridges or using rifles of some sentimental value. There are lots of bowhunters in the woods too. The challenge of short-range or primitive instruments is a worthy one, but hardly at odds with the choice of a deadly centerfire cartridge. Challenge defines the sport; without challenge there is no sport.

You will find as you shoot more deer that shooting deer becomes less an imperative in hunting deer. You can still enjoy fine rifles, accurate and effective cartridges and the prerogative of the shot even when you don't take it. You can always handicap yourself to fulfill personal obligations to your sport. How, is up to you; you need no help with that.

Choosing a cartridge is amoral, something you do after you've decided how you will hunt. Here is where to start:

Consider game regulations first. In Montana you can use almost anything you want to use. In other states there's a caliber requirement—commonly .243 Win. or larger. Regulations shouldn't affect your choice of cartridge, because the best deer cartridges are legal everywhere centerfire cartridges can be used. But it's a must to know your state's rules about this.

Some people think that there is a variety of deer cartridges because deer hunting is done in different places and each cartridge was designed to fill pretty narrow requirements. That's true, but only for a few cartridges. The best cartridges are successful just about everywhere you can hunt deer, and you don't have to own several rifles chambered for different cartridges to be well equipped.

The cartridges best suited to hunting black-tailed and mule deer are those with a bore diameter of .243 Win. (6mm Rem.) to .308 Win. Surely the more powerful .22 centerfires will kill deer, and some of them—the Swift and the .22-250 Rem.—do it handily. Winchester's forgotten .358 is a fine deer cartridge, as is the wildcat .338-06. But the .22s have lighter bullets than you need for penetration on deer angling away and for shooting long distances in the wind. Bores bigger than .30 caliber, meanwhile, have heavy bullets, but to make them shoot flat requires lots of powder in big cases—cases bigger than the .30-06 and .308 Win. The result is a heavy recoil and more bullet than you need.

In brush, say some, you need heavy bullets and you don't need chalk-line trajectory. They claim that big bullets clip twigs like pruning shears, while little bullets whine away. They make a case for specialized deer cartridges, recommending some for the thickets and some for open country.

They are drawing lines where none exist.

Your job as a deer hunter is to direct a bullet through the vitals of the deer. To do that you'll fire one shot, one that you're sure will do what you intend it to. If, when you hunt in the woods, you see deer you'd shoot at with a .358 but not with a .308 Win. you're making shots where none exist. If the 150-grain bullet in the .308 Win. is unlikely to reach the deer, there's enough chance the 250-grain .358 bullet won't either.

There is no such thing as a brush bullet. All bullets fly best when they miss brush. Expecting the bullet to clear its own path is expecting too much, no matter what its diameter. A big part of your job as a rifleman is choosing a path to the target and directing the bullet along that path.

There are differences in the way bullets act when they hit brush. But the ones that pay least attention to obstructions, the ones that fly straightest after contact, might not be the ones you suppose. Weight seems an obvious factor: the heavier the bullet the less it will be deflected. That's true only if velocity, bullet diameter and rifling twist help out. Tests show that a short, fat bullet, one with low sectional density is more apt to be deflected than a longer, slimmer bullet of the same weight. But tests also show that velocity is more important than sectional density and bullet shape in determining bullet stability in brush. Bullets driven at a modest velocity—2,400 to 2,600 feet per second (fps)—work best. Oddly

The .308 Win. (7.62 NATO) is one of our most efficient deer cartridges. More powerful than it looks, it trails the .30-06 by only 100 feet per second. And it is accurate.

enough, big, slow bullets often deflect as badly as smaller, fast ones.

Rifling twist must be right for the bullet. Long heavy bullets require sharp twist; if the bullets are too long and heavy for the twist they are easily upset in flight.

If you were to figure on clipping your way to a deer at each shot there would be a compromise to make: the 2,500 fps speeds, which are best in the brush, would be less than you'd want from your bullet in open country. If you owned a .308 Win. you'd want to use 200-grain bullets for the thick shooting, and perhaps 150-grain loads where the trees didn't grow. But the .308 Win. with the 150- or a 165-grain bullet works superlatively in both places. A change in bullet weight is unnecessary if you agree that bullets should pass between twigs, not through them.

My deer cartridges are chosen with open country in mind. They work well in timber too; but the logic won't reverse. It's best that

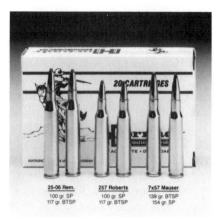

Here are three good light cartridges for deer, each with two good deer loads. More power and heavier bullets are seldom necessary.

25-06 Rem.   257 Roberts   7x57 Mauser
100 gr. SP   100 gr. SP   139 gr. BTSP
117 gr. BTSP   117 gr. BTSP   154 gr. SP

you choose your cartridges this way, with the long shot a priority. Short ones are easier. It doesn't matter that most deer are shot at short ranges. A lot are missed at long distances. You want the cartridge that will work for all the shots you might have, not just most of them.

My favorite deer cartridge is the .270 Win. It could just as easily be the .280 Rem. or the .30-06. I've shot more deer with the .270 Win. than with any other cartridge, and the .270 Win. rifles I've owned have shot very well. I'm comfortable with the .270 Win. If I had reason to change I'd change to the .280 Rem. or .30-06. It would be nice to finger something exotic, something nobody else uses. But there just isn't much you can do to improve on these three cartridges. Each, in a good rifle, is capable of hitting small targets and killing deer farther than you are. Each is pleasant to shoot, easy to load for and accurate in most rifles.

All the popular mule deer cartridges are good cartridges: the .243 Win., 6mm Rem., .240 Wthby Mag., .250 Sav., .257 Roberts, .25-06 Rem., .257 Wthby Mag., 6.5 x 55, 6.5 Rem., .264 Win., .270 Wthby Mag., 7mm-08 Rem., 7 x 57 Mauser, .284 Win., 7 x 61 S&H Mag., 7mm Rem. Mag., 7mm Wthby Mag., .308 Win., .300 H&H Mag., .308 Norma Mag., .300 Win. Mag., .300 Wthby Mag. Some are more popular than others, and I've omitted several excellent wildcats that are as useful as any cartridge here. But nothing listed or unlisted can beat the .270 Wthby Mag., .280 Rem. or .30-06 for an all-around deer cartridge.

There are several reasons for having so many cartridges. The first is evolution. The .30-06 spawned the .270 Win., the .300 H&H Mag. all short belted magnums. Both parent rounds are still useful, though the lovely .300 H&H Mag. requires a long action and is not as efficient as its offspring with modern powders.

Another reason is pure competition. There isn't enough difference between the 7mm Rem. and 7mm Wthby Mag. to justify having them both, but they're here.

Cartridges also proliferate because gun enthusiasts want them to. One or two rifles may be all you need to hunt all the big game you'll ever hunt, but it's more fun to have lots of rifles, each for a special kind of hunting. There is nothing wrong with this, though a shooter who does a lot of shooting with but one rifle is usually a very accurate shooter.

There are two good reasons why we have so many deer cartridges: One is that deer and elk seasons overlap in some states, and your choice of a pure mule deer rifle may not be the best choice for a combination hunt. The 7mm and .30 magnums work nicely for both animals.

The second reason is that some rifle actions are short and can't accommodate cartridges that may be ideal in all respects but too long to fit these rifles. The .308 Win. is really just a short .30-06, performing nearly as well and feeding through lever rifles and short bolt-actions. The .284 Win., a fat cartridge with a rebated rim, was designed as a short-action .270 Win. or .280 Rem. Short cartridges don't mean much to me because I hunt with bolt rifles and single-shots that readily swallow long cases. Still, some short rounds have proven useful; a lot of them are more efficient than longer cartridges. The .308 Win. is one of the most accurate and efficient. It was the parent case for Winchester's .243 Win. and .358.

If you don't want a .270 Win., .280 Rem. or .30-06 you'll do well with a .25-06 Rem., 7mm-08, 7 x 57 Mauser or .308 Win. These are my second choices. The .25-06 Rem. shoots fast and flat, but not appreciably faster or flatter than the .270 Win. with heavier bullets. The 7mm-08 Rem. and 7 x 57 Mauser lack the case capacity of the .280 Rem., so they drive the same bullets slower. It's about the same situation with the .308 Win. and .30-06, though I have chronographed 180-grain .308 Win. bullets at 2,700 fps from a 24-inch barrel. Those were stiff loads, but equaled factory data for the .30-06.

I've not owned a .284 rifle, but case capacity is about the same as that of the longer .280 Rem. A fat case with little taper gives the

The .30-06 is still one of the best mule deer cartridges. The author's favorite is Remington's 165-grain Core-Lokt.

extra room but also can hamper feeding. Bullets in the .284 must be seated deep in the short actions the case was designed for.

You see little written about the 6.5 x 55 anymore, but when lots of surplus rifles were being made into hunting rifles the little Swedish Mausers in this chambering were popular. The 6.5 x 55 is a good cartridge when handloaded: efficient, accurate and effective on deer. You might think of it as a .270 Win., shrunk just a little. I don't think the .270 Win. needs shrinking.

Ned Roberts' original .257 Roberts was the 7 x 57 Mauser case necked down and given a gentler shoulder. The commercial version retained the steeper 7 x 57 Mauser shoulder, and that's better. I've shot deer with a .257 Roberts and found it adequate. It and the 7 x 57 Mauser should be handloaded. Neither is well suited for long-range shooting at big bucks.

The .250 Sav. lacks a margin of power far away but is a fine cartridge for most shooting. I think the same about the 6mms.

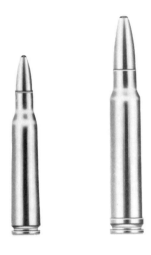

The author has used both the .257 Roberts (left) and the .338 Win. Mag. on deer. The .257 Roberts is adequate, unless you're hunting elk at the same time. Then the .338 Win. Mag. is the better choice.

Though they retain velocity better and are deadly if you have a broadside presentation, their light bullets at ranges of over 300 yards make angling shots risky. Nobody likes to take these shots regardless of rifle, chambering or skill. But if you want to and decline because your cartridge is not up to it or, worse, shoot and cripple, you've failed.

Some people make a big thing out of meat damage. That's not something to make a big thing about. If you shoot a deer where you should you'll not ruin much meat with any bullet. If you choose to shoot one in a bad place because you have no other place to shoot and don't want to decline, you'll have to ruin meat to kill. Bullets at high velocity open more violently than those moving at a slow velocity, given the same construction. The cartridges that drive bullets fast are more destructive. They are also flatter shooting and better mule deer cartridges. If you like, you can handload them to lower velocities with stronger, heavier bullets. You'll castrate them this way, but you'll save meat. The argument against high velocity need have nothing to do with meat.

Nor should it hinge on recoil. If you shoot well you'll shoot well with any cartridge that's a reasonable choice for deer. You don't have to shoot very often. Once a deer should be enough. On the range you can pad your shoulder with shot bags or a folded towel. If you're planning to carry a light, short rifle, recoil may become bothersome, but before it does you'll have another problem. That has to do with barrel length.

High velocity is generated from big cases with relatively small bullets and lots of slow powder. The powder needs time to burn and the bullet needs time to accelerate. Long barrels give them that time. It's foolish to mate a cartridge like the .264 Win. or the .25-06 Rem. to a carbine. If you insist on short barrels, choose a .308 Win. or 7 x 57 Mauser, something with a larger bore in relation to case capacity, that works well with faster powders and will shoot efficiently in short rifles.

The word magnum has no real significance. With centerfire rifle cartridges it has come to mean big cases with a belt in front of the extractor groove. But magnum handgun cartridges have no belt, and there are lots of unbelted rifle cartridges bigger than the belted magnums. You certainly can't define a magnum in terms of energy or velocity, because the .240 Wthby Mag. produces less energy than a .30-06, and the .458 Win. produces less velocity. For that reason magnum doesn't necessarily mean more recoil. In evaluating cartridges it's best just to forget about that word and pay attention to performance charts. You can remember the belt if you like, because it has some significance.

The belt on magnum cases serves to headspace the cartridges; that is, it stops the case from going farther into the chamber than it should. The forward edge of the belt contacts a recess in the chamber and holds the case back against the bolt face. The shoulder on a .30-06 case and the rim on a .30-40 Krag serve the same purpose. Rimless pistol cartridges are headspaced from the case mouth. Excessive headspace means the measurement from the bolt face to datum line—the chamber groove arresting the belt in magnums—is too great. Then the cartridge can stretch or separate on firing, spilling gas into the action. That can burn a ring in your chamber, destroy your stock, ruin your face. A critical thing, headspace.

. Some people think belts on magnums do more—that they act as a reinforcing ring. While they do increase the thickness of brass in front of the extractor groove, belts really don't strengthen the case. The .308 Win. and .270 Win. unbelted, operate at pressures exceeding 52,000 copper units of pressure (cup)—the approximate level of modern belted magnums. The European 6.5 x 68 and 8 x 68 cartridges are roughly the same size as our short magnums, with about the same performance. They lack belts. The strength of a

.240 W.M.   .257 W.M.   .270 W.M.   7mm W.M.   .300 W.M.

Weatherby's lineup of cartridges includes five suitable for deer: the .240 Wthby Mag., .257 Wthby Mag., .270 Wthby Mag., 7mm Wthby Mag. and .300 Wthby Mag.

case is determined inside, primarily by the shape and thickness of the web.

Belted magnums aren't necessary for deer; all but the .240 Wthby Mag. are just too much. Too much noise, recoil, case stretching and powder burned for velocity gained. Few are as inherently accurate as standard rounds like the .30-06. The one thing the bigger magnums give you is versatility; they really do work better on elk than the cartridges we've just reviewed. As with deer, elk can be killed with guns smaller than you likely will carry. But if you want to make the best of every opportunity for a shot, powerful cartridges are a good idea.

The .264 Win. and the 6.5 Rem. have never been popular. Yet, of the modern belted cases these two are the most suitable for deer hunting. The reason for this contradiction is that a lot of hunters who buy magnum guns buy them for something other than deer hunting. While both of these 6.5s shoot fast and flat, they were designed for bullets of 120 to 140 grains. Most hunters like something heavier than that for elk, and they don't see a need for the big, fat, belted case just for deer.

I've never shot the 6.5 Rem. but I've done some range work with the .264 Win.; I've hunted with it and killed deer with it. It's one of those cartridges you think ought to do great things. While burning lots of powder behind small, fast bullets the .264 Win. eats away throats relatively quickly. My .264 Win. is still very accurate. And I've exceeded 3,300 fps with 140-grain bullets. This cartridge works best loaded pretty stiff with slow powders. It is a superlative long-range cartridge in long-barreled rifles.

The successful 7mm Rem. Mag. was designed as a two-purpose round. Weatherby's 7mm Wthby Mag. performs identically. Both are among the best open-country cartridges for deer and elk.

Thirty-caliber magnums date from 1925, when Holland and Holland introduced the Super 30, a derivative of the popular .375 H&H Mag. The Super 30 was a graceful-looking cartridge, long, slender and slick-feeding. It did require a magnum-length action. When Winchester started making short magnums in the late 1950s, reducing body taper and neck length and steepening shoulders to get magnum powder capacity in stubby cases, the Super 30—by this time the .300 H&H Mag.—suddenly looked old.

There are several .30 magnums loaded by factories now. All of them are pretty good cartridges for deer and elk. Most are better for elk hunting than deer hunting; you simply don't need that much power to kill a deer. With bullets of 150 to 165 grains the .30 magnums shoot as flat as a .270 Win. with 130-grain bullets. The biggest, the .300 Wthby Mag. will do that with 180-grain bullets.

The best commercial belted .30 case is, to me, the .308 Norma Mag. The .30-338 is very similar but not the same. Both are of reasonable powder capacity for the bore and work through standard-length actions. The popular .300 Win. Mag. holds more powder, but its neck is quite short. Bullets have to be seated well into the case. This arrangement makes the case seem ill-planned. How much it affects accuracy I don't know. Obviously, powder displaced by the bullet can't be used to drive it, so velocities aren't that much higher than what you can get with a .308 Norma Mag. I've shot several elk and deer with the .300 Win. Mag., and it killed them. I've had poor luck getting tight groups from any of the four commercial rifles I've used.

The handsome .300 Wthby Mag. requires a magnum-length action. A fine all-around big game cartridge, it uses 80-odd grains of slow powder to launch a bullet. The .300 Wthby Mag. is inefficient for deer because it is more than you need.

The Holland cartridge, the one that started .30 magnums, is still a pretty good choice for deer. The case was designed for cordite powder, and its Coke-bottle shape doesn't work too well with modern propellants. If you forget about that, and its length, this is a fine deer cartridge. I've found it more accurate than sharp-shouldered .30 magnums, and more pleasant to shoot. It has a 200 fps edge on the .30-06; 165-grain bullets can be driven over 3,100 fps.

There are several wildcat cartridges around that work well for deer. Necking down the .30-06 to .25 caliber produced what was for years a wildcat cartridge. Remington started loading the .25-06 Rem. in the late 1960s. Though not as efficient as other deer cartridges, it gives fine results to extreme range.

There's something fun about making your own cartridge, and if you choose to hunt with a .260 AAR or a .277 ICL you'll add a new dimension to hunting. Wildcatters generally shoot more than hunters who buy a rifle just for hunting. That extra shooting makes them skilled and able marksmen.

Bullets And Ballistics

More important than the case design or powder capacity of your cartridge is the bullet. The bullet does the work. Whether it mikes .264, .277 or .308 doesn't matter. What does matter is its shape and weight, its concentricity and construction. Bullets must be accurate and must upset reliably in the animal to kill it humanely.

The concentricity and uniformity of bullets is not the problem that it once was. Most makers of hunting bullets manufacture them to close tolerances. That's the main reason hunting rifles are more accurate now than they were a few years ago. You don't have to worry about bullet dependability because rarely will you find one defective. If you want to be fussy you can measure runout with a dial indicator and weigh each bullet to the tenth grain. Unless you have a very accurate rifle, though, with a minimum chamber,

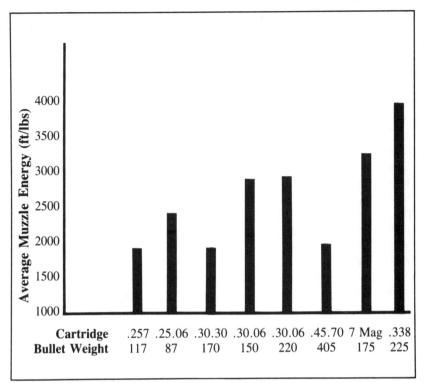

Cartridge	.257	.25.06	.30.30	.30.06	.30.06	.45.70	7 Mag	.338
Bullet Weight	117	87	170	150	220	405	175	225

Average muzzle velocity for common deer cartridges.

fooling around with such things is polishing bird seed.

Bullet weight is important. Light bullets can be shot faster than heavy ones, but will not penetrate as far. But there's more to it than that. The first is the twist of the rifling in your barrel. If it is standard and you're considering only bullets in the middle of the weight range for the cartridge, you can forget about twist. If the barrel is a custom barrel designed for heavy bullets the twist will be too sharp to stabilize light bullets properly. Barrels built for light bullets have slower twists and will not stabilize long, heavy bullets. Velocity makes some difference; the faster the bullet, the less pitch is needed to stabilize it. Pitch, or twist, is measured as the distance a bullet travels in one revolution. A 1:12 twist means the bullet goes 12 inches while revolving once.

Sometimes more is made of twist than is necessary. Mostly, the cartridges that work best on mule deer work best in barrels with a 1:10 twist. That includes standard rounds like the .308 Win. and belted magnums like the .300 Wthby Mag. There are exceptions.

The .264 Win. and 7mm Rem. Mag. call for a pitch of 1:9 to stabilize hunting-weight bullets relatively long for the diameter. While the 7 x 57 Mauser does well with modern bullets in a 1:10 barrel, European standard pitch is 1:8.66. This was to accommodate long, heavy bullets when the rifle was developed as a military weapon. Some chamberings are routinely offered with different twists by different makers. Browning's 78 rifle in .30-06 has a 1:12 twist, Ruger's 77 a 1:10. Sometimes, standards change. Remington's .244 Rem. was chambered in rifles with a 1:12 twist. Word got around that it worked with light bullets, but that 100-grain bullets suitable for deer would not stabilize. The .243 Win. came in rifles with 1:10 twists and outsold the .244. Remington renamed the .244 the 6mm Rem., changed the twist to 1:10 and sold more rifles. I think this was all sort of phony. I owned a .244 and liked the way it shot with all bullet weights up to 105 grains.

Very quick twists have been tried: 1:5.5 to stabilize a 125-grain bullet in the .226 Barnes wildcat and a 200-grain bullet in the 6.5 Barnes. Barrels in .257 Condor have been rifled 1:7 to stabilize 160-grain bullets. Very slow machine gun powder is required to keep pressures down, and there's great strain on the bullet jacket. Spin speeds don't get much attention, compared to bullet velocity. But the twist and resulting spin affect not only the accuracy of a bullet but its performance in a deer.

Consider that a 7mm bullet fired through a 1:9 twist at a muzzle velocity of 3,000 fps rotates 4,000 times in the first second of flight! When it hits something and the jacket ruptures that spin is still at work, tearing the bullet apart with terrific centrifugal force. And bullet spin does not drop off as fast as velocity. That is why tests of 200-yard bullet performance cannot be made near the muzzle with the bullet loaded to 200-yard velocity. The spin is not the same as with a bullet started faster far away.

Because most deer bullets work well in barrels of standard twist, you can forget about twist if you want to. If you don't and want to know a quick way to calculate proper twist, try this formula. It was worked out in 1879 by Briton Sir Alfred George Greenhill. The twist required in calibers equals 150 divided by the length of the bullet in calibers. This applies only to projectiles with a specific gravity of 10.9—that of a jacketed rifle bullet. Pure lead has a specific gravity of 11.35. To illustrate:

A .30-caliber 180-grain spitzer bullet is 1.35 inches long; 1.35/.30 = 4.5 calibers; 150/4.5 = 33⅓ calibers or that many times the diameter of the bullet; 33⅓ x .30 = 9.99 or, to be practical, 10. The proper twist is 1:10.

More relevant than twist to most deer hunters is bullet weight. The best deer bullets are those in the middle of the weight range for the caliber. The exceptions would be 6mm Rem. and .25 cartridges. There, the heavier bullets are best—because bullet diameter is small and because middle- and light-weight bullets are designed to expand quickly on light game. They lack both momentum and the construction necessary for penetration in big mule deer at oblique angles.

Likewise, heavy, medium-bore bullets are ill-suited to mule deer. The 220-grain .30-caliber bullets, for example, hold together all too well to be effective on deer. They will kill deer but not as quickly as lighter bullets because they open more slowly. Deer are thin-skinned, light-boned animals, vulnerable to the explosive opening of high-speed bullets in their shallow chest cavities. A bullet should be fairly quick to open on deer, but not so frangible that it doesn't penetrate.

The recommendations of one self-proclaimed expert: 220-grain bullets in the .30-06 for hunters who want to be sure the deer goes down and stays down. Maybe his deer stays down, because the .30-06 with any bullet is more than enough cartridge for any deer at ranges deer are commonly shot. But they go down quicker and stay down just as long if struck with lighter, faster bullets.

You can err the other way, though. I recall an elk I shot with a 130-grain .270 Win. bullet that killed deer instantly. The same bullet blew up on the rib cage of the elk, lacerating the near lung with shrapnel. Luckily, the bull had not seen me and I was able to shoot once more before he made cover.

Some of the deer you see will give you a broadside presentation, but others will be angling toward or away. I don't take ham shots and am disgusted with people who do. But a raking shot through the rear of the rib cage or an oblique frontal shot into the shoulder are good shots. To make them you need a bullet that will stay in one piece for two feet of travel in soft tissue, and will hold its course and weight on contact with the heaviest bones and joints in a deer's front end.

Bullet construction is really more important than weight in accomplishing what a bullet is supposed to accomplish. But construction is linked to weight because bullet makers know what weights are practical for deer and they build bullets in those weights for deer hunters. In the .243 Win. consider bullets of 100

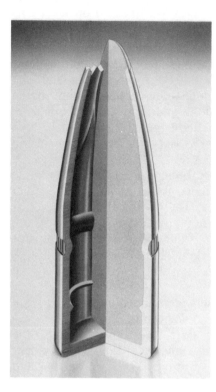

Bullet construction is important. You want the bullet to expand but not fragment. This Hornady has two inner belts locking core to jacket.

and 105 grains, in the .257 Roberts 100 and 120 grains, in .264 120 and 140 grains, in .277 130 and 150 grains, in .284 140 and 160 grains, in .308 Win. 150 and 180 grains.

Thirty caliber bullets are now made as light as 110 grains. Such a bullet will surely kill deer as well as a 100-grain .243 Win. But there are two reasons why light bullets in the larger bores are poor choices. First, light, small-diameter bullets are designed for quick expansion on fragile game. Second, bullets that are short in relation to their diameter have a low sectional density and, consequently, a low ballistic coefficient. These two things affect bullet performance in the air and in the deer. They should affect your choice of bullets, steering you to the middle of the weight range.

Light bullets have low sectional densities and ballistic coefficients; the heaviest bullets have high sectional densities but because their noses must be blunt to stay within length limits imposed by twist, magazine and throat, they have lower ballistic coefficients than even light spitzers.

Sectional density (w/d^2) is a three-place decimal expression of the weight of the bullet in pounds (w) divided by the square of its diameter (d). The higher the sectional density, the greater the inertia and momentum of a bullet in flight. Bullets with high sectional densities retain their velocity better and penetrate deeper than shorter bullets of the same caliber. But sectional density doesn't include the bullet's shape; a round-nose bullet and a spitzer bullet of the same weight and caliber have the same sectional density. They do not fly the same. The difference is in the shape, in their ballistic coefficients.

Ballistic coefficient is a mathematical expression, another three-digit decimal, of the way a bullet battles the air. In a vacuum a 150-grain .30-06 bullet fired at 2,700 fps at an upward angle of 45 degrees has a range of nearly 43 miles. But the same bullet shot at the same velocity and angle through the atmosphere goes less than two miles. The retardation caused by air resistance is over 56 times as strong as the force of gravity on this bullet. The higher the velocity, the stronger the drag.

This is an important thing to think about, and some pretty bright people have thought about it. Isaac Newton, after dropping glass spheres filled with air, water and mercury from the dome of St. Paul's Cathedral, concluded that drag was proportional to the square of the velocity. Later experimenters found this to be true only at low velocities.

In 1881, Mayevski found drag to be proportional to some power of the velocity within a range of velocities. Mayevski based his study on firings done by Krupp in Germany using a projectile three calibers long with an ogival head of two caliber radius.

At the same time in France the Gavre Commission found that it wasn't quite so simple. Their firings, at velocities to 6,000 fps, showed a sharp rise in retardation at the speed of sound. Instead of proposing a formula, the Gavre Commission produced a table of drag values derived by experiment. It was the first ballistics table. By 1909 the British had a similar table, in 1929 another. Each was valid only for a projectile of specific form.

The Ingalls tables, developed later by U.S. Army Colonel James Ingalls, best approximate drag for hunting-style bullets. Ingalls used a bullet shaped much like that of the one-pound, one-inch projectile with two-caliber ogive the British fired in their early experiments. The Ingalls tables are complete only to a velocity of 3,600 fps; from that point the British 1909 tables must be used.

There's more to this than is appropriate in a deer hunting book. The application is that the ballistic coefficient of your deer bullet is a measure of how that bullet will penetrate a barrier of air to get to the deer. You can determine ballistic coefficient mathematically this way: $C = w/id^2$. C is the ballistic coefficient. W is the weight of the bullet in pounds. I the bullet's form factor. D is the bullet's caliber. You can determine form factor by shooting if you know both initial and terminal velocities.

You can also get to your ballistic coefficient this way, without knowing the form factor. The easiest route to ballistic coefficient, though, is through a loading manual, where the work has been done for any bullet you'll likely use.

Hunting mule deer calls for bullets of a high ballistic coefficient, bullets that retain their velocity and energy at long range, that shoot flat and hit hard. This means round-nose bullets are out and semi-spitzers are only OK. Spitzer bullets are certainly the best of the shapes available. Those with flat bases have lower ballistic coefficients than those with tapered heels or boattails, but there's not much difference in performance at hunting yardages. Boattail bullets excel only at very long range.

The most efficient bullets for drilling air are not the best for killing mule deer. You must compromise. The 190-grain .30-caliber and 168-grain 7mm match bullets have high ballistic coefficients and buck the wind nicely. But they are not built to expand on deer, penetrate deer or do any of the other things a deer bullet should do when it gets to a deer. Look at bullets with ballistic coefficients above .370, but don't try to match the match bullets in the upper .500s.

Bullet shape and weight also affect the way wind works on the bullet. Heavy bullets are less affected by wind than light ones, but they travel slower. Fast bullets buck wind better than slow bullets, provided they retain their velocity. There's something called lag that determines wind drift. Lag is the difference in velocities at muzzle and target. A 110-grain .30-caliber bullet with its low sectional density and ballistic coefficient would have lots of lag. It can be started at high velocity, but it slows down quickly. A 165-grain .30-caliber bullet would have less lag because even though it starts slower, it loses less velocity in the air. It is less affected by the wind.

A bullet that pierces wind well is easier to hit with. Because of

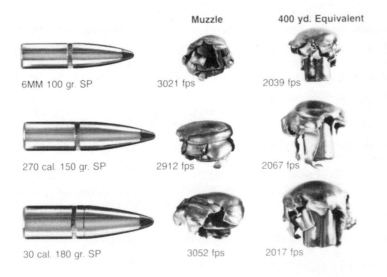

	Muzzle	400 yd. Equivalent
6MM 100 gr. SP	3021 fps	2039 fps
270 cal. 150 gr. SP	2912 fps	2067 fps
30 cal. 180 gr. SP	3052 fps	2017 fps

Perfect expansion is most often seen in a recovery box. But most modern game bullets open nicely and stay together. That they do so consistently in varied mediums, at wildly different linear and rotational velocities is a wonder.

its high ballistic coefficient it will also retain its velocity at long range. This is important. Velocity is what ruptures the bullet jacket on impact and starts expansion. At low velocities jacket rupture may be incomplete, or may not occur at all. The bullet will act like it was designed for heavier game, zipping through the deer without doing much damage. This used to be a bigger problem than it is now.

From time to time you hear complaints about bullets not performing as they should; we're pretty spoiled. Most deer bullets work quite well. We demand a lot from a bullet: to open quickly at 300-yard velocities yet hold together after a solid hit just feet from the muzzle. There are some very clever jacket and core designs around, and no matter what ranges you shoot or with what cartridge, you should find a bullet that will do what you want it to when it hits a deer.

While bullet performance is more important to humane kills than bullet energy you hear a lot about energy. Most of what you hear is meaningless because there are several ways to measure energy. Here are two.

The traditional approach is to calculate energy in foot-pounds like this: $E = wv^2/2g$ where w is weight in pounds, v is velocity in feet per second and g is the acceleration of gravity (32.16 fps per second). There are 7,000 grains to a pound so you must multiply the 2g by 7,000 (to equal 450,240).

Because the velocity is squared in this equation it figures very heavily in determining foot-pounds of energy, too much, in fact, for some people. They suggest a simpler equation: the pounds-feet formula. Here, $E = wv$; w is weight in pounds and v is velocity in feet per second. Multiply the weight and velocity. Divide the wv by 7,000 to get from grains to pounds. This equation is kinder to shooters who use heavy bullets at low velocities.

Mule deer don't study these things, and you needn't fret over energy calculations. The important thing velocity does is get your bullet to the deer in a short time with little deviation from your line of sight. At the deer it provides impact that ruptures the bullet jacket and enough momentum so the bullet carries on through the vitals. Really that's what matters.

A cartridge like the ones listed, with a bullet of medium weight, a sleek profile, good sectional density and ballistic coefficient ratings, driven at velocities between 2,600 and 3,200 fps will serve you nicely.

The only other thing to consider is accuracy. It's not just a function of the rifle. Your choice of cartridge and loads for that cartridge determine how tightly the rifle groups and how confident you are when you're shooting at a deer. A premium bullet that doesn't hit is like a Ferarri without a steering wheel.

Handloading Hints

Factory-loaded ammunition is much better than most shooters will admit. It's nonsense to say you can always better your rifle's performance by handloading. You may find a handload that will group tighter, and surely you can concoct one that will shoot flatter than any factory load. Once in a while you'll discover one that will do both. But you'll not beat the reliability of factory loads, in feeding or ignition—though your handloads will work as well if you put them together properly.

The primary reasons for handloading big game ammunition are to save money, expand your choice of components—especially bullets—and have fun. There's satisfaction in handloading, and in shooting deer with loads you've developed.

Handloading for hunting is different than handloading for the target range because there's no provision for an alibi. Your ammunition works or it doesn't. If it doesn't you lose your shot.

Most neglected by hunters when metallic reloading is cartridge functioning. That is, the load may be accurate, powerful and put together with the best of components, but if it hangs up on the feed ramp or does something you don't want it to do before you get it in the chamber it is a worthless load. Prevent misfeeding by using clean brass, new or full-length-sized or neck-sized from that rifle. Discard brass with dings, crumpled mouths or shoulders, prominent stretch marks in front of the belt, damaged rims or loose primer pockets. Trim hunting cases just a little below recommended length; keep them within SAAMI specifications for length, checking each time you reload.

Clean your dies with bore solvent before you load hunting ammunition, then wipe them dry. Accumulated sizing lube can retain grit that will score your cases.

All cases wear out, some quicker than others. Belted magnum cases are a special problem. Keep track of the number of times you use a batch of cases. When stretching becomes a problem relegate the whole batch to the practice pile. Any with a definite white ring in front of the belt will separate soon. Throw them away. Because of a magnum's headspace on the belt, chamber dimensions in front are usually more generous than they need be. So the case will be loose in the chamber. Firing pushes the brass to the front, causing a stretch ring to appear in front of the belt.

To see if there is a stretch ring on your cartridge, bend a short hook in the end of a straightened paper clip. Insert it in the suspect magnum cases. Scraping the hook against the inside of the case near the belt will enable you to feel a depression caused by the flow of brass forward. Full-length sizing pushes the case back to original dimensions but does not replace the brass where it has pulled thin. Another firing will repeat the stretching, and the case will eventually rupture, releasing hot gas to cut your chamber like a torch. Separation may occur, leaving the case head on your bolt and the rest in the chamber.

You can prolong the life of magnum cases by neck sizing only. Turn the die down till it contacts with the shellholder. Then back it off the thickness of a dime. This way it will squeeze down the neck to hold your bullet, but won't set the shoulder back. The next time you chamber that case it will fit tight all the way to the front and you'll have little stretching. This is practical if you're using the cases in only one rifle because chamber dimensions vary. It's also

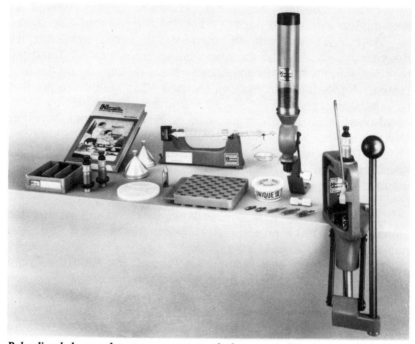

Reloading helps you become more aware of what ammunition is supposed to do. It also extends the good times you have with your deer rifle, gives you a wide choice of components and loads and draws the best performance from you rifle. It can save you money too.

a good idea to make sure your chamber is round. If oblong in cross-section, it won't easily accept a neck-sized case oriented a different way than when it was last fired.

Rimless cases that headspace on the shoulder don't have this problem. Some, however, are prone to neck splits after several firings. I've had a lot of neck splits in .243 Win. cases. They're caused by a hardening of the case and occur when the neck is no longer ductile or malleable enough to spring out and back to release the bullet. You can keep cases soft by annealing them. Set a batch of unsized empties upright in a shallow cake pan in one-half inch of cold water. Space them a couple of inches from each other. Then, using a butane torch, heat to a dull cherry the neck and shoulder of one case. Tip it over in the water. Do the rest the same way. Unlike steel, brass gets soft if it's heated and suddenly quenched. You will melt a few cases before you learn how to direct the flame, but the ones you save will not split.

Even with rimless cases, I neck size only. The less working of the brass the better.

When you handle your cases, be sure your hands are clean, and keep a rag handy at the bench so you can keep them dry. The sweat on your hands will etch a case, weakening it. Before I put cases or cartridges away after handling them—especially if I've taken them on a hunt—I wipe them with a clean cloth.

In resizing, use only enough lube to ease extraction from the die. Too much will deform your case. Case mouths need lube too, or the expander button will pull them, stretching the case. You can use powdered graphite for this; it's dry and won't contaminate the inside of the case. I use liquid case lube, applied with a nylon bore brush. I wipe the insides of the necks dry afterward so the powder doesn't stick there when I charge the case.

I don't clean primer pockets every time I reload, though it surely is a good idea. I do check them. A plugged flash hole can cause a misfire, and too much debris in the pocket can keep the primer from seating fully and cushion the striker blow.

Keep your fingers off primer faces, loading the tube or cup carefully after washing your hands of any case lube and wiping them dry. A hand seating tool will give you a good feel for the pocket, but you can also develop a sensitivity with the press handle. Primers that go in too easily mean you should discard the case or use it only for practice. Primer pockets can become enlarged by shooting, but bulged pockets primarily result from high chamber pressures.

You can use just about any large rifle primer without affecting the accuracy or reliability of your handloads. Only the best loads in the best barrels shoot tight enough to show variations in primer type. Magnum primers increase pressures slightly, but their hotter, more persistent flame ensures ignition in big cases with 65 grains or more of 4350 or slower powder.

Remember when choosing a primer that your bench work will likely be done on summer afternoons. Igniting the same charges in a subzero November dawn is harder. Recently a hunter worked up some accurate hunting loads using special Remington cases punched for small rifle primers. Though the ammunition functioned perfectly on the range it failed on the hunt—not just one round, but all of them! The primer was not hot enough for sure ignition in the cold. It was a good primer, misapplied.

I've not had a standard rifle primer misfire or fail to ignite a charge in cold weather, though I've used standard primers in cases as big as the .375 H&H Mag. against 81 grains of H4831. Still, big cases and slow powders call for magnum primers.

You can use many powders for the bullet and case you choose. But the powders that your manual lists as providing the highest velocities for your cartridge are best. If two look about the same I usually choose the one that most nearly fills the case. Full cases generally give more uniform results because the powder is always in the same position, perhaps just slightly compressed.

You shouldn't have to worry about undercharging with slow powders if you're loading for deer. But here's a warning: In big cases with small-diameter bullets do not reduce charges of slow powder below those suitable for standard hunting loads. Rifles have been blown up by reduced charges of H4831 in cartridges like the .264 Win. Why this occurs is still not clear. That it occurs has even been argued. But there's danger in experimenting. If you must use reduced loads, choose a relatively fast powder, one recommended for the bullet with velocities you want.

It's best to weigh hunting charges by hand, on principle. You can dip a .270 case in a keg of H4831, brush it level with a card, seat a 130-grain bullet and hunt deer. If you're so pressed for time that you must handload like that you're better off with factory ammunition. Period. It will be more accurate and safer. A powder scale is much slower than a measure, but for hunting you need only a few loads. Use the scale.

Keep your fingers off powder, as you kept them off primers. Powder is extremely hygroscopic: it absorbs moisture. You want dry, clean powder in your case.

After I charge a batch I check each case to make sure that each has powder and powder levels are the same. An extra-full case could mean that I measured wrong or that there's an obstruction in the case.

Bullet seating is important because over-long cartridges can impair feeding, even jam the rifle. Short cartridges function OK, but best accuracy comes when bullets are seated out almost to the lands. Deep-seated bullets also encroach on powder space.

To find the best seating depth for your rifle, back out the seating stem on your die until, at the top of a press stroke, the bullet is inserted one-quarter inch into the neck. No bullet should have less bearing in the neck than this; in fact, an old rule says the bullet should be at least bore-diameter deep in the case. That means a quarter inch is barely deep enough for a .25 bullet, not deep enough for a .30-caliber bullet.

Next, carefully chamber the cartridge. If it goes in without resistance to bolt closure pull it out and look carefully for land marks on the ogive of the bullet. Probably there are none. This means your rifle has a long throat and you have no idea how long it is. How long is academic, though, because you seated your bullet as far out as is practical and probably farther than your magazine will accommodate. The next step is to check it in the magazine. If it won't go, screw in your seating die and reseat the bullet until the cartridge just barely fits in the magazine. Then assemble a few more cartridges and fill the magazine. It may be that there's more room on top and that you'll have to shorten your cartridges still farther to guarantee reliable feeding from the bottom. Don't let bullet points scrape the front of the magazine box. Better that you have a little clearance here. Function is vital!

Chances are that after seating a hunting-weight bullet only one-quarter inch into the case neck you'll not be able to close the bolt, that the lands will engage the bullet and give you some resistance. If so, back the cartridge out slowly as soon as you feel the tug of the lands. Seat the bullet just a little deeper after checking to see the land marks. Try again.

For a third and fourth attempt use another cartridge so you can identify the engraving of the lands each time. Close the bolt when you feel resistance only in the downward locking stroke. If you see land marks now you know exactly how long your throat is and how short your cartridge must be to clear them. It must be a little shorter because you do not want any marks on the bullet.

If your bullet meshes slightly with the lands, pressures will be higher because the bullet cannot get a start before it encounters the resistance of the lands. Accuracy can be good, unless the pressure is very high. Excepting loads that are top-scale to begin with, the pressure jump from a bullet touching the lands will not be dangerous. The problem with a bullet engaged by the lands is that it may pull out when you try to extract the loaded round, spilling powder into lug recesses and magazine and leaving the bullet in the bore. Every round you chamber at the range gets fired. Not so hunting! Cartridges must feed and extract smoothly.

A good seating depth for most bullets is .1 inch shy of the lands when the cartridge is chambered. That's enough to give the bullet a start; it still puts the bearing surface close to the lands and keeps the bullet base as far out of powder space as is practical. Provided your magazine accepts bullets seated to this depth, it is a good place to set your seating die.

Some rifles, notably Weatherbys, are designed with an ample throat—freebore, they call it. Freebore lowers pressure initially. That way cartridges can be loaded hotter than would be possible if the lands engraved the bullet sooner. The tradeoff is accuracy. No match rifle has an ample throat. For hunting, though, Weatherby Mark V rifles shoot well. In fact, those I've shot have been extremely accurate. With these rifles, magazine length determines seating depth.

Be aware also of the two-diameter bullet—some but not all bullets for the .264 Win., for example. By making the front of the bullet the diameter of the bore and the rear or seated portion the diameter of the groove, pressures can be held down without having to lengthen a rifle's throat. The bullet stays centered because the front is tight between the lands, if not engraved by them. Trying to seat a two-diameter bullet out until you get land marks is futile. Developing a load for a two-diameter bullet, then switching to a single-diameter bullet without checking throating or reducing the charge slightly is dangerous. If in doubt about your bullets, measure them with a micrometer.

When adjusting your seating die and stem be sure you're moving the right component. The die body should be no closer than the thickness of a nickel to the shellholder. If you adjust the die body instead of the seating stem and run it down too close to the shellholder you'll likely buckle a case at the neck, or bulge it slightly at the shoulder. If the damage is small you may not notice it until you try to chamber the cartridge. For this reason—and because other little problems can go unattended—it's imperative that you cycle every round you intend to hunt with, from the bottom of the magazine through the chamber and out. Testing just one cartridge from a box is assuming all are the same. They may not be. It's foolish to bet your hunt on it.

It isn't necessary to crimp bullets in deer cartridges. If your necks are properly sized, neck tension is enough. Crimping can impair accuracy.

There are ways that you can make your hunting ammunition the best it can be. Unless your rifle is more accurate than most, the results will be small. You can separate cases into lots by weight, chamber case mouths, turn necks, drill and de-burr flash holes, clean primer pockets, check bullets for runout with a dial indicator. All this makes some difference in a bench rifle, very little in a sporting rifle.

It is still good to do. It teaches you things.

Developing a load for your rifle is engaging because *you* get to design the cartridge you will hunt with. Only the case dimensions are established. You have a grand selection of components to choose from. It would take you a long time to try all the combinations available for even one popular cartridge. So you start with a couple of powders and arbitrarily choose one brand of cases and primers. The real testing is with bullets.

The most accurate bullets, like the bullets with the best ballistic form, are not the best bullets for deer hunting because they were not designed to kill deer. Still, many deer bullets are acceptably accurate. Accuracy is important in hunting; so is proper expansion. The bullet you choose will be a compromise.

Not long ago I was trying to put loads together for a hunt. The rifle was a new one. I tried a variety of loads, and finally found one that shot much better than any of the others. The problem, was that I didn't like the bullet. It wasn't built for what I had in mind. I kept experimenting with other bullets, hoping one would shoot as well. None did. I decided to hunt with the bullet that grouped. Luckily, the shot I got was one where accuracy counted more than bullet construction. I was happy with my choice.

You needn't shoot half-minute or even one-minute groups with your load. It's nice if you can, but a minute and a half will do just fine for deer out to 400 yards. Groups bigger than a minute and a half are not so good. It doesn't matter how your bullet performs in a deer if you miss because your bullet won't hit the deer. Sometimes you'll find that changing powder type or charge will help, that you won't have to use a bullet you don't like after all.

Developing a load is a chicken-and-egg sort of thing. The bullet is the most important part, but you can't assess the performance of a bullet in the air or a recovery box until you have a powder charge that will drive the bullet at the velocity you want with no pressure problems.

Usually I choose a bullet I think will work, or one I want to work, then test powder charges until I get what I want or decide to switch bullets. The way I start with powders is to pick one, two or three that in the loading manuals generate the highest velocities for that cartridge. Then, with a charge five percent under the maximum listed, I start shooting. For hunting I want loads that are powerful, loads that will function in all conditions but that give to the bullet the most velocity practical for the cartridge.

I increase charges two grains at a time until I get signs of high pressure. Generally just below this point I'll find groups as good as at any pressure level. When trying charges at or near maximum I vary the charges a grain at a time. I've not found it profitable with large-capacity hunting cartridges and slow powder to split loads closer than a full grain in weight.

It's important to recognize pressure signs. Extruded primers are among the best known, but I've seen primers crater with mild loads. The striker face, spring and striker hole in the bolt face affect the way primers look after firing. Primer extrusion is not a good indication of pressure.

Just as obvious but more reliable is the shine on a case head that indicates the brass has been forced into the ejector recess. A sticky bolt lift is another sure sign of high pressure. Either of these means you should back off. Pressures are not just high; they're too high.

The best way to measure pressure, though, is with a micrometer caliper calibrated to .0001 inch. With this, straddle the case body just ahead of the web on rimmed and rimless cases. If a new case shows .0010 inch expansion after firing, back off one grain to get a safe but maximum load. With belted cases .0015 inch expansion on the rear of the belt means the same thing. It is of no use to develop a load that's too hot to be safe or reliable.

Your load testing will be more meaningful and easier if you have a chronograph. Chronographs are expensive. But you'll do well to buy one. My Oehler lets me compare factory ballistic claims to factory ballistics, one handload with another. It tells me the price in velocity of short barrels, how much I gain by pushing pressure limits. A 130-grain Speer bullet, it says, leaves the muzzle of my .270 at 2,940 fps if powered by 59 grains of H4831. Although that might still be my favorite deer load without the chronograph, I would know less about it.

Paying attention to things like ballistics and handloading techniques won't put a big buck in front of your rifle. But you will be prepared for any buck that steps there.

6

Rifles For Hunting Deer

For roughly 80 years there's been little improvement in cartridges and only minor improvements in rifles suitable for deer. The .30-06 is still adequate for any deer hunting you have in mind, and a better round than you need most of the time.

Only sights have improved a great deal since 1906. More on that later.

The important thing about hunting deer is finding one you want to shoot.

The important thing about shooting deer is hitting that animal in the right place.

There are good reasons to think about rifles and cartridges for deer. Hunting rifles are part of deer hunting, and many people who hunt do so because they can use the rifles they like. If they had to borrow a gun or were issued one, or for some reason lost interest in guns, they'd probably not hunt as much.

Another reason to study rifles, cartridges and ballistics is that you then have a better feel for the tool in your hand. Think of it as an extension of your hand. While shooting, like hunting, can be done by following an instruction manual, you'll neither shoot nor hunt well unless you poke around in peripheral subjects. You may never have to shoot at 400 yards, but understanding what your bullet does to get there will help you become a better rifleman at all ranges. You won't need a rifle that nibbles one hole with five

The Ruger Number One is an accurate, dropping-block single shot. It is particularly handsome in the "S" configuration, but its barrel-band forward swivel, under sling tension may affect point of impact, the author says.

shots, but knowing what makes rifles that accurate will help you make yours as accurate as it can be.

An analogy: You can drive a car without knowing anything about what makes it run, but you'll not see the car's potential. If anything goes wrong you'll not have what it takes to make the car work again. Lots of things can go wrong while hunting. Wind, long distances, your own heavy breathing, a running buck, steep angle, rain, snow, dust, cold, heat, thick brush—these and other things make shooting deer a challenge even for experts.

About Actions

The rifle actions most suitable for mule deer hunting are the dropping-block single-shot and the bolt action. Slide, lever and autoloading rifles are, generally, less accurate. Their triggers are not as good, and they have a much narrower range of chamberings. The advantage of fast follow-up shots is of little value. Your first shot is your best. If you need more, you probably took the first when you shouldn't have or did not take enough care with it.

If you want a single-shot rifle the Ruger Number One is a fine choice. Browning's discontinued 78 and its newer 1885 are good too. In the Ruger, the 1B is probably best. While the 1A and 1S look very nice, the barrel-band front swivel is a liability. A tight sling will affect accuracy and you'll frequently shoot with a tight sling. Better that the swivel is on the forend.

Accuracy in the Number Ones can be very good or pretty bad. I have two in the same model and caliber; one shoots well and one doesn't. Forend tension has a lot to do with how these rifles perform, and you may have to do some minor fitting to get the most from your Number One. The trigger and stock design are exceptional.

Besides its aesthetic qualities a single-shot rifle has the advantage of a very short action. One with a 26-inch barrel has the same overall length as a bolt rifle with a 22-inch barrel. Longer barrels, generally, give higher velocities.

Most western deer hunters use bolt-action magazine rifles. They're the slowest of repeaters but the most accurate. Accuracy is far more important than speed.

Bolt-action rifles are strong; almost all have front-locking lugs that engage with the simple door-bolt movement adapted to rifles by Nikolaus von Dreyse in his early 19th century needle gun. Peter Paul Mauser developed a much better mechanism in 1872, and followed it with the German-built Spanish Mauser of 1893—the first modern bolt rifle.

There's ample camming power in a bolt action, all provided by your hand. Oversize cartridges that wouldn't feed in other actions can be crammed into the chamber with a bolt action. Bolt actions are simple, with mechanisms that are easy to take apart and clean. A one-piece stock and finely adjustable trigger enhance accuracy.

Although some will disagree with this point, it doesn't make much difference which bolt action you buy. Remington's 700, Ruger's 77 and Winchester's 70 comprise most of what you'll see in the field. All are good; Weatherby, Sako and traditional Mauser actions are too. The firing pin on a Kleinguenther action has a fall of only .158 inch, roughly a quarter that of the 98 Mauser. A short fall makes for fast lock time. That's good because the rifle moves less between the time the trigger breaks and the primer detonates. Wichita's action was designed by bench shooters in the U.S. and closely resembles the Champlin. These, and the domestic Dubiel, are made in small numbers.

Belgian's Dumoulin, the British BSA, Danish Shulz & Larsen and early Czech BRNO are among the better sporting actions that have been imported. Military as well as commercial 98 Mauser actions are still used in some of the best hand-built rifles. Several really good actions are no longer made, notably the early Winchester 70. The machining and fitting on these were nice, but the modern Kimber and Grisel actions are in many ways better. Even inexpensive models like the Savage 110 perform well. Many familiar rifles now shoot tighter than those collectors prize.

Some new actions, however, have features of little use to deer hunters, including roller cams and barrels that can be changed at a whim. Such things cost extra and can be liabilities if they compromise a crisp trigger, fine accuracy or dependability, or if

Clean lines and thoughtful detailing characterize the Kimber action and stock. Note the three-position safety, Mauser extractor and borderless multi-point checkering.

they add weight or impair the balance of your rifle. Every feature of a rifle should contribute to quick pointing and an accurate first shot.

You can get a custom-made rifle today that is better than any made years ago. The artists who machine, engrave, stock and checker custom-built rifles now are the best there's ever been. They have tools and techniques the first gun craftsmen didn't, and, except perhaps for stock wood, better materials. Depending on what you want in your custom-made rifle, price tags start at about $2,000. Without baubles like gold inlays a rifle of the best quality is $2,500 to $4,500. That's a lot of money, but little enough for the time and talent invested. Besides fine workmanship and flawless performance, you get a stock that fits you perfectly.

If you want a fine rifle for less than the price of a hand-built, the Kimber Big Game Rifle might appeal to you. Made in the image of the early Winchester 70, it has a much better stock and some improvements in the action as well. It is nicely fitted and finished but still a woods rifle that is made to be used. Kimber guns reflect a great deal of thought. This one is everything a hunter could want. The price is higher than that of most production models, but this rifle will leave you wondering how it could be improved.

Another excellent bolt rifle is that marketed by Dakota. This small firm combines the talents of stockmaker Don Allen and metalsmith Pete Grisel. Their Dakota 76 is built on Grisel's action and is impeccably fitted and finished. Priced a bit higher than the Kimber, it's still reasonable.

There are others, like the Wichita, built the same way. You usually get a better rifle if you pay more money for one, provided you pay attention to the fundamentals.

When I started hunting I couldn't afford even a cheap sporting rifle. My first deer was shot with an iron-sighted .303 SMLE I'd bought for $35 and cobbled into a hunting rifle. It worked. Although you have to pay more than $35 for even a battered surplus rifle these days, some sporting rifles are built to sell cheaply and perform very well.

Both Remington and Winchester offer economy-grade guns: the Sportsman 78 and Ranger rifles respectively. These are built on 700 and 70 actions. The only significant compromise is in the uncheckered hardwood stocks. This makes the rifles look homely, but doesn't affect the way they shoot. Sights on the inexpensive guns are not what they are on the better models, but since you probably will use a scope that's of little concern. You'll have a narrower choice of calibers in the 78 and Ranger rifles, but both offer the .270 Win. and .30-06—two of today's best-selling western deer calibers.

The Parker-Hale Midland is another rifle built to a price and still worth taking afield. Savage's 110E is too. On used gun racks you'll find Remington's 721 and 722 rifles, long- and short-actioned forebears of the 700. You can actually buy them for very little, and they make good deer rifles. I owned a 721 in .270 Win. and a 722 in .244 Rem. Both were very accurate. The triggers in 700 rifles aren't much different than what was in the 721 and 722; they were good enough not to change. Another Remington you can get second-hand is the 788. A rear-locking, short-action rifle, this was one of the most accurate for the money ever offered. I used one in .308 Win. to shoot metallic silhouette matches. The original price was $99.

Remington's discontinued 600 and 660 carbines have a good reputation in the woods, and those in .350 Rem. fetch high prices. The barrels are too short for me, but in .308 Win. or .350 Rem. Mag. these little rifles serve nicely in blacktail cover.

Rifles last a long time. A used rifle should perform as well as a new one of the same model for as long as you're likely to hunt deer. The only reason to buy a new rifle is to get something you can't get with a used one—a new chambering, for example. But the lower price of a used gun is only a bonus if the rifle is in other ways just what you want. Compromising performance for price is poor economy. Within the limits of your budget, price should never be the thing that attracts you to a rifle. That rifle is important! You'll do well to buy exactly what you want, not just something you think will work.

What matters in your rifle are those features that help you quickly put a bullet in a small target every time you shoot. Because extra weight helps you do this, you'll have to figure on a compromise so you can still carry that rifle up the mountain. On other features, resist compromise. Your rifle should never cause you to miss what you shoot at and should never do anything you don't expect it to do.

A rifle action, bolt or single-shot, must work smoothly. The buttery glide of an early Mannlicher bolt and the silky tracking of a prewar Winchester 70 are hard to find on factory rifles. But that's OK because bolts don't have to be as smooth-working as these. If they don't bind, if there are no hitches, that's enough. If the safety works freely but positively, the trigger predictably and cartridges feed surely, yours is a useful action.

Little problems you can handle yourself. Fine abrasive paste on the bolt body can smooth the action if you run the bolt back and forth fast for a few minutes. Most triggers can be adjusted; those that can't or don't give you what you want can be replaced with an aftermarket trigger like the excellent Timney. Safeties can be replaced, usually with the trigger. They're hard to work on, but you can usually quiet a noisy safety or free one that sticks. My favorite is the Winchester 70 safety. It's positive, accessible and easily pushed off. The middle detent lets you open the action while the sear stays blocked. That's handy.

There are other things to look for in rifle actions. Most are details that distinguish one rifle from another. Some are worth considering before you buy a rifle because they affect performance.

One detail you don't have to worry about anymore is how to mount a scope. Most every factory-built rifle is drilled or grooved for a scope. Some will accept only mounts made by the same company. Sako is an example—though not long ago Leupold started making rings that would fit the tapered dovetails of a Sako receiver. Ruger has offered its rifles drilled for standard mounts or machined for Ruger rings. Lots of rifles now come without iron sights, which is fine for most shooters because irons just get in the way if you're using a scope.

The Remington Mountain Rifle, available in five premier deer chamberings, is finely balanced and very light. This one sports a Kevlar stock which is stable in all weather.

Many shooters prefer all steel parts in their rifles. I do. But to kill deer you don't need all those steel parts. In fact, you may like your rifle better on the mountain if it has lightweight parts of aluminum, rubber and plastic. A steel butt is nice looking, but a rubber pad is more comfortable to shoot and takes abuse better. There's nothing wrong with an aluminum triggerguard or floorplate assembly, and they cut ounces from your rifle. They look clunky, that's all.

Stamped parts are like that. A lot of magazine followers are stamped now; they work just as well as followers that aren't, but don't impress people you want to impress. The stamped steel guard and floorplate of the 721 and 722 Remingtons supposedly made them homely and then obsolete.

More likely the new 700 Remington just replaced them. The 721 and 722 were made to perform better than other rifles of the same price, not to look pretty. They were good rifles and sold well for a time.

Stampings and investment castings, plastic, alloy and web slings are hard to get away from if you look at new rifles. Not appropriate on fine hand-built rifles, they make mass-produced rifles affordable. They work when they're supposed to, probably as much as machined steel parts.

There's a considerable fuss about the Mauser extractor now: that long spring-steel claw that rides on the side of the bolt and hooks around its face. A strong, positive extractor, it pulls out any case that isn't melted to the chamber walls. It controls the next cartridge too, gripping it once it pops free of the magazine. The Mauser extractor looks and is expensive. It makes the rifle action look muscular because it makes the bolt look bigger. If every bolt-action rifle had a Mauser extractor they'd all have good extractors.

They don't all have Mauser extractors, though. Even the Ruger 77, which looks like it has one, doesn't. A Mauser extractor won't permit a recessed bolt face like Remington's or Weatherby's and won't work with a plunger ejector. A Mauser extractor is more costly than the little hook used by Winchester and Sako and the beryllium clip in Remington rifles. A Mauser extractor is probably the best, but to get one you'll have to forget about some rifles that have a lot going for them.

Extractors used by most gunmakers are dependable. I've not had any fail. While I like controlled feeding from the magazine, I also like the accuracy I get with Remington and Weatherby rifles. It bothers me to have a plunger ejector jam a fired case against the chamber wall as the extractor drags it back, then pop it over the side as soon as its mouth clears. But I can live with that problem, or take the ejector out if it bothers me enough. Truly, any proven extractor will clear the chamber and any proven ejector will clear the breech. In hunting, that's all you need.

The number of locking lugs that a bolt has doesn't matter. The Krag-Jorgensen rifle and Britain's SMLE each had only one in front, and that worked fine. One lug is probably insufficient to bottle the higher pressures of modern cartridges. The 98 Mauser has two; that's plenty. Most Remington, Winchester and Ruger bolt rifles are patterned on the Mauser and have two lugs. Weatherby rifles have nine. That doesn't make them more or less able to bottle pressure. For one thing, each of the nine lugs is pretty small. And each lug must bear its share of the load. On rifles with two lugs one almost always bears most, and sometimes all, of the thrust. It must be at least as hard to mate nine lugs so they all bear evenly. All locking surfaces and mechanisms on current sporting rifles are stout enough.

Schultz and Larsen rifles and, later, the Remington 788, had locking lugs in the rear of the bolt. This wasn't supposed to be as good as front lockup because headspacing couldn't be as precise and there was talk of bolts stretching and shrinking. Both rifles shot well, though, and the bolts stayed the same size.

Some shooters are concerned with how many cartridges they can stuff in a magazine, but that's not important. Your first shot is the shot that will kill most of your deer; those rounds in the magazine are just in case things don't go as you expect them to. It isn't often that you'll need them quickly, and I can remember only once having to use them all. Usually I load three cartridges in the magazine, whatever its capacity.

Quick-change box magazines work OK but have no particular advantage over integral magazines.

The floorplate assembly of most sporting rifles is hinged, with the release button in the trigger guard. This allows you to dump your cartridges at the end of a day or before you get in a car without running them through the chamber and banging up bullet tips. Rifles built to sell cheaply have blind magazines (cavities routered into the stock) and no floorplates.

While hinged floorplates are useful, they can be troublesome. If the latch is not secure they can dump your cartridges on recoil. That happened to me once and it made me feel very foolish. Hunters after dangerous game have wrapped duct tape around the floorplate and up the sides of the stock just in case things come loose. A blind magazine is not a bad idea, provided it's well finished for smooth feeding. With a blind magazine you don't have to worry about scratching an aluminum floorplate or sweating the blue off a steel one.

Most rifles come equipped with sling swivel studs. They used to have swivels, but detachable swivels are more popular now than fixed swivels. It's easy to install studs on a rifle that doesn't have them. They cost little, plus a hunting sling is most useful!

Recoil pads are good, even if they're thin. The rubber grips well and protects the stock. It's not easy to install a pad on rifles with epoxy-type stock finishes, because to make the pad fit you have to sand it flush with the stock. That means stripping the finish on the entire stock and refinishing. That's hard. You can get a pretty good fit by doing all the pad shaping on a grinding wheel, and using a sanding block to smooth the surfaces. Most of the time you must cut the stock to install a pad—to square it up if not to shorten it—because plastic and metal buttplates are usually curved. Be careful. Even with a band saw, splintering can occur when you cut. Resale value drops if the stock is shortened. It's best to install the thinnest pad you can so the stock looks its original length even if it's not. A thick pad won't reduce recoil much more than a thin one. Felt recoil depends mostly on stock shape.

The Stock: Your Rifle's Handle

Stocks are much better now than they were even a few years ago. The first bolt rifle stocks, like that on the Springfield, had too much drop. On firing, the rifle pivoted up and smacked your

Low combs and those that slant down sharply at the heel kick your face on recoil. This early Winchester stock has too much drop.

cheekbone hard. The Springfield was also too short. That's why shooters who learned to shoot with the Springfield keep their right thumbs to the side of the grip instead of on top of it.

The first sporter stocks were also low at comb and heel. That wasn't as big a problem, because most shooters used iron sights. But it was a long time after scopes came out before stocks were changed. In the 1950s you could buy lace-on and glue-on pads for the comb of your rifle so your face would rest in line with the scope. These are still available. Later stocks were made with raised cheekpieces and what was called a Monte Carlo comb. Most didn't look very good, but they kept your face from being battered.

When Leonard Brownell went to work for Bill Ruger to design a stock for the new Number One and Model 77 rifles in 1977, he brought great talent for shaping useful and beautiful stocks. The straight comb of these stocks is trim but supports your face. Ruger stocks have clean lines, are quick to point and comfortable to shoot. The classic stocks offered by most gunmakers are similar.

Early on, the main advantage of a hand-built rifle was the wonderful way it fit you. Stocks on modern sporting rifles are so good that unless you have a special style or size, you'll have trouble improving on them.

This comb, on a later Winchester, is better. Stock shape does more to accentuate or tame recoil than rifle weight or buttplate material. And it certainly has much to do with speed of handling.

Sophisticated shooters aren't supposed to think like that. They're expected to talk of shaving a fraction of an inch here and there, adding spacers to butts and dishing out combs. You can do these things and profit by them. But many shooters change their stocks before they learn how to shoot well. So, the changes are not always good ones. Unless you have a great deal of shooting experience, you probably don't know enough to do much changing. Better to buy a rifle that feels good when you snap it to your shoulder, shoot it for some months, then think about its fit. You may well decide you like it as it is.

To be a good marksman in the woods you must adapt to different shooting conditions. You'll not always wear the same clothes, so the ideal length of pull will change. Some of your shots will be uphill, some down. Some will be from the sitting position, some standing, some kneeling, a few prone. You'll use a sling when you can, but often you won't. These and other factors affect the way you hold your rifle, and the way the rifle feels. But your rifle will be the same all the time. You must adapt to it.

This is contrary to the thought that stock fit makes you hit or miss, and that fitting the stock to you like a pair of hand-built boots is imperative. Truly, you cannot fit a stock to you unless you shoot from the same position all the time. That's why target rifles built for position shooting have so many stock adjustments. You change the stock when you go from prone to sitting, again from sitting to kneeling, again from kneeling to offhand. If one set of stock dimensions would work, such fuss would be futile.

One fellow I shot with in smallbore matches had slimmed the grip of his rifle, then plastered on a big gob of bedding compound. While it was still soft, he got into position and held the rifle as he would on the line until the goop hardened. His was a grip made to fit, but it worked only because this was a prone rifle, shot from the same position each time. In the woods with a hunting rifle you don't have that option. You must take your shots as they come, and your stock must be one of many compromises. It should fit you imperfectly in any position—but almost perfectly in all positions. Many factory stocks will.

You don't have to measure a stock to see if it fits. Measurements tell you little. Just throw the rifle to your shoulder a few times. Do it with your eyes closed, then open them. Are you looking down the sights? Is the rifle pointed where you thought? Does your eye center the scope or fall in line with the sights? Try aiming the rifle from other positions, with and without a sling. Hang it from the sling on your back. Carry it cradled in front of you and down at your side with your hand about the balance point. Do everything you would expect to do with it in the field. If it feels good it should work for you.

The comb must put your eye immediately in line with the sight. Better one that's a bit too low than one that's too high because in the excitement of the hunt you'll likely not get down hard enough on a high comb and your shot will go high. You can correct this situation by skimming wood off the comb or using higher scope rings. I like low rings, so would alter the comb.

A comb that slants down from the comb to the heel will kick your face harder than one that's straight. Weatherby's distinctive comb slants forward. It doesn't look good to some shooters but it's functional. Rather than angling toward your face on recoil, the Weatherby comb angles away. That's good for your face. Most modern combs, even the conservative-looking ones, are designed for scope shooting and are quite comfortable.

As important as comb dimensions, stock pitch also affects the way your rifle points. Pitch is the angle of butt to bore. Most rifles point well with one to two inches down pitch—that is, when the

No matter what rifle you choose to hunt with, get another in .22 rimfire that feels almost the same. How well you shoot is more a function of you than of the rifle. Practicing with that .22 will help you shoot deer.

rifle is stood with its rear bridge against a wall and the butt flat on the floor the muzzle will be an inch or two away from the wall. Too much pitch will cause the rifle to recoil hard against your cheek as it pivots up on your shoulder. The rifle will naturally point low. Too little pitch will direct recoil in a straight line, but off-hand you'll feel the toe of the stock biting into your shoulder. The rifle will naturally point high. Cutting the stock is the only way to change its pitch.

Grip angle, radius and the size of the grip in cross-section are all important to fast shooting. I have big hands and like a long open grip. But I like a slender grip too, one that feels more like a baseball bat than a coffee can. I don't want the comb to be in the way of the heel of my hand, and I don't like palm swells. Grip preference is a personal thing.

The rifle's forend should taper slightly from magazine well to the forend tip. That makes for good looks and fast handling but still allows your left hand to control the muzzle and absorb some recoil. I like a forend almost round in cross-section, just a tad flattened on the sides and bottom, as if someone has tried to squash it but failed. Flat-bottomed forends or those too thin for my hand to control are of no use to me.

As for aesthetics, it's a matter of taste. I prefer straight-combed stocks with no cheekpiece, a shallow sweeping grip and a long forend—with all lines straight or parts of a circle. Either a checkered steel or brown rubber pad looks good on the butt, a smooth steel cap or no cap at all on the grip. I like dark, dense wood with moderate figure and no forend tip. There are plenty of stock styles that will work for shooting deer.

Checkering is the only feature you might add to a well-shaped stock to make it prettier. Checkering is also functional, and can improve your grip. I like point-pattern checkering, 24 lines to the inch. But you can't get that on most factory rifles. Production-grade American walnut is too soft to hold fine checkering. What you'll see most is 16- to 20-line checkering. That's OK too. It's not as pretty but can be more functional. If dirt or snow gets on your rifle you'll appreciate the coarse checkering with its deep grooves.

Skeleton gripcaps and buttplates, with checkered insides, are pure decoration, a mark of the stocker's ability. Gary Goudy stocked a .300 H&H Mag. for me in dense English walnut. Inside the skeleton grip cap, checkering is cut 32 lines to the inch.

Bedding has a lot to do with accuracy, and if your rifle doesn't shoot well with one of several loads it's a good idea to check the bedding. Groups strung vertically suggest bedding is at fault. If you can't easily spring the forend away from the barrel it's too tight. Lampblack on the barrel or in the barrel channel will show high spots.

To fix barrel bedding you can float the barrel. That's easy. But it doesn't always give the best accuracy with light barrels. A slight up pressure at the forend tip can be good, provided it stays the same. From there back to an inch in front of the recoil lug the barrel can float unless there's a forend screw you want to engage, like on the early Winchester 70s. A small brass shim just behind the forend tip is an easy way to get some pressure out there after you float the barrel. It's best to shave the channel evenly and add the shim, rather than trying to leave a lump of wood. When you open the barrel channel you don't have to ruin the fit of metal to wood by gouging a bunch away. The thickness of a piece of heavy paper is gap enough.

I like to glass the recoil lug in its recess and leave a pad of glass in front of and behind that recess. I pour a pad at the rear of the receiver too, near the guard screw. These glassed areas stabilize the action in the stock. The glass recoil lug abutment keeps the stock from splitting.

Synthetic stocks are supposed to make all this unnecessary. They stay inert under the metal, no matter what the weather. If they were poured around the rifle, as glass bedding compound is, they'd fit just right and you'd not have anything more to do with your stock. But even the stocks that are supposed to fit without fitting don't. Weatherby's fine Fibermark rifle, for example, has pads of glass on either end of the action, though the synthetic stock is made specifically for that rifle. One Fibermark I shot was exceptionally accurate. If Weatherby goes to the trouble of glassing its own synthetic stocks, it seems logical that glassing aftermarket stocks is a good idea too.

Synthetic stocks are made of several materials; fiberglass is only one. Some synthetic stocks are much lighter than wood, but others weigh close to the same. They're all stronger than wood, all more stable. None look as nice as a figured piece of walnut, but on a rifle made to shoot deer that doesn't matter.

Barrels To Help You Hit

Perhaps the most important part of a rifle is its barrel. Unless you're looking at used guns, though, most barrels appear pretty

Winchester's Winlite stock is well shaped for shooting. This and other synthetic stocks are more stable and durable than wood.

much the same. You can't see little problems in barrels so you can't tell if the barrel is good unless you shoot the rifle. Most barrels are good enough for deer hunting. If you want a very accurate rifle it's best to have a Hart, Douglas, Shilen or MacMillan premium barrel fitted to a sound action. Have the bolt face squared, the lugs lapped and the chamber cut just a little under SAAMI dimensions. But then you'll have to take other steps with bedding and ammunition too.

The best accuracy comes at a high price. It's easy to get most rifles to shoot into a minute and a half, but beyond that you must work hard to tighten groups. If your rifle can shoot into 1½ inches at 100 yards you can shoot deer at any reasonable range.

Reliability is just as important as accuracy, and if doing things like cutting a minimum chamber impairs feeding it's best not done. Most alterations you'll make to factory rifles won't make them any less reliable.

About barrel length: longer is better until it gets in your way. There's a trend toward short barrels now, because they're lighter than long ones and make for handier rifles. In thickets short barrels are OK, provided they're chambered for efficient cartridges with powder charges consumed quickly in the bore. If you'll be hunting blacktail with a .308 Win. or a .350 Rem. you won't need a long barrel to get most of what these cartridges can offer ballistically. In blacktail cover the short barrel will get you on target quickly and enable you to slip through brush easily.

In most deer country though, a long barrel is better. It puts more punch in your shot because the powder has more time to accelerate the bullet. Each extra inch of barrel adds 20 to 40 fps to your bullet, depending on bore, powder charge and original barrel length. A long barrel also puts more weight out in front to steady your hold. And it reduces felt recoil and muzzle blast. That also helps you shoot better.

Long and short are relative. In modern sporting rifles a long barrel is 24 inches or more; short barrels are less than 24 inches. Most shooters will accept that arbitrary break. In the time of lever-action rifles, before 1900, there were carbines with 20-inch barrels and rifles with 24- and 26-inch barrels. Some were even longer. When cartridges went smokeless following the .30-30 Win. in 1895, barrels got shorter. Though Savage's 99 and Winchester's 71 were offered with 24-inch barrels through WWII, most lever rifles were shorter.

Bolt-action rifles came to life as military weapons and had barrels up to 30 inches long. The standard Springfield barrel was 24 inches. Because hunters started shooting bolt rifles with the Springfield, this barrel length was pretty well accepted for a long time. Most of Winchester's 54 and early 70 rifles had 24-inch barrels, as did Remington's 721 and 722. Some 70s had 25- and 26-inch barrels. Many rifles of that day were also sold as carbines, with 20-inch barrels. In the case of the 70, the carbine was just like the rifle except for barrel length. It looked like a dubbed-off rifle.

In the 1950s Winchester introduced its 70 Featherweight with a 22-inch barrel. Remington's first 700 had a 20-inch. Since then standard-weight bolt rifles have been offered with 22- and 24-inch barrels. Lightweight models mostly have 20-inch barrels. Carbines have 18-inch barrels. Winchester has dropped the 25- and 26-inch barrels it once installed on the .338 Win. Mag. and .375 H&H Mag., and those on the .300 H&H Mag. and .264 Win. Only Weatherby offers a 26-inch barrel as standard now.

I like barrels 26 inches long. I dislike barrels shorter than 24 inches. Most rifles balance poorly with barrels under 22 inches. Rifles with 18- or 20-inch barrels must be designed as carbines to be useful. Teaming a short barrel with an action and stock designed for a long one is absurd. But that's how many lightweight rifles are put together.

Getting good performance out of your cartidge means getting a barrel of proper length. Accuracy isn't affected by length; bench rifles that shoot into less than a quarter minute have barrels only 20 inches long. But these rifles are chambered for cartridges like the .222 Rem. and .308 Win., cartridges that hold modest charges of medium- and fast-burning powder. It's ridiculous to chamber a 22-inch barrel for the .264 Win. (which Winchester did in 1962) or

The Weatherby Vanguard VGL typifies lightweight rifles currently popular. The author prefers longer, heavier barrels.

a 19-inch barrel for the .270 Win. (which Sako now offers). There's no rule here, but for belted cases of .33 caliber or less I like a 26-inch barrel. Cartridges like the .270 Win. and .30-06 work well in 24-inch barrels, as do short-action rounds like the .243 Win. and .257 Roberts. Stubby cartridges of .30 caliber or more work fine in 22-inch barrels.

Rifling twist in factory-built rifles needn't concern you because twist is usually determined for bullets of medium weight for the cartridge. Those are the bullets you'll use for deer.

Barrel weight once was pretty consistent for all sporting rifles. Most makers used similar contours and you didn't have much choice. Now there are featherweight rifles, ultralight rifles, heavy-barreled varmint and heavy target rifles. A standard-weight barrel is still a good one. While light barrels carry well, your purpose is to shoot a deer and light barrels are generally not as accurate as heavy ones. If a rifle is too light you won't be able to hold it steady when you're breathing hard or if there's a wind.

Even normal rifles are made lighter than they used to be, and the lightweight rifles are light indeed. Weatherby's Vanguard weighs 7 pounds 14 ounces, the Vanguard lightweight only 6 pounds 8 ounces. A thinner, shorter barrel is mostly responsible. Remington's 700 weighs 7 pounds 4 ounces, in wood or synthetic Rynite. In fiberglass it weighs a pound less. The glass-stocked Model Seven is a pound lighter still! Winchester and Ruger offer light rifles stocked in wood, as do other makers.

My deer rifles average a little over 7½ pounds empty. Loaded

Better than barrel-mounted open sights are aperture sights like the Redfield here. If the aperture is small take out the insert and use the big threaded sleeve as your sight. It's much faster, nearly as accurate and lets you shoot in dim light.

with sling and scope they weigh about 9½ pounds. That's just right for me. I wouldn't have them lighter. Sometimes they seem heavy, but they shoot well and I can hold them pretty still.

Sights, Scopes, Slings

Your rifle is a big mechanical tool with a simple function: to release the energy in the cartridge and spew the bullet in one direction. It can only direct the bullet one way because the barrel is fixed. It's your job to move the gun so the barrel points at the spot on the deer you want to hit. You can't do that without sights; you can't do it well without good ones.

There's nothing wrong with iron sights for hunting mule deer, and in blacktail coverts especially, irons may be the better choice.

The most useful iron sights comprise a trim receiver or aperture sight with a big hole and a prominent round or square bead in front. The bead should be angled to catch skylight but flat on the surface so it doesn't reflect light to the edges. Size depends on barrel length. The longer the barrel the smaller the bead will appear. A ¹⁄₁₆-inch bead is fine for barrels of 22 to 24 inches. While big beads are easy to find, they obscure small targets. A patch of deer in a thicket or the shoulder of one across a field can disappear behind a bead, spoiling your aim. The bead is best kept as small as you can find quickly against brush. Gold is a good color, better than silver. White is OK if there's no snow.

The rear aperture should be big. Your eye will automatically center the bead in the area of most light: the aperture's middle. I like a ⅛-inch hole with a ¹⁄₁₀-inch rim. A smaller aperture lets in too little light for woods hunting, and a bigger rim obscures too much of the target. Little holes in big disks are useful on the target range, where bull's-eyes are black on white, and the lighting is good and there's plenty of time. While deer hunting you'll need less precision and more light to your eye.

There used to be several receiver sights available, but as scopes became popular many have been dropped. Williams Gun Sight Company still offers its excellent Foolproof sight, which is good for hunting because it has nothing on the deck except the aperture. The Williams 5D is similar, but without micrometer adjustments. Both are mostly aluminum, compact, sturdy and available for many rifles.

Lyman made several receiver sights at one time but now markets only an aperture designed for muzzleloaders. I used a Lyman sight on a 94 Winchester to shoot a fine blacktail buck. The deer was running, close up, and there wasn't much time. I'd have been handicapped with a scope. The short little rifle was as ideal as the sight, and the .30-30 Win. bullet adequate.

Open rear sights aren't as useful as apertures mounted on the receiver, cocking piece or tang. Part of the reason is that there's not much distance between an open sight and the front bead. This short sight radius makes small errors critical. A receiver sight just about doubles the open-sight radius.

Another problem with an open sight is that it's far enough from your eye that you must focus on it to see it. That would be OK if you didn't have to focus on the front sight and target as well. But to align the sights with the target you must see all three clearly. Your eye can't focus on all three, and compromises by focusing on the bead, keeping rear sight and target in fuzzy perspective. Because you can forget about the rear sight when looking through an aperture close to your eye, the aperture sight makes hits easier.

A barrel-mounted open sight is supposed to be the fastest sight available. It can be, provided it's shaped right. The best configuration is a shallow V, like the one the Williams people used and called the African. I used this sight to shoot deer. It was as fast

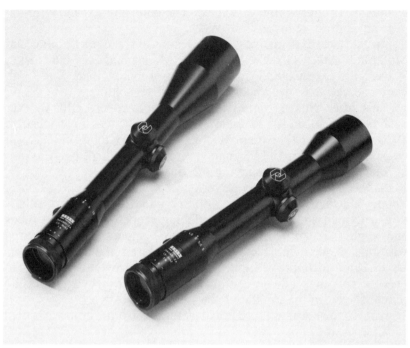

Expensive and heavy, the Zeiss Diatyl and Diavari scope have incomparable optics, and click adjustments that the author has found among the most predictable.

as it looked, and more accurate. It is faster than the traditional V or U notch. For me, it is the only open sight as fast as a receiver sight with the aperture disk out.

Buckhorn and semi-buckhorn open sights with their big ears have been ruthlessly maligned for some time. They deserve it.

Today, most hunters have scopes on their rifles. The big advantage with a scope is that it displays your target in the same plane as the cross hairs. There's no focusing problem because deer and reticle seem to be the same distance from your eye. A scope has other advantages: it gathers light so you can see better at dawn and dusk, defines detail so you can see better what you're shooting at, and magnifies your target so it appears big and the reticle does not obscure it.

Scopes date back to the Civil War, but receiver-mounted scopes for sporting rifles are of the 20th century. Though Zeiss marketed a 2x prism scope in 1904, it was some time before Rudolph Noske introduced a scope built in America. It was a 2¼x with a ⅞-inch steel tube. Eye relief was six inches! Noske eventually offered a line of scopes. The company expanded in the '30s but did not recover from World War II.

In the late '20s, as Noske was testing his scope, Belding and Mull put together a 3x scope called the Marksman. Like the Noske, it was quite expensive: $57.50 was a lot of money then. Still, both were cheaper than the imported Zeiss or Hensoldt.

Just after Noske started marketing his scopes, Bill Weaver designed one to undersell them. The 2¾x 330 was introduced in 1933. In the next five years Weaver offered six more models, all on ¾-inch tubes. In 1937 Lyman countered with its 2½x Alaskan, a ⅞-inch scope that was among the finest ever made.

After WWII several scope makers sprouted. Bausch & Lomb, Leupold, Unertl, Bushnell, Kollmorgen, Redfield and others joined Lyman and Weaver in producing scopes with bigger tubes and higher magnification. Complicated mounts with external adjustments were replaced by compact bases and rings. Lenses were coated to improve light transmission, nitrogen was added to prevent fogging, adjustment mechanisms were changed so the reticle stayed in the middle of the field.

As scopes became more popular imports from Europe and then Japan arrived to compete.

Today, a variety of scopes are made in Japan. European firms like Zeiss, Schmidt-Bender and Swarovski offer excellent scopes at high prices. Heavier and bulkier than American scopes, some have 26mm and 30mm tubes. Optically, they're superb.

Variable scopes have been around for nearly 40 years. One of the first was Weaver's KV, a scope that could be set at 2½x or 5x but nothing in between. On early variables the reticle got thicker as the power was turned up—just the opposite of what you'd think logical. Now reticles stay the same size. Before when you changed power, you'd lose your zero; groups shot with a scope set at 4x would be in a different place than those shot with a 9x setting. Then if you turned the power back to what it had been the bullets might go to another spot! Modern variables, the good ones, maintain their zeroes.

Most new scopes are variables. In a survey of elk hunters, 144 of the 205 scopes used were variables. Deer hunters prefer them too. I don't. I like low-power, fixed-power scopes for my deer hunting. I've used variables but almost always left the power ring at one setting. I can't recall ever taking the time to change magnification when I saw a deer. There were times I could have, but didn't. And that made me wonder if I needed a variable at all.

Last year on a rocky slope above timber I wished for a bigger scope. Just briefly I wanted the little deer I'd stuck the cross hairs on to look bigger. Then I squeezed the trigger and the deer fell down. The range was roughly 300 yards and the deer wasn't small and the bullet had hit where I'd wanted it to. Though my 3x Lyman wasn't ideal for such long shooting, it worked.

That little 3x, the Lyman Alaskan I carried on the same ridge two years before and the 4x Leupold I used to shoot a buck at over 400 yards all worked well. Maybe bigger scopes would have helped me place bullets more precisely, but I don't think so. At those distances wind, my wobbles and the natural deviance of shots from zero make precision hard to guarantee—even if holdover is perfect!

By sticking with small scopes I was ready for the fine mule deer buck I shot in a thicket at 18 yards. A 2½x scope helped me shoot the biggest blacktail I've hunted, and a 4x the biggest mule deer.

One nice thing about a fixed-power scope is its simplicity. There are fewer moving parts, fewer seams than in a variable. That means there's less chance of something going wrong. While variables are quite dependable, tenaciously hold their zero through power changes and don't fog, they can't, by all logic, equal the ruggedness of fixed-power scopes.

Besides being a bit more foolproof than variables, the little scopes I use are compact. They don't compromise the handling of my rifle. At the same time they're lighter than variables because they have less glass and machinery inside and a smaller objective bell. My rifle isn't top-heavy, like some I've handled. Many new rifles made light for the mountains are married to big variable scopes. That's ridiculous.

Some variables, like Leupold's compact line, are of sensible size and mate nicely to short, light rifles.

Another benefit of fixed-power scopes is that there are fewer air/glass surfaces inside to reflect and absorb light. The best variables are bright scopes. But the best fixed-power scopes can be made brighter.

My choice would be a 4x for most mountain hunting and a 3x for blacktail coverts. I've used and liked 6x scopes for deer hunting in places where the shots are almost sure to be long. Because I always carry binoculars, I never depend on my scope to tell me about size or antlers. A scope is for aiming. That's all I use it for.

There are three reasons to favor low magnification over high.

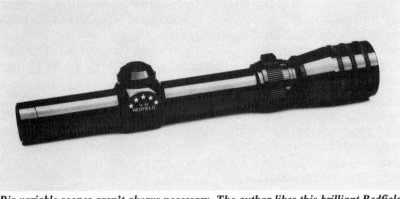

Big variable scopes aren't always necessary. The author likes this brilliant Redfield 1-4x for deer.

One is that low-power scopes are smaller and lighter than high-power scopes. Another is that low-power scopes have a larger field of view. For example, Bushnell's 1.5-4.5x Scopechief has a 74-foot field at 100 yards when set to 1.5x. At 4.5x the field is only 24 feet. A 2.5-8x Scopechief has low- and high-end fields of 45 and 14 feet, a 3-9x 39 and 13 feet, a 4-12x 29 and 10 feet. There's no standard for field of view for deer shooting. Long shots, deliberately taken, can be made with any scope. Occasionally though, you'll have to shoot close and fast, perhaps at a running deer.

Most of the time a field of 30 feet will be adequate. It will let you find the deer quickly and stay with it even if it runs—at least at distances beyond 50 yards. For close shooting bigger fields are better. Among the most useful variable scopes are those starting at 1.5x. They give you a big field for close shots and enough magnification for long ones. Bausch and Lomb's 1.5-6x would work for any kind of deer hunting.

The final advantage of low-power scopes is their brightness. While many factors affect the brightness of the image, the relationship of magnification to objective lens size is among the most important. If the objective lens is big and magnification is low your image will be bright. As magnification increases or objective size decreases the image becomes darker. There are numbers to make this clearer.

The first is the objective diameter in millimeters. Some scopes have a light baffle around the objective, so you can't very well measure it and must accept the maker's specifications. The next number is the magnification of the scope. Dividing objective diameter by magnification gives you the exit pupil. Squaring the exit pupil gives you relative brightness. Multiplying objective diameter by magnification, then getting to the square root of that number leaves you with the twilight factor.

Here's how that all works:

A 2.5x scope with a 20mm objective has an exit pupil of eight (20/2.5). Relative brightness is 64 (eight squared). The twilight factor is seven (20 x 2.5 = 50; the square root of 50 is approximately seven). You can do the same calculations with any scope or binocular.

Exit pupil is the pencil of light you see in the scope when you move your head back, farther from the scope than it would be if you were shooting. Your eye has a pupil too, one that dilates and constricts in bright and dim light. In bright sunlight your pupil will be about 2.5mm wide. In shadows, at dawn or dusk or when the sky is overcast it will dilate to about 5mm. The biggest it will ever get in the dark is 7mm. An exit pupil bigger than 7mm in the scope is useless to your eye. One bigger than 6mm is almost useless. If you can sacrifice field, it's better to have higher magnification with an exit pupil of 5mm. Your target will be easier to see in most light. That's where the twilight factor figures in.

While relative brightness values give an advantage to big objectives and low magnification, the numbers only tell you about the light that's coming in. They don't tell about what your eye can use. Because they exaggerate differences between exit pupil values, they mislead many people. Although valid for comparison, they are not always useful to hunters.

The twilight factor is useful because brightness alone does not give you good definition—brightness and magnification do. As magnification decreases, twilight factor values decrease, and your ability to see objects gets worse. That's just the opposite of the relative brightness trend. As long as the exit pupil is big enough to give your eye all the light it needs, the twilight factor will increase with magnification. As soon as exit pupil values drop below what your eye can use, the twilight factor drops back too.

A 6x scope with a 42mm objective gives you a 7mm exit pupil and all the light you can handle. Its twilight factor is about 15. An 8x scope with a 56mm objective gives you the same size exit pupil, and the same relative brightness, but a twilight factor of 21 because it magnifies your target more. Both have higher twilight factors than most scopes of less than 6x, because the exit pupils of these scopes are bigger than necessary. This doesn't mean any scope below 6x is worthless. Field of view is also important!

Compact scopes gather less light than scopes with bigger objectives. This gets bothersome only when magnification is high.

The price of scopes varies a great deal and there's not much apparent difference between a cheap one and an expensive one. But there are differences that make expensive scopes good buys.

There are three to seven different types of glass in a scope, each with a different chemical makeup and refractive index. Each lens is ground to a precise curve and polished smooth, to the point that you won't notice the bumps and flat spots. But good, expensive lenses are held to closer tolerances than cheap lenses. That's what makes them both good and expensive. One lens maker keeps his curvatures to within two light fringes, or twenty one-millionths of an inch!

Another difference is in the makeup of lenses. While most scopes have four to seven lenses, some lenses comprise two lens elements, usually glued together with clear epoxy. The types of glass comprising each lens and the quality of the bond affect light transmission through the lens. Since about 1960 new ways to make lenses and lens materials have generated lenses with sharper, more precise curves. These make possible smaller scopes of higher resolution, and bigger price tags.

When you look at, instead of through, the ocular and objective lenses, you'll notice an amber, blue or purple tint. This tint is the coating of magnesium flouride used to increase light transmission through the lens. An uncoated lens loses about four percent of incident light to reflection and absorption. If a scope has 10 lens elements it can rob you of 40 percent of the light striking the objective lens! For a long time no one knew what to do about this. Then, in 1935, Professor A. Smakula of Zeiss Works in Germany developed an anti-reflection coating. It immediately became classified information because of its value to the military.

During WWII, Germany continued to research and develop lense coating products. The Schott Glassworks in Germany developed a two-layer coating by 1939 and a three-layer coating by 1943. These were of different fluorides, each with different reflective properties.

After the war, everybody was coating lenses, mostly with magnesium flouride.

The layer of magnesium flouride on a lens is pretty thin: six one-millionths of an inch. If all air/glass surfaces in a scope are coated, as much as 90 percent of incident light can be transmitted. Coating is something that's easy to fudge on, because you can't tell by looking at the scope whether or not the internal erector lenses are coated, or the quality of the coating, if any.

Zeiss currently uses as many as seven layers on its lenses. Multiple coating is not common in the U.S., though it's proven to increase light transmission. One multi-coated 3-9x variable transmitted 97 percent of incident light in a test. An identical scope with one layer of magnesium flouride transmitted 82 percent.

Scope tubes, generally, are made of black anodized alloy. Weaver and some European makers still use blued steel. There's little difference in strength, weight or cost.

The mechanics of a rifle scope are straightforward, but precise machining and fitting are required for adjustments to move predictably. Backlash in adjustments is a measure of the fit of their parts. In variable scopes the play between the erector cells and cam tubes must be as close to zero as possible. Leupold allows a one ten-thousandths of an inch tolerance, a tight standard. Not only moving parts, but joined parts must be fitted tightly. A scope is similar to a fine watch in that it has many lightweight and delicate parts. There's no room or purchase for big screws to hold things together, but the instrument as a unit must stay tight, solid and take punishment. In the case of the scope, it has to withstand repeated explosions right underneath it. Watches aren't jerked around like that.

Besides the scope's quality, finish and mounting of the glass, there is its coating to consider. And the fit of moving parts. And the fit of stationary parts. Finally there's the willingness of the maker to scrap every scope that doesn't meet recoil and submersion tests. There are many techniques to inexpensively manufacture a scope, but most compromise performance.

That's not to say that you must pay $600 for a rifle scope—though you can. Inexpensive scopes are poor bargains. You shoot as you see, and your scope determines how well you see. Buy the best you can.

Mounting your scope is much easier now than it was when few rifles were drilled for bases and when mounts carried windage and elevation adjustments and when bolts and safeties got in the way of anything on top of the receiver. But the best mounts have been in use for some time. Today they're better, and cheaper.

Redfield's rotary dovetail idea was first used in a scope mount in 1916. It was an expensive item for many years. During the

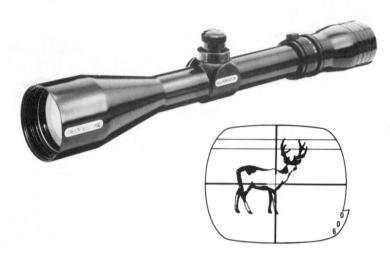

To shoot far you need good optics. Redfield obliges with its Illuminator scope with rangefinder. You can even dial your way to zero.

Depression, for instance, it sold for $25. You could buy a Model 70 Winchester then for $61. A Redfield mount today looks much like it did then, and costs about twice as much. The Model 70 costs $444.

Weaver's QD top mounts came in 1950. They're aluminum and pressed steel and work very well. They're one of the most inexpensive mounts you can buy, and one of the most functional.

Several other mounts were available in the early days of scopes. Mostly they were complex, heavy and expensive to make. Few survived the war. The excellent Bausch and Lomb scopes' without internal adjustments needed mounts with adjustments, so some of these held on into the '50s.

Now Redfield, Leupold and Burris market mounts on the old Redfield design, and they're fine mounts indeed. Leupold's latest dual dovetail mount is particularly trim, lacking the rear windage screws that aren't necessary for modern scopes. Conetrol makes a slick mount, with vertically-split rings capped so neatly at the top they don't look split at all. Beuhler's is a proven mount. Kimber, Ruger and Sako rings designed just for those rifles also work well. Williams' Streamline mounts are useful; the rings can be reversed to clear scope bells and turrets.

Leonard Brownell's detachable mounts, now marketed by

Kimber, are among several expensive models that look good on nice rifles. But today, there's little need for a mount that can be quickly taken off.

The best mount is one that puts your scope low over the bore—as low as the scope will permit. If it's high or offset you will have to crane your neck to peer into it. Your cheek won't be where it's supposed to be. You'll be slow getting on target and less apt to hit what you're shooting at. The closer the scope is to the rifle the better the rifle will feel in your hand.

Mounts that let you see the sights under the scope are bad business because they put the scope too high. The comb will put your head in the proper place for only one line of sight. If you try to look along another axis parallel with the bore you'll have to move your head. The time to decide whether to use iron sights or a scope is before you buy the scope. Iron sights are only useful on an uncluttered deck. Their single advantage is speed, and if you have to take even a fraction of a second to decide between the irons and the scope, and just a wink to find them under the scope, you'd be better off with a low-mounted scope.

If your rifle has sights screwed to the barrel it's best to take them off when you mount a scope.

Backup sights are seldom useful when hunting deer. My Winchester 70s, the old ones, have forged ramps in front, so I can't remove those sights. On the rear of some of my Redfield bases there is the provision for a folding aperture made long ago called the Little Blue Peep. I've put a couple of these on. I expect I'll never use them, but they don't interfere at all with my low scope mountings. This is the only kind of backup sight I'll tolerate.

Most of the rifles in my rack have Redfield or Leupold mounts, but there are some old Bausch and Lomb mounts too, with early Bausch and Lomb scopes. A couple of Ruger Number Ones have Ruger rings on them. A Kimber has Kimber rings. One of my favorite deer rifles, a battered .270 Win. Model 70, wears a set of very low Tilden rings holding a 3x Lyman. The Tilden hasn't been made for a long time. It was a svelte, finely machined mount.

The only item you'll need on a deer rifle besides sights is a sling. A strap won't do; you must have a shooting sling. The sling is not just so you can carry the rifle on your shoulder or hang it on a peg at the cabin. A sling can help you shoot. It can steady your rifle so much you'll not believe the difference until you try it. I've shot most of my deer from a sitting position with a tight sling.

There are several types of slings around. The most useless is the wide carrying strap. You can see these in any sporting goods store. They're usually embossed with scenes of deer or pine trees or sunsets. If you buy one of these slings, you'll like it because it distributes the weight of your rifle nicely. If it's padded it will feel extra nice.

But shoulder your gun, and try to pull your forend into a steady position with one of these slings. You'll soon find out that they're too bulky and too awkward to give an accurate hold.

Military slings with double hooks are OK. You can shoot with them and they are adjustable. But the hooks, generally brass, can gouge your rifle stock if they bang against it. A military sling is heavier than it needs to be.

Long ago Townsend Whelen recommended a sling that later came to be known by his name. There's some confusion now as to just what a Whelen sling is, because there are none marketed as such. A while back, I bought a Whelen sling. It works quite well.

My Whelen is a single strap 1¼ inches wide. It has a double claw hook on one end, which comes forward from the rear swivel and engages holes in the sling about one-third of the way to the front. Where you put the hook determines the overall length of the sling. The front of the sling has no hook. There's one leather keeper that slides on the front part of the sling to size the loop. Though this sling is a good one, it's not perfect because there's still a claw to ding your stock.

The only shooting sling without a claw is the Latigo offered by Brownell's. It's the sling to buy. The only hardware on the Latigo is a brass loop and a two-piece brass button. Both are kept from contact with the stock when the sling is put together. One leather keeper runs forward of the button, which determines both sling length and loop placement. My Latigo slings are an inch wide, as I prefer. They're narrow enough to be light and quick into action, and wide enough to make shooting and carrying the rifle easy.

7

Life Outside

In the ad he'd read that nothing was needed except a sleeping bag and personal items. That meant he'd bring clothes, binoculars, rifle and ammunition, a little bag of toilet articles, matches and a flashlight. The rest was to be provided. When he got to camp, it was. He was miserable.

Things can make us neither happy nor unhappy. Without certain things we may be uncomfortable, without others imperiled. But nothing has in it contentment. Happiness is an attitude.

Bringing more than you need or can manage on a hunt will impair your ability to hunt. How much you should bring depends on your camp. To an outfitted camp you needn't bring much. If you bring more because you are provided a horse and a big tent you are acting the dude. Hunters bring what they need. Dudes bring what they think they might want.

If you pack in yourself, or make day hunts from trailhead, the weight of your pack becomes crucial. But you needn't sacrifice comfort or safety. Just be sure everything you carry has a purpose vital to the hunt or your survival. Certainly you can be as happy as the fellow with panniers full of fluff!

The Outfitted Trip

Choosing an outfitter is more important than deciding what to take on an outfitted hunt. That's the first thing you do, and you must do it well in advance. A year is good lead time. If the outfitter is competent he'll be popular. If he's popular he'll be fully booked each year, mostly with returning hunters he talks to during hunting season. So this year, before hunting season, is the time to sift information on outfitters, contact references and narrow your choices to three or four camps for a hunt next year. That way you can talk with outfitters before hunters this year confirm plans for next.

The state you want to hunt likely has an outfitter organization. Contact the state game agency for the address and phone number of this organization or its president. Then write or call for a list of members. You might briefly tell what you're looking for in a hunt and ask the secretary to indicate on the list which outfitters best provide that. If you've already gathered a batch of outfitter names from the "Hunter's Connection" in *North American Hunter*, check to see that they are members of the state group. They should be, or should be able to give you a good reason why they're not.

Next, send for your free *NAHC Approved Outfitter & Guides Booklet*. This is a state-by-state listing of outfitters and guides that fellow NAHC members have used and recommend to other NAHC members. Write: NAHC Approved Outfitters and Guides Booklet, 12301 Whitewater Drive, P.O. Box 3401, Minnetonka, MN 55343.

Then, send postcards requesting literature to NAHC approved outfitters you think offer the kind of hunt you want, in the area you want. You ought to consider at least a dozen. Forget any who don't respond.

The quality of a brochure sometimes reflects the quality of the outfitter. Good outfitters like to be thought of as professionals. But it's best to take the outfitter's brochure as you would an introduction to someone by his friend you don't know. Read it. Make notes of questions to ask. Then forget it. Your choice of an outfitter should hinge on your talks and written correspondence with him and his former clients.

The first step is to write the outfitter, listing the questions you have by number and keeping a copy for yourself. That way the outfitter, who is probably busy, can answer each question quickly. He'll appreciate your business-like approach. In this letter introduce yourself. Be succinct but thorough and polite. Tell what you want from a hunt, when you prefer to hunt and when you could hunt. Tell him how old you are, your height and weight and physical health. He needs to know about you, just as you must know about him and his operation. While details can wait, things like a horse allergy or your vegetarian diet are important to mention. If you're a woman with a name like Terry make sure he knows you're a woman. If you're a bowhunter wanting a hunt during rifle season make sure he knows that too.

Some hunters look at outfitters like they might a carton of cabbages in the produce section of a supermarket, fingering this one and that until they find one that might work in their slaw. While few outfitters have the luxury of choosing their clients like that, all would relish the prerogative.

After the money is paid the relationship of client to outfitter is curious, unique. It is a business bond. It is a comradeship. It is tight, controlled by the agreement and the isolation of camp in the woods. But it is loose, too, because the outfitter is to provide not only game but congeniality and a good time for the client who expects one. The chemistry between outfitter and client must be right if the hunt is to be a good one. The way his business works, though, the outfitter has little to say about what kind of hunter he gets. That's a paradox, because the outfitter knows what is to come. Most hunters have little idea what a pack trip entails, what human relationships mean when people are corralled together in camp. Still, hunters decide.

Among your questions in that first letter is a request for references. Ask for references who are NAHC members. If the outfitter has none or hedges on supplying them, whether NAHC members or not, go elsewhere. If he gives you a list, call at least three people—in different parts of the country. Let them know your situation, that you are an NAHC member. Ask them to be candid, try to find out what they didn't like about the hunt or the outfitter. Remember that the outfitter would probably not have given you these names if he didn't think he'd get favorable treatment. If after talking with these people you think they've been honest with you and all have recommended the outfitter, follow up with a call to the outfitter to see what kind of a fellow he is to chat with.

Some outfitters don't service their clients directly. They may have several camps, with guides, wranglers and a cook in each. If that's the case ask for the phone number of the guide you will hunt with. The outfitter may stall here, and with reason. It's hard to assign guides one year in advance. He won't know the make-up of his camps for months, and many western guides are seasonal; the crew might change year to year. If you can't get a commitment it's still good to speak with one guide. He may tell you things other hunters can't and the outfitter won't.

By this time you'll have spent some time on the phone and will have eliminated some outfitters. Only three or four should still be on your list. Now is the time to write these people with specific questions, questions like:

1) If I booked with you in the next two weeks can you guarantee me a hunt October 4 through 11 next year?

2) What is the total cost of the hunt and what is the deposit?

3) In what drainage will the camp be?

4) How many miles will we ride to get there?

5) How many hunting days are there, excluding days in and out?

6) How many other hunters will be in camp?

7) Do you have other camps? Where?

8) Must I share a guide with someone else?

9) Will horses be available in camp for hunting?

10) May I hunt alone if I choose? On horseback?

11) Do you provide hunting scabbards?

12) What do you recommend I take for clothes?

13) What arrangements have you made to pack meat out and preserve it in warm weather?

14) What is your policy should I be forced to cancel my trip?

15) What is your policy should game regulations change and a deer tag be unavailable to me next year?

There are other things you might want to ask. And at this point it's a good idea to tell your outfitter anything he might want to know about you. Be very candid with your physical condition. Completely cover all medicines and other special needs. One hunter didn't and almost died in a camp that couldn't provide the prescription heart drug he'd forgotten to bring.

Most outfitters are proud of the food they serve on hunts, and you'll probably be delighted with the menu. I've been treated to fresh pies and puddings, roast turkey and baked ham, pastries and salads and vegetables of all sorts. Fine steak is standard. But if you have specific wants tell them about it well in advance. Outfitters buy groceries in bulk. They don't have time during the season to make unscheduled trips to town for food. Besides, small western towns may not have what you want in stock anyway. Nobody is going to saddle Nell in the dark to ride for lox; to be sure of having Turkish mustard, bring it yourself.

It's good to let the outfitter know what you want for a deer too.

At least one year in advance, sift through information on outfitters and guides, contact their references and narrow your choices to three or four camps. That way, you can talk with outfitters before hunters this year confirm plans for next year.

Score doesn't matter to me, though I usually hold out for an old buck. If you want to specify score or antler width, do it in the early stages. One outfitter was approached by a fellow who wanted a 30-inch buck. The outfitter patiently explained that mule deer in his area didn't have wide antlers, but there were some huge bucks with thick, high racks. The prospective client hung up the phone. From one point of view his was a silly demand—lots of antlers that measure 30 inches are pretty shallow and skinny. But the outfitter was spared the headache of a client who likely was unreasonable in other ways. At least the caller was clear and direct in telling what he wanted.

If you are serious about killing a very big deer tell the outfitter that. If he promises a big deer, especially one that meets record-book minimums, take your business elsewhere. No legitimate outfitter can guarantee that. What you want is an outfitter who tells you that your chances of finding a mature buck in his area are excellent if you work hard, but that you'll not find a record deer unless you're very lucky. In Colorado, the state with the most deer in the record books, the odds that you will take a deer that will make the books are 12,905 to 1. Part of the job of locating big deer is yours. Before you contact outfitters you should know which areas yield big bucks. If your standards are high you must do more homework, expect a harder hunt no matter whom you go with.

After you commit to an outfitter stay in touch with him. He'll appreciate your interest and you'll stay apprised of your investment. You can and should get to know each other well. As soon as you find out who will guide you it is a good idea to introduce yourself by mail. Just before the hunt ask the outfitter if there's anything he'd like that you can bring from your part of the country. Doing him this favor costs little and is both thoughtful and good business.

The equipment you bring to an outfitted camp depends on the outfitter, the country and the season of the hunt. Here is my standard list of items for a backcountry hunt in the Rockies:

1) Scoped rifle with sling in hooded leather scabbard.

2) Twenty rounds of ammunition, 8-round leather cartridge pouch.

3) Binoculars.

4) Two folding knives with 3-inch blades.

5) Fanny pack with survival kit: matches, firestarting tablets, two flashlights, compass, watch, disinfectant and bandages.

6) USFS and USGS maps of the area.

7) Plastic canteen.

8) Gun and lens cleaning supplies: bore cable or Hoppe's short-section rod, brush, solvent, patches, lens fluid and tissue.

9) One pair cotton trousers, two pair light wool trousers, two heavy leather belts.

10) Two flannel shirts, two wool shirts.

11) Two turtleneck pullovers.

12) A change of underwear and cotton and wool socks for each day.

13) Gaitors.

14) Filson wool jacket.

15) Light rain parka.

16) One pair insulated high-top leather boots, one pair uninsulated boots, one pair camp moccasins.

17) Two wool watchcaps.

18) Down sleeping bag with hip-length ensolite pad.

19) Two cameras with 55mm macro, 28mm lenses, 10 36-exposure rolls of Plus-X black and white and Kodachrome 64 color film, aluminum tripod.

20) Billfold with money, hunting licenses and tags.

All but the rifle and scabbard can go in one bag. I use a military surplus duffle bag. It rides easily on a horse, can be roped to the side of a pack horse, or simply thrown on top between two light pack boxes. Once in a while I'll include a packframe so I can camp away from base camp or carry a deer out from where a horse can't go. The frame can be lashed anywhere. If I want to take photos I'll include more film, 300mm and 80-200mm zoom lenses. All the camera gear except the tripod then goes in a plastic Pelican case that's packed separate from the duffle.

A word about camera gear: you don't need as much as I take, but you'll do well to take more than you think you need. One camera is enough, and if you must have only one lens a 28-60 or 35-70 zoom will work. The macro or close-focusing feature is useful. Don't spare film. It's pretty cheap and the photo opportunities are expensive. Take shots of the country, the people, the stock, camp activities, funny things, moody things and things that strike you as odd. Certainly you'll take photos of your deer; take lots of them. Use the tripod and self-timer instead of depending on another person. Good photography takes time, and you may find your guide getting impatient as you load your third roll of film. Forget about your guide. The moments after the kill are part of the trip you paid for. Use them to experiment with different angles and exposures. The pressure of the hunt is off. Get some smashing photos!

It's a good idea to let your outfitter know of your interest in photos before you go. He can suggest subjects you might not think of, direct you to places you don't know about.

When you get to the trailhead or the outfitter's lodge or wherever you have agreed to start the hunt, have your gear ready to go on the horse. The outfitter will appreciate it and respect you as a hunter.

You can also make a good impression by offering to help do things. You are the client and don't have to work. But if you are cheerful and willing, you will be the kind of client the outfitter will try hardest to please.

There's a limit to how helpful you can be, though; once you offer to help let the workers decide what you can do. Maybe it will be throwing hay to the horses or holding a lead rope. It's best to leave currying and saddling to the wranglers. They know which horse each saddle fits, which to pack and which to ride, which kicks or bites.

Mules are more intelligent than horses, surely more thoughtful. They will quickly spot you as a dude. Leave mules alone unless someone asks you to help with them. While horses like a scratch between the ears from time to time mules don't like anyone fooling with their ears. There are other differences. Outfitters use mules because they are strong and sure-footed in the mountains, not because they behave sweetly around clients.

After you're assigned a horse, ask about it so you can know it. Be firm but gentle with it. You can always get stern if you must, but starting out that way makes a bad impression on the horse and the people who are to be your companions. An outfitter can tell a lot about a hunter by the way he handles a horse. Ignorance is not a problem. Bravado and brutality are.

You'll probably be assigned a saddle. If you have a choice make use of it. Stay away from deep, short saddle seats or those with a lot of dust on them. If they've not been ridden there's probably a reason. Picking a saddle is a pretty straightforward thing. Look for one that's well padded, with a seat dish roughly the size of your bottom. Be sure the stirrup adjustments work, because you'll use them. Ask a wrangler which he'd choose if given the selection you have.

Pay attention to the way your horse is saddled. Saddling is not your job, but someday you may want to do it or have to do it. Adjust your stirrups yourself. It's easy. The wranglers will appreciate you for this because they'll be able to do something else. Standing straight-legged in the stirrups you should have a couple inches of space between your crotch and the saddle.

There are many ways to attach a scabbard to a saddle but most of them are wrong. The only way I'll hang my rifle is on the left side, scope up, with the butt to the rear and angled up about 20 degrees from horizontal. The front part of the scabbard rests against the horse, stirrup outside. The natural bend of your leg at the knee will accommodate the bulge of the barrel.

This carry has several good things about it. It protects the rifle completely; nothing is sticking up or out. If your horse runs away your rifle will probably still be snug and undamaged when you catch up. There's no binding of the scope either, no pressure on it at all. A horizontal carry prevents debris from falling into the open scabbard and one on the left side makes the rifle easy to reach as you dismount. If your horse bolts all you have to do is grab the stock and let the horse run with the scabbard.

Strangely, few outfitters rig their scabbards this way. A lot of rifles ride vertically in front of the right leg. This is a poor carry, even for an iron-sighted carbine, because the stock sticks up where it can catch brush when your horse runs away without you. Without a hood—few scabbards supplied by outfitters have hoods—the vertical scabbard funnels rain, snow, leaves, twigs and dust into the scope and action of your rifle. This arrangement transfers weight to the objective bell of your scope too. In thick timber you may find the vertical carry annoying because the rifle stock gets in the way when you bend low to avoid tree limbs.

A horizontal carry on the right side is OK. But it doesn't allow you to quickly grab your rifle as you dismount. Right side carries are popular with some hunters because the weight of the rifle counters the tug of mounting and dismounting. This advantage hardly equals that of quicker access to your rifle, though. You can always load your right saddle bag as a counterweight.

A rifle hung butt-forward is also slower to reach than one hung with its butt to the rear. If your horse is hard to handle you may not get your rifle out at all. Because a horse dips its rump as it lunges away from you, a rifle pointed forward comes out of the scabbard pretty easily. With the stock to the front, you must lift higher because the horse naturally keeps its shoulders up as it backs away from you.

Hanging the rifle upside down is foolish because then you're putting a lot of strain on the scope. The rifle bounces up and down on the rims of the objective and ocular bells, springing the scope tube.

My scabbard was built to my specifications by a saddlemaker. It is heavy, unlined leather with a hood that buckles down with straps on both sides. I keep the hood on most of the time. Less its hood, the scabbard covers all but the grip and buttstock of the rifle. Its bottom is open so it can drain. I designed it to fit snugly a Winchester Model 70 with a 26-inch barrel. It works for shorter-barreled 70s and other bolt rifles as well. I bring it whenever I pack in or hunt with horses because I want the best protection for my rifle all the time.

Your scabbard and saddle may need adjusting a short time down the trail. That's OK. Your packs will also have to be shifted and tightened. Loading a mule is different than tossing things in the back of a pickup.

On the trail keep your horse at an even walk, the same pace as the horse in front. Stay on the trail. Horses like to wander through meadows and take shortcuts on switchbacks. A lot of horse traffic like this scars the land, ruining vegetation and cutting ruts. Let your horse drink at stream crossings, but keep it from muscling in beside other horses. This can lead to tangled lead lines, jostled packs, a kick, a bite and finally what is known as a wreck. Wrecks make more work for everybody, a late supper at camp and surly wranglers.

There's not much more to do your first day on the hunt. What there is your outfitter will tell you. The rest of the trip you can offer to split wood, get water, start fires, fuel lanterns and feed horses. That's not what you paid to do, but the hunt will be more enjoyable if you take an active role in camp. Being helpful and considerate is a different image than most people have of hunters. Sadly, it's different than what most outfitters think of hunters. Break the mold.

If something in camp becomes a problem for you let the outfitter know right away. You haven't the time to let things correct themselves. His responsibility is to satisfy you; he can do that only if you keep in close touch with him.

Whether you kill or don't kill on a guided trip depends on the weather and luck—things you can't control. It also depends on how hard you hunt and how much the outfitter or guide is committed to getting you a shot. Presumably you've chosen a good outfitter and are serious about hunting, so there's nothing to prevent you from killing except the things you can't prevent. If the weather turns sour or someone has an accident or the horses get loose and run away, smile. Dour hunters spoil a camp. While your objective is to kill a deer, the reason you're on the trip is to have a good hunt. You will if you decide to.

Outfitters work under pressure at camp. It's like running a resort but much harder because of the primitive conditions. You'll make his job easier and camp more pleasant for everybody just by being cheery.

Remember that your outfitter wants you to kill a deer. If you're happy, he's happy. You may be happy not killing a deer and that's OK. But the outfitter feels better when he packs meat out. It's a measure of his professionalism and skill. He also appreciates a kind word now and then, especially if he's trying very hard and has been unable to show you the buck you want. It's a measure of your maturity as a person, your stature as a hunter when you thank him for the extra effort and acknowledge with a grin the bad luck you've both been having.

Short Notes On Short Hunts

Black-tailed and mule deer are pretty easy to hunt without an outfitter in some areas. You can find the deer close to roads, close to places where you can shower and get your food at a table. You can hunt them after work or on a Saturday if you live close by. If you don't, you can stay in a comfortable motel and hunt them daily from road's end until you tire of the sport.

You can hunt elk like this too, but elk are bigger than deer and after you shoot one you must find a way to get it out of the woods. You can carry a deer, boned, in one ambitious trip. An elk takes four. The last three aren't fun.

If you hunt by yourself close to roads you need only your rifle, a magazine full of cartridges, binoculars, canteen, proper clothes for the weather, your fanny pack with its survival kit and a lunch. Lunch for me is usually a couple of bagels, a chunk of cheese, several boxes of raisins, two granola bars and an apple or orange. I don't eat this as a lunch but nibble on it throughout the day, stopping to eat the bagels at 10:00 a.m. and 2:00 p.m. That way I stay nourished but am never full. I don't like bagels as well as homemade biscuits, cornbread or bran muffins. But the bagels hold together like tough little tires in my pack.

Day trips like this are fun because you can concentrate on

You don't need to carry a backpack on day trips, but be sure to carry a fanny pack for snacks, water and survival gear.

hunting instead of camping. You sleep well at night and eat good food that somebody else fixed. The only problem with day trips is that you have to walk past areas where other people have hunted to get to country where big bucks haven't been disturbed. You have to do that every morning and return every evening. The hikes get boring.

One way to counter boredom is to hunt areas that have no backcountry but still have deer, areas where the deer are smart enough to grow old in spite of hunting pressure. In these places you needn't make the long hikes because the deer are just a short distance from where you start in the morning. They are there because they don't have anywhere else to go; but they are also there because they were too smart for the hunters who came before you.

Deer that live nearby are popular deer with hunters who like short hunts and hunts that don't require much of them physically. There are a lot of these hunters around and you might think the pressure would be too great for good hunting. It is too great if you want some solitude and a chance to find your deer undisturbed. But if you just want to shoot a deer, you can do that in some pretty frightful crowds.

I recall a morning I encouraged my partner to rise early and go with me to a little place just out of town to shoot a buck. We knew this place had been hammered by hunters the past week, opening week. But my friend taught school and had to be in class by 8:30, so we couldn't go to most of the places we thought would be better.

Working slowly parallel through some pretty open woods, we moved uphill against the thermal drag. The sun would come up behind us. It was cold and not yet very light. In the shadows I saw movement. It was a long time before I was sure it was a deer, and then I couldn't see antlers. The deer slipped away.

A few minutes later I heard Vern shoot. At 8:20 he was in school and I was caping his fine four-point buck.

One opening day while I was hiking ridges up where the snow stayed, a farmer shot a crackerjack mule deer with non-typical antlers in his garden.

This is not to say shooting deer is hunting deer. It isn't. But mule deer are often killed in places they've been pressured. It's a good idea to hunt these places if your time is limited. Don't give up because someone said they hunted a covert, even if you know they did a pretty good job. When you can't hunt wilderness the close places are better than staying home. Often they're more productive than remote deer country.

Unless you just sit at clearing's edge waiting for a deer to come out, hunting mature bucks that live close to settlements is as hard, or harder, than hunting them in a wilderness. It is easier physically, but the deer are uncannily adept at avoiding hunters. They've learned under intense pressures how to survive the hunt. Those that don't learn are quickly shot. Hunting the easy places, you're hunting the hard bucks. In everything you must be more careful than when you're in wild country. The deer will probably be comfortable in timber and reluctant to leave it. They'll forage almost exclusively at night, and be aware of what's going on around them. They won't be caught not expecting people to be around because people are around all the time. Don't look for tame deer. The hunters before you shot them.

When I hunt close country early I like to do it in running shoes. They're quieter than boots, and comfortable in most places. Otherwise I wear the same things I wear on a hunt far from roads: wool except in very hot weather, soft, loose cotton slacks or shorts and a cotton shirt when it's warm.

Even when you plan a short hunt, carry a canteen. I drink a lot of water even when I don't feel like it. In cold weather especially, or when the going is easy, you don't get thirsty. But then you need water just as much as when you climb a steep hill on a hot day. Close to settlements, I'm careful about drinking from creeks. I do it all the time up high and have never been sick. The parasite Giardia is more and more a problem though. I fill my canteen in town or from springs at their source.

Maps help you just as much when you hunt close by as they do in remote country. Besides USFS and USGS maps you might find useful a county map or one produced commercially by Pittmon or Metsger. They show less topographic detail but more roads than government maps. Carry a compass and tell someone where you're going. Common sense is appropriate no matter where you hunt.

Binoculars are too. Some hunters carry them only on long hunts or in open country. This is foolish. If by using binoculars you spot a buck that you would not have seen otherwise, what does it matter how long the hunt is?

Binoculars are very important, in thick cover. Peering into a tangle of branches with binoculars can bring you details you'd miss with your eye alone. Maybe you'll see the tip of an antler or the glint on a buck's nose, those little things that are so easy to

Drink plenty of water when hunting, even if you're not thirsty. A canteen will let you continue hunting rather than searching for a stream.

overlook and walk past. Big bucks get bigger watching hunters walk past.

There are a variety of fine binoculars available. As with scopes, they have coated lenses. The barrels are carefully collimated, or aligned so they're parallel, to prevent eyestrain. Both porro-prism and roof-prism glasses are right for hunting deer. Roof-prism models are more compact but weigh no less.

You can get binoculars with center-focus or individual-focus adjustments. Center-focus glasses have a focusing wheel between the barrels that moves them both at once. Only one of the barrels then is adjustable by itself. To focus this kind, pick an object to view. Cover the front of the adjustable barrel (usually the right hand one), and look through the other barrel as you normally would with your left eye. Use the center wheel to focus. Now cover the left barrel, look into the right barrel and adjust only that barrel's focus. Now both barrels are set for your eyes at the distance you selected. To change focus for different distances turn the center wheel only. Both barrels will move, retaining the relationship you set when you first adjusted them.

Binoculars with individual adjustments have no center wheel and each barrel moves independently. These are not as quick to adjust in the field but are a bit simpler. Leupold's new binoculars have click detents in their individual adjustments, so it's easy to move them right away to where you need them.

Pocket or compact binoculars are popular, but I prefer bigger ones. An exit pupil of four is as small as you'll want for deer at dawn and dusk, five is better. In darkness your eye can use a 7mm exit pupil, but binoculars with objectives that will give you such light-gathering power are too bulky for hunting. The best binoculars for deer hunting range in power from seven to 10, with eight a fine choice. Objectives of 30 to 42mm will work, depending on the power. An 8x40 glass has an exit pupil of five.

To protect them from bumps, more and more binoculars are being offered with rubber "armor." This is a good idea because it protects your rifle and scope as well as the glasses. Often during a stalk my binoculars swing into my rifle—though the glasses are on a shortened strap. There's a noise problem when that happens, and the rubber dampens the noise.

The only problem with rubber is that it's heavy and makes the binoculars heavier by about four ounces—bulkier too. I've cushioned my 7x35 Bausch & Lombs with a strip of deerskin taped around each objective lens housing. It weighs almost nothing and

Compact binoculars are handier, but bring less light to your eye. These Leupold 7x20s are among the brightest of compacts. Click-adjust focusing makes them easy to use.

pads the part of the barrel most likely to bang into something.

Binoculars with good lenses are expensive. But money spent for good binoculars is well invested. Nothing save your rifle is more important to carry afield for deer. Inexpensive glasses will tire your eyes, discourage you from using binoculars as often as you should. Bright optics quite literally give you a new world to explore as you hunt. They find things for you, identify them. They tell you whether the buck is there, whether he's as big as you want to stalk. They can help you pick your route to the buck, spot other deer that might see you, judge yardage. Binoculars make your strongest sense even stronger.

When hunting, keep your binoculars tied short around your neck so they don't swing but can be raised comfortably and with little hand movement to your eyes. Keep your fingers off the lenses; use only lens tissue or a soft clean cloth to wipe them. Take care not to breathe on them in the cold because they will fog. Carry your binoculars outside your coat except when you must protect them from dust or moisture. Body heat and sweat will cloud the lenses, and the friction of your clothes may turn the focus wheels.

Far From The Roads

Hunting deer on your own needn't mean just short trips to places where other hunters swarm. You can get far away, and enjoy it even more than you might a pack trip with horses and a plush camp. Going solo into remote places is an effective way to

Top-quality binoculars like these Leupolds help you hunt. Once you use them, you'll feel naked without them.

hunt, but you need special gear and a special attitude.

Packing a camp in with your own stock is fun. It lets you take things you wouldn't carry on your back and makes the trip in and out easier. Horses limit you, though. You have to think of what they need instead of what you're doing. Hunting effectively is a selfish job; if you have to consider much more than yourself and your quarry you won't hunt well. Camping where you can set a hitch line, giving grain and water to your horses, hobbling them, catching them, doctoring them, seeing to it that they don't damage the meadow, all of these worries you're better off without. Sometimes and in some places you'll need horses. When and where you don't it's best to go on foot, carrying camp on your back.

When you hike to remote places you need the same clothes you would for an outfitted hunt in the backcountry. You have weight limits, though, and can't take as much. I usually carry a light pair of wool trousers, wool shirt, turtleneck pullover, a change of underwear and socks for each day, a pair of wool gloves, my Filson jacket and a wool watchcap. What I wear on the trail depends on the weather. Sometimes it's shorts and a T-shirt, other times light wool trousers and a wool shirt. I wear the sturdy Vibram-lug leather boots I'll hunt in because extra shoes are too heavy to carry. I sometimes pack a light rain poncho.

Wool is heavier than many synthetic fabrics, but I wear wool when I hunt because it insulates well when wet, is quiet, durable and not bulky for its warmth. Weight is important when you backpack, but utility is even more so. You may have to wear the same clothes a couple of days in a row during a storm. Maybe you won't be able to start a fire. You need good clothes. As for changing underwear each day, it's hardly a luxury if you want to get close to deer. Staying clean, if it means packing extra briefs or breaking creek ice to take a bath, helps keep your own body scent from ruining your hunt.

While jogging shoes are comfortable to stroll in, they give little ankle support. Your feet tire quickly in light shoes under a heavy pack. Boots protect as well as support your feet and ankles, cushioning bumps against rocks and deflecting branches. For packing and hunting in remote country boots are best.

I've worn several kinds of boots by several makers and prefer a simple uninsulated leather boot for most deer hunting. I like 8-inch tops, a smooth one-piece toe, a 1½-inch heel. Vibram lug soles, stitched to the uppers outside and inside, are best. Floppy speed-lace eyelets are better than hooks. If the weather is cold or there's lots of snow I like this same kind of boot, but insulated. In warm weather low-top hiking boots, built like my 8-inch boots, work fine. I frequently wear them with shorts. The only thing I don't like about them is that trail dust and plant seeds glom onto my socks and work their way down. In the high country that's no problem; in sagebrush it is. Better there to wear light cotton trousers over high-top boots.

I don't care for synthetic windows in boot uppers. They collect dust and snow and then don't breath as well as the leather. Synthetic braided laces, though, last longer than leather laces.

Glue will not hold shoe parts together under hard use. If it is not sewn it will eventually come apart. Boots that don't cost very much aren't worth very much. The best boots cost more than $150; that's cheap for the only transportation you have in the backcountry.

I dress lightly when packing in on a trail, even if it's cool. A hike uphill under a loaded pack warms you quickly. Put your canteen where it's easy to reach, and carry snacks in your pockets. Drink and eat often. It's better to take a slower, steady pace than to move quickly and stop a lot to rest. There's a rhythm to your walk. Find it, swing with it and let your body move naturally.

*The author prefers raisins, bagels, apples, granola bars and cheese for lunch.
Packets of oatmeal and soup make for quick hot food in the morning and evening.*

Your camp is a sleeping bag, a tent and a little stove. While there are a variety of sleeping bag fills available, goose down is still my choice. It's lighter than any other fill and packs tighter. The only problem with down is that it is useless wet. To keep mine dry on the trail I wrap it in the thin hip-length ensolite pad I sleep on and strap it under my pack. As soon as I make camp I pull the bag from its stuff-sack and bat it around so the down lofts and any moisture can escape. I do the same thing each morning, leaving the bag open to release body moisture.

Down was meant to insulate by itself. Don't try to help it by putting things on top of your bag. Once on a snowshoe trip my partner and I spread a reflective survival blanket over our bags at night, just to hold in a little more heat. What the blanket held in was moisture, soaking our bags and making them all but useless. We had four days left on the trail.

The best bags have outer shells of rip-stop nylon and are stitched so the down is trapped evenly in little compartments. These compartments overlap so that no seam runs the depth of the fill. That way there are no cold spots. Be sure your bag is put together like this. Get a size longer than you think you'll need and be sure it has a hood. Either a mummy or semi-mummy shape will work. Rectangular bags are bigger than you'll want. To be comfortable in the cold they must have more fill than a bag contoured to your body. That means extra weight, bulk and expense.

The cost of a bag depends on the shell construction and fill material. My extra-long bag has 3½ pounds of goose down and I've slept, if not comfortably, at 26 below zero Fahrenheit. It's much better to get a bag that's a bit too warm than one not warm enough. There's a bit to consider when selecting a sleeping bag but it's pretty easy to understand. After you've looked at a few you'll find all but the most expensive unsuitable for deer hunting. You'll not regret buying a good sleeping bag. A cheap one will remind you it's cheap, hunt after hunt.

In some deer country, during some seasons, you may not need a tent. I've slept without one and enjoyed it. Still, a tent gives you confidence that if the weather changes you can keep hunting. If you hunt the northern Rockies or other high places in fall a tent is part of your survival gear. Weather changes very fast, to extremes.

Two years ago a freak September storm buried the basin I usually hunt the first week in October. I went up anyway, struggling through thigh-deep snow. The deer had left.

Last season I hiked into the same basin on the same date in shorts.

The canvas pup tent used to be standard for a one-man camp in the wilderness. It's been supplanted by better tents. They weigh less, breathe better, are stronger and more stable and pack tighter. The smallest is the cocoon-type shelter. It's offered by several makers under different names. It's a good tent for bicycle camping in summer but doesn't work well on a deer hunt. There's no room in it for your pack or rifle, and if you have to spend some time in it during a storm you'll find it confining. A two-man tent is better when you're going alone. For yourself and a partner choose a three-man tent.

Most backpack tents are shaped like domes or like pup tents. There are other designs, as good but none better. All backpack tents that I know about are stable enough for hunting and roomy enough, provided you consider your gear as one man. It's a good idea to look at a tent set up before you buy it. Dimensions don't tell you enough about how a tent will feel from the inside.

More important than shape are construction and materials. Nylon taffeta is commonly used for tent walls, roof and fly and, in a heavier weight, for the floor. It's good. Better is ripstop nylon. A urethane coating makes both repel water. Some tents have a coated fly and an uncoated roof for better air circulation. Don't buy any tent without a fly.

Seams on good tents rarely give way under normal use. All seams should be brushed with a sealer to waterproof them. Fine mesh or no-see-um netting, at the doors and windows is standard. The best zippers are heavy nylon. They're less affected by cold than metal zippers. Poles on inexpensive tents are metal-tipped fiberglass; on the best tents poles are of expensive aluminum alloy. The aluminum lasts longer. Most poles now are shock-corded together for quick setup.

If the tent comes with pegs they're usually skinny metal ones that work pretty well in solid ground but aren't much good where the soil is loose. I have a set of thick plastic pegs. They cost and weigh little, but their I-beam design works in all soils and in packed snow.

Put your tent in a wind-sheltered spot but not right under a tree, on level ground but not in a bowl or floodplain, far enough from where you intend to hunt that you won't move the deer out but close enough that your hikes at dawn and dusk will be short. Remove sharp objects from the tent site so they don't puncture the floor. Don't ditch dig around your tent. It does little good, and leaves an ugly scar. Make sure poles are fit snug, pegs are tight and tent surfaces free of wrinkles. Stow tent and sleeping bag stuff sacks where you can find them easily. Always put up the rain fly.

A two-man tent should weigh less than your rifle. Six to eight pounds is about right. It's hard to get a tent that will work in severe weather much lighter than this. Three-season tents, for spring, summer and fall, are lighter, but the weather in mule deer country in fall is often winter-tough.

When I'm going alone on a short hunt and expect the weather to stay nice I take a tube tent of sorts. It's not the disposable plastic kind most people think of as a tube tent but it sets up the same way: with a rope lengthwise through the top as ridgeline and pegs at the corners to tighten the sides. At only three pounds it's lighter than a real tent but has a little more room than a cocoon-type shelter. It loses its shape in the wind because there are no poles, only pegs stretching nylon against a rope that also stretches, and that's tied to trees that sway. The biggest problem with this little tent is that you need trees and soil to make it work. The high country I like to hunt has few trees, and I don't recall ever finding two that were the right distance apart with level ground between them. Where there are trees that will work the ground is steep or rocky; often I have to weight the corners with rocks instead of using pegs. That wears the fabric and makes the tent smaller inside.

But I still carry this tent because it's so light. Everything you take on your back must be as light as you can make it. Your rifle, tent, sleeping bag and camera will be your heaviest items. A stove weighs about one pound—the same as your binoculars. Butane stoves weigh about the same as white gas stoves, are quicker and easier to use and don't make you smell like fuel. They're a bit bulkier though, and you can't tell how much butane is left, so you must either start with a full cylinder (wasting fuel) or carry a spare—an extra 10 ounces that you'd probably rather take as food. Below freezing, butane doesn't work as well as white gas.

You need little in the way of utensils afield. I make do with one aluminum pot with a bail. In it I cook my standard hot dishes of oatmeal, soup and macaroni and cheese. I eat with a plastic spoon.

My diet during backcountry hunts is simple. I cook little packets of oatmeal in the morning. During the day I eat bagels, cheese and raisins—the same stuff I carry on day trips but without the fresh fruit. At night variety means a different soup flavor.

When hunting in deep snow and cold temperatures, bring a four-season tent, snowshoes and a collapsible saw.

Many hunters eat tastier food than I do. You can. My provisions stand up well in all sorts of weather, are easy to fix, clean to eat and keep me in good health. I avoid canned things not only because they're heavy but because they leave me with a can that I don't want to pack out or leave as litter. Most canned goods are smelly too. I like sardines and they're good for you, but you won't do well stalking the woods smelling like a fish.

I usually drink just water on a hunt.

My fanny pack and its little survival kit go on every hunt. Some people like rucksacks or, as they're called now, daypacks. I don't like them because the shoulder straps get in the way when I want to shoot. Rucksacks carry more than I want to take when I'm hunting, so they aren't very efficient for me. Another thing I don't like about rucksacks is that they make me just a bit top-heavy. That's of little importance most places, but I've been on some ledges where I wished the weight hanging from my shoulders was on my belt. And when I run, I run much more easily with the day's provisions on my waist. I use rucksacks when taking pictures in the summer because they hold more camera gear than a fanny pack. But a fanny pack is better on the hunt.

To carry your clothes and camping equipment up a mountain, across a desert or into the woods you need a pack. Most people call anything you strap on to carry something else a pack and don't bother to define what they're talking about. A fanny pack is easy to imagine. You probably have some idea of what a rucksack or daypack is too, even if you never thought much about it. But the most important pack of all is still called a backpack. One label is as meaningless as the other because many types are available.

For deer hunting you need a packframe with a bag that fastens to it. Call the frame a frame, the bag a bag. Because everybody else does it's probably best to call the whole thing a pack.

The frame can be internal or external. Internal frames are pretty new. They comprise aluminum or spring steel stays or polyethylene plates that flex to conform to your back but are stiff enough to give the pack some shape and support loads up to 50 pounds or so. Internal-frame packs have shoulder straps and a belt.

External frames have been around a long time. Some people still refer to them as packboards. When bags were hung on them they became frames. They used to be wood but are now made of lightweight metal alloy. External frames can handle more weight than internal frames and are the only kind to consider for deer hunting in remote areas. Even if your camp is light, you must think about packing the deer out. An external frame pack is the answer.

The best frames are of aircraft tubing, heli-arc welded at the joints. They have thickly-padded shoulder straps and a wide padded belt that can be tightened to take some of the weight off your shoulders. That belt is essential for heavy loads! There's an adjustable web across the lower frame to keep the frame from rubbing your back and to let air circulate under your load. Some frames have a shelf to help support the bag, and some are adjustable for length so you can add a sleeping bag or other gear on top. Stays and crossmembers keep the frame from buckling.

There are several bag designs. The most expensive bags are well designed. I've just worn out a bag that carried camp in and deer out on many hunts. The zippers are shot and there are too many holes in the fabric to patch up. The frame is still good. I got the pack secondhand for $15, 17 years ago. It had been carried through the Alps and other places high and cold. I don't know what brand it is because there's no name on it. It has four horizontal compartments, the biggest at the bottom. My wife sewed a couple straps to the outside of the bottom pouch so I could carry my sleeping bag. In the bottom three compartments I can stuff 100 pounds of meat, leaving the top pouch free for camp. One-hundred pounds is all I want to carry. That's more meat than most deer have.

I have a new pack now, one that should be better designed for deer hunting. It has one big pouch with a vertical divider in it that you can push out of the way. I plan to use the divider to separate meat and camp. The huge opening at the top will make it easier for me to reach in and to look for things without unloading. There aren't many external pockets on this bag; there were none on my old one. I don't use external pockets much. A map pouch I like. The fewer zippers the better.

The best bags are big ones made of nylon pack cloth double stitched at the seams. Good bags attach to the frames with D rings. For any part that can get lost, always carry spares. My old bag had grommets that just snapped over studs on the frame. Its own weight kept it from riding up and over the heads of the studs. I liked not having to worry about things coming off or getting lost. The only spares I carried were a pair of shoulder straps. A few 100-pound loads left the originals ragged where they hooked to the frame and I felt better with extras. I never needed them though.

When you load your pack, put the heavy objects at shoulder height, as close as possible to your back. Pack tightly and balance the load side to side. Rather than having just a little in each compartment fill any you can and tie the empty parts of the bag against the frame so they don't snag brush.

Be careful with a full pack. If you fall the weight acts as a lever to bend your body ways it wasn't meant to bend. Once when stooping to drink at a creek I slipped on a mossy rock and fell. The pack wrenched my back to the side and dislocated a vertebra. I was in the hills for several days after that, and what could have been a fine trip was a painful one.

Packframes can wear holes in your clothes and mar your belt. Unless you get used to them gradually they can also raise welts on your back. Break in a new frame gently, with light loads. If you carry a rifle by its sling on your shoulder the rifle or scope will likely bang against the frame. I carry my rifle in my hands when wearing a pack.

A compass and at least two maps go with me in new country. Usually I take two compasses, in case I want to discredit one. The maps are 7½- or 15-minute quadrangles from the U.S. Geological Survey, and a Forest Service (USFS) or Bureau of Land Management (BLM) map. Sometimes a Pittmon or Metsger or other commercial area map is useful, but mostly just for roaded places. You can get USFS or BLM maps at local offices. USGS maps must be ordered from: Map Distribution, U.S. Geological Survey, Box 25286, Denver Federal Center, Denver, CO 80225, or call (303) 236-7477.

The compasses are inexpensive and lightweight. I don't use them to chart a course, only to tell me where north is. To get where I hunt I usually take established trails. After that I go the way I think will help me find deer. The compass is a check, something to keep me aware of where I am in relation to everything else. I'm hunting, not orienteering.

When you hunt tell someone where you're going and when you'll be back, someone who cares enough about you and is responsible enough to do something if you don't return. If you hunt with a partner you'll not only have a cheerier camp, but there will be less chance of an accident becoming a serious problem.

I like to share a camp with someone else, to talk over a fire and share adventures. I prefer to hunt alone. Finding a good hunting partner or campmate is hard. Sometimes it's better to go alone than with someone you can only tolerate. Hunts can spoil established friendships; the isolation of a hunting camp precludes escape or even distraction. Little things that wouldn't bother you in a place with many people suddenly bother you when there's just one person. A partner who makes each trip pleasant for you is one to be prized and deserves to be pampered.

Properly equipped, you can have fun far from other hunters. Outfitting yourself is pretty easy. The reason that hunters don't have fun by themselves is that they've not learned how to keep themselves company. They wouldn't enjoy being isolated in town; they don't enjoy it in wilderness. This has nothing to do with hardship imposed by the outdoors. Rather, it is a psychological thing, a product of living close to people and depending on them every day.

Having fun is important. It is the reason you hunt; it is also a requisite if you are to hunt well. The fear of being alone, the feeling of being small, can overwhelm you in the backcountry. But the experience gives you a fresh perspective and helps you see that you are not at the center of life but only one of its many forms. It exposes what is pretentious in you, what is phony. Only real things matter in the wilderness. There is nobody to impress.

You must take that approach, look at your hunt not just as a way to kill a deer but as a lesson in self-reliance and a chance to see things you couldn't see before. You must look on it as an adventure, an opportunity, something positive in your life. Being alone in truly wild country is a privilege most people will never have. It is important for you to acknowledge that.

If you do, if you choose to make your attitude right, the hunt will be fun, you'll hunt well and have plenty of good memories. If the loneliness doesn't subside, you'll at least accept it. If there's still some fear, you will control it.

What you think on a hunt is far more important than what you bring or what you kill.

8

Readying For The Hunt

Y ou can hunt deer without preparing, just as you can run a marathon without training. But to succeed at either, you'll work hard beforehand. Both are tests of what you've already done. You don't always have to kill game to enjoy hunting, just as you don't have to win marathons to have fun running. But you'll be happier if you do well.

Preparing Yourself

Doing well on the hunt means being satisfied with your performance. You set your own standards; it's futile to assume someone else's. Doing well shouldn't have anything to do with killing, because you may hunt very well and not see game, or have the chance to kill and decline. Don't burden yourself with a mandate to kill. You haven't enough control of those things that make killing possible. Luck operates, even when you do everything you can to eliminate it.

Setting standards is one of your first jobs as a hunter. If that sounds regimental and stuffy, consider that even when you're out for exercise and take the rifle as an afterthought you've set a standard. Some people call it purpose, but standard is better. Hiking new territory to explore and stretch your muscles cuts your chances for success; you're more apt to kill in areas you know well. But some days you don't want to hunt old territory, and don't care if that compromises your success. Standards are ways to define our desires. They can be levels of achievement or personal goals that have nothing to do with recognition by others.

There's big-time fuss about scores now. Don't let that influence your hunt. It takes more persistence to consistently kill big bucks because you have to pass up lots of lesser deer. In that respect, scores can be a measure of the hunter. But scores are, quite simply, a measure of the bone on a deer's head. If you make more of them than that you probably won't enjoy hunting very much.

Scores fuel contests between hunters when the only sensible contest is that between the hunter and his game. Not only does luck figure heavily in someone getting a record-scoring animal, but the race draws people who may poach for prizes. Awards given by the Boone and Crockett Club are in recognition of outstanding big game specimens, not outstanding big game hunters. Scoring simply decides which specimen is better. It is an arbitrary thing, hardly a basis for boasting.

To build your dreams on scores is to set yourself up to fail. Big bucks are old bucks, and there are more old bucks where hunting is limited by the landowner. Private lands with big bucks can be expensive to hunt, and many capable hunters cannot afford that opportunity.

On public land there are bucks that score well, but not as many. Genes and nutrition contribute to differences in antler development. Also, season dates have a lot to do with the vulnerability of big deer. Lastly, antler anomalies affect score, and a magnificent old animal might measure poorly.

If you hunt well the score of your deer is immaterial. It's best to forget about measuring tapes and think about deer.

What you think about deer and deer hunting is important. It shapes your attitude during the hunt, and attitude is one of the most important things you carry with you. It can help you or hinder you. It's difficult to abandon an attitude. You might as well make sure that when you start yours is a good one, one that will enhance your trip and better your chance for success. If you're optimistic—tense and excited but not taut to kill—and have set realistic standards for yourself, you'll like the time you spend afield. Eventually you'll spend as much time as you can out there. That will help you shoot deer. If you're preoccupied with things like score, or intent on besting a local record or taking the first deer to the locker, hunting will become a chore. You'll miss a lot of good times. You'll be frustrated and as a result won't hunt well either.

What I'm getting at is that your perspective must be right: right about hunting and right about the hunt. You can be eager to go, keen for the kill and hardly able to hold your energy. Or you can take the corncob-pipe approach, shuffling into the woods to escape from time and pressure or to shed ambition. High-strung or mellow, you can share with others this thought:

The success of my trip is in the hunt, not the kill. There is a tension here, and there may be a climax. I'll enjoy both. I'll learn what I can, and in everything I'll do the best I can. That way I'll be satisfied with this hunt. I'll push myself when I want to, but pain is not a requisite. I'm competing with no one. If I test myself it's because I choose to and not because I must prove something. There is nothing to prove or lose on this hunt, only something to gain. To that end I apply myself.

It's a good idea to write yourself a little note about deer hunting, a little paragraph like this one that expresses what you feel about hunting. Writing makes you organize your thoughts and make sense of things you never had to make sense of before. It clarifies perspective, and that helps understanding.

Hunting requires skills you don't use in other activities. Some of these, like climbing hills, are physical. Some, like reading trail sign, tap your mind. Others, like shooting, have both mental and physical parts. To do any of these things well you must practice. Because you can't hunt year-round your practice must be something you design, start and continue. It won't be as much fun as hunting, but if you neglect it you won't have as much fun hunting.

While hunting deer is different in many ways than competitive sports, there are parallels. One is the need to stay mentally and physically sharp. Lots of people like to play basketball but only a few like the calisthenics, shooting drills and play memorization needed to become effective. Determination is the first requisite for anyone who wants to excel. Determination to do well is the difference between proficient hunters and those who trust luck. It's what makes practice possible.

Getting ready mentally is the first part of practice. Practice starts with the idea that you'll be as successful as you are prepared. You'll accept luck as part of the hunt but will rely on skills to harvest a deer. Again, *success is not a dead deer;* it is a good hunt. The shot is the climax, your tagged buck the result. Success is neither a measure of your prowess or of the hunt. Many shots are fired and many deer killed by people who know very little about hunting.

To be a good hunter is to be a naturalist, a rifleman, an athlete. Your practice is best aimed at those jobs.

Learning about deer and their environment is something you can do in a chair at home. There are scores of deer books, and some are good. Use the reading list at the back of this book, continue in the NAHC Hunter Information Series book club and visit your public library. Prowl used bookstores in big cities and the wildlife research section of your state university library. Subscribe to magazines that feature deer regularly. If someone scoffs at your approach, pay him no mind. You're drawing on the experiences and research of hundreds of intelligent people who were interested enough in deer to learn and write about them.

Reading about deer is a big job. You must go beyond the hunting stories and the record books and get concerned about deer biology and habit. If you don't know local plants you're handicapped because deer surely do, and they go where they find their favorites. Plant taxonomy is important to learn. Another area to research is the deer management plan for your state or the state you want to hunt. Every state game agency should have a long-term proposal for managing mule deer. The data supporting that plan, as well as the plan itself, can be very useful.

Plowing quickly and deeply into deer research and even popular deer books and articles can sap your enthusiasm. You'll learn most by reading in pieces over a long period.

You must also spend time in the woods. Think of it as the lab session of a science course, or a field trip to illustrate what you read. When you go—and it shouldn't be only during hunting season—be observant. Look for details. Ask questions. Try to think of what you'd need to know if you were a deer. What would you have to know to live here, in this timber? What would you do first every day? Where would you look for food? Where would you drink if things got dry? What would you do in a storm? Where would you lie down to stay concealed? What does the wind do here and how would you take advantage of it? What does this place look like in winter? What would you do then? How would you evade a hunter over there? And there? Where would you go to cross to the next drainage?

Background work on deer and deer habitat can serve as scouting for the hunt. When you scout you'll also learn about deer behavior that can be applied anywhere you go. When you're afield,

To be a good hunter is to be a naturalist, a rifleman, an athlete. Your practice is best aimed at those jobs. You must also go beyond the hunting stories and the record books and get concerned about deer biology and habit.

carry a pencil and paper. I like to draw maps of new areas—especially where detailed U.S. Geological Survey maps aren't available. I do this even if I don't intend to use the map, because sketching my perception of the country helps me memorize it.

It's a good idea to take notes too. Carry a little spiral pad and jot things down as you see them or think of them or wonder about them. Read the notes when you get home. You'll be surprised at how much you noticed and considered, and how much you forgot. Notes make you more observant because you're looking for things to record.

Being in the woods helps you in ways less tangible. It teaches you the rhythm of wild things and soon you find yourself fitting in. To be a good hunter you must fit in. A hunter out of tune with the woods is easy to spot and easy to avoid. He moves awkwardly, quickly, with no purpose. He fidgets with his watch and compass and clothes and, forever, with his rifle. His steps are loud and he walks where he shouldn't. He steps on things instead of over them. He scrapes things, cracks things. He's so preoccupied with himself that he cannot see other creatures. When he looks for them he looks in the wrong places. He may smell of tobacco or gasoline or bacon or sweat. Usually he smells like a mixture of these.

But it's impossible not to smell like a human. You can, however, do lots of other things that will help you become part of the woods. These are best practiced on your off-season trips, where the object is to learn and the pace is slow and mistakes don't cost anything.

Getting familiar with your equipment is as important as getting accustomed to the woods. Weather during most deer seasons varies considerably and you must be prepared to accommodate those changes. That means having worn every combination of hunting clothes in some off-season trial. Boots get plenty of attention from people who advise beginners, but boots are only a part of what you wear. Certainly, all footwear and every item of clothing should be tested before the hunt.

You'll want to carry a small pack filled with the things you'd take hunting. You might not use them, but you'll notice something that could be left home, something else that was left at home but shouldn't have been. You'll find your pack comfortable or uncomfortable, too full or too big. You'll adjust your pack and binocular straps, find a better way to carry your coat in warm weather, pad something that rubs, move things around on your belt. Field trips are great shake-down cruises!

Being in the woods gets you used to looking in the right places for deer and recognizing deer when you see them. Most people look too high. Everybody knows that, yet most people still look too high. Most of a deer is lower than your navel, so look navel-high. You'll still spot the occasional ear twitch.

It's good to take your rifle afield whenever you can. You get used to carrying it and quickly learn the most comfortable and efficient way to hold it. It becomes part of you. You'll be aware of that barrel jutting above your shoulder as you crouch under a limb; you'll know what to do with the rifle when climbing a cliff where you need both hands; you'll swing it up when you need to without fumbling; you'll make final sling adjustments. It's also helpful to practice getting into sitting, kneeling and prone positions with that sling.

Estimating range is a hard thing to do in unfamiliar country, but it's something you can practice in the off-season. Especially important for bowhunters and black-powder and handgun shooters, it's a rifleman's job too. An animal 40 yards away doesn't look much different than one at 50 yards—but an arrow shot for 50 yards will completely miss a deer standing at 40 yards. A 300-yard shot with a rifle will be a miss if the deer is actually 400 yards out. Flat country makes the animal appear closer than it is; rough country, especially an intervening canyon, makes it appear farther. When you're out learning about deer you can become a better shot just by pacing off yardages after guessing the distances.

If you live near where you hunt you can scout while you study deer. Some hunters never scout. Others scout just before the opener, frantically looking for tracks and hurriedly glassing the hills. They don't learn much more than the people who don't scout at all.

For one thing, you must be in an area several times, at different times of the day and in different weather, to get a feel for it. You must not be in a rush; you must be observant.

Secondly, tracks found just before deer season tell you little in the West. That's because dry weather has preserved week-old tracks and quickly desiccated droppings. If you don't find any tracks you're in a poor area indeed! But those you see are no guarantee that deer are still around, and they don't tell you how many there are or what their travel patterns will be on the opener. Besides, intense scouting just before the hunt alerts deer and many change their behavior.

Take your rifle afield whenever you can. You get used to carrying it and quickly learn the most comfortable and efficient way to hold it.

Scouting is best done year-round. Serious whitetail hunters do it that way and mule deer hunters should too. If you live far from where you hunt and can't scout you'll be at a disadvantage, but not a great one. Given that you've learned a lot about mule deer biology and habit and have spent some time in the woods with your deer hunting clothes and equipment, you should fit right in to a new hunting area. In a few hours you'll be hunting effectively, and in a couple of days you'll know the area quite well.

When scouting, or on the first day hunting a new territory, pay attention to these things:

1) Exposure of the dominant ridge.
2) Exposure of finger ridges.
3) Vegetation by species as elevation and exposure change.
4) Water sources, especially the little ones.
5) Trails, thin ones in thickets as well as thoroughfares.
6) Saddles, places deer cross ridges.
7) Tracks and droppings, especially big ones and fresh ones.
8) Beds, bedding cover and escape routes in that cover.
9) Wind patterns during the day, thermal shifts.
10) Signs of intruders, cattle, sheep, dogs.
11) Human activity, logging, construction, vehicles.
12) A sense of time in moving from place to place.

Just being aware of these things isn't enough. You must interpret what you notice and put it with other things you've learned to get an accurate picture of the area and local deer habits. In the off-season you can predict what the deer will do come fall.

Spending time reading books and poking around in deer cover takes determination—if not at first, then later when other things call for your time. Getting your body ready takes even more determination. There's a lot of effort and time involved. While being fit is a good feeling, getting fit is not. There is no shortcut. The best way is to start slowly, and gradually increase your exercise load.

You're physically deteriorating if you're past your mid-20s. The only good news is that you have company and that the deterioration can be slowed. Slowing it means eating properly, exercising and getting rid of things that make you ill at ease—like stress. These things are good to do even if you don't hunt, but many people don't do them because there's too much effort involved. Who knows, maybe hunting is the excuse you need.

There are plenty of diets and health programs available. Some work. But none are magic. All require that you stick to your plan.

You can't hunt well if you're grossly overweight. If you convince yourself of that, any sensible diet will not only make you a better hunter but a happier person. Because I have no professional training in dietetics or medicine I'll not pretend to know much about either. I can tell you what kinds of eating habits work for me.

One thing I do is limit animal fat in my diet. I don't try to eliminate it; that would be unpleasant if not impossible. But I don't eat bacon or sausage anymore unless it's rude not to, and I substitute cottage cheese for sour cream on potatoes. I resist butter, mayonnaise and ice cream when I can. I still eat cheese because I like cheese and a little is good for you. It's easy to change from whole milk to one-percent. A lot of deep-fried food is cooked in animal fat because it's cheap. I avoid them.

Vegetable oil is better for your body than animal fat but is still high in calories. Some vegetable products like palm oil, coconut oil and avocados are also high in cholesterol, something that isn't good for you either. Primarily, cholesterol is an animal fat.

Processed sugar is another thing I shun. Unlike animal fat, it won't clog your arteries, but it makes you heavy. I keep sugar off my cereal and out of my tea and scrape the frosting off a birthday cake. On hunts I've replaced candy bars with dried fruit. The fruit is high in fructose; maybe I'm just fooling myself. Anyway, it has some food value. I eat bran muffins. But butterhorns are out.

Limiting fats and sugar doesn't mean living like a lemming and eating like a rabbit. Cut back gradually and you'll hardly notice the change.

Some things I eat a lot of: green salads with vinegar dressing; macaroni casseroles; boiled rice, potatoes and vegetables; oatmeal; bran cereals; whole-grain bread; raisins; soup. Once in a while a piece of pie sneaks in or a ginger cookie. But if I eat the right things I can eat a bunch and not gain weight. I like that.

If you're exercising a great deal you can eat anything and stay thin. Cross-country cyclists gnaw constantly on candy bars and cookies and peanut butter sandwiches *and lose weight*. Their bodies use more calories than they consume. Most of us haven't the luxury of eating like that because we don't use much energy while making a living. On a photography assignment last summer I hiked 27 miles in mountainous terrain and over four passes in one day. That wasn't far, but the hot, dry weather and my burden of camera gear made it seem so. Though I ate plenty of high-calorie foods that day and the day after, I lost six pounds. They returned after a few meals and a couple of days at the desk.

Being in good physical shape makes hunting more fun, and more productive.

The best exercise for hunting is aerobic exercise—the kind that demands a lot of your heart and lungs. You can get technical and monitor your anaerobic threshold, but that's not necessary. If you exercise until you feel uncomfortable and sweat you'll be doing yourself some good. As your body responds to the strain, it will condition itself to combat it. You'll find that what made you uncomfortable two weeks ago will seem easy. To keep improving your condition you must gradually increase the duration or intensity of your exercise. How far you go with this depends on your fitness goals.

Physicians advise that you start any exercise program slowly so you don't damage yourself. That's good advice, and a good reason to start exercising long before your hunt. As you get older it takes longer to put yourself in shape. Better that you keep yourself in shape with a year-round program.

There are all sorts of machines available to help you. The treadmill, ski machine, rowing machine and stationary bicycle are all good for your heart and lungs. I get bored straining on a machine in a small room, so I jog or ride a bicycle. Both are easy to do in most areas, and both give you fresh air in the bargain. Jogging is especially good because you need only a pair of shoes. You can do it from a motel room as well as at home.

Swimming is excellent exercise, but I don't do much of that because I don't have a pool and winters here are cold. Jumping rope is good too.

Several fitness guides recommend that you exercise at 80 percent of your maximum heart rate for 20 minutes every other day. Somebody has figured out that that's ideal. It isn't for me; I try to exercise an hour a day. I don't know if I go at 80 percent of my maximum but when I'm done I'm tired and feel good.

On those days that I jog I go four to eight miles, then do 60 situps, 60 pushups and 30 exercises for my lower back, which has been weak since birth. Sometimes I play basketball or ride a bicycle for an hour. Games like basketball make exercise more fun, but it's good to do things that don't require other people because then you'll not be tempted to skip exercise when nobody is around.

If you want to jog eight miles but haven't jogged recently, it's best to start with what's comfortable—maybe a mile or two. Do that for a week every day, then add a mile. In eight weeks you should be able to comfortably jog eight miles a day. If you ever feel that you're straining yourself or not recovering well in a day postpone adding that extra mile until your body is ready.

With strenuous exercise, it's important to warm up and cool down. I do this by stretching, walking and doing calisthenics. If you pop out of bed and into your shorts and career down the driveway and into the road doing a five-minute mile for eight miles, and then sit down right away, you'll be stiff and sore. Warm up and cool down, it's that simple.

My exercise program takes all the time I can afford to give it and I'm satisfied with the condition my body is in—most of the time. It's not top condition, but other things in life demand my attention too.

Your program may be more or less intense. What suits you is what is right. The deer are always more fit than the hunter. The question is: How much advantage will you give them?

Desire, optimism and a rational perspective—these and a good diet with plenty of exercise will ready you for the hunt. You've studied deer and walked where they live. You may have scouted the area you'll hunt. On field trips you've tested pack and clothes so you'll be comfortable. The only thing left is your equipment.

Preparing Your Equipment

Equipment means binoculars, rifle and knife. It can mean peripheral things like your vehicle. It might include a tent. You won't have to do much to prepare your sleeping bag for the hunt, but it's a good idea to check it and that foam pad for rips. The tent, if you use one, is best pulled out and set up. Check the end of each pole, especially fiberglass poles. Splintered ends or aluminum poles that are bent should be replaced. Plastic tent stakes cost almost nothing; if you're missing a stake or using one that's battered, replace it. On the hunt you'll want everything to fit and work properly all the time.

Take good care of your vehicle. Here are some things to do and check:

1) Change the oil and filter before a long trip.
2) Clean or change the air filter.
3) Check and gap each spark plug and buy an extra set to carry.
4) Buy spark plug wires, examine the distributor cap for cracks.
5) Check transmission and differential oil levels.
6) Pack front wheel bearings after every 40,000 miles.
7) Check the fan belt and buy an extra.
8) Fill battery cells to the proper level and test the battery.
9) Check antifreeze level and strength; it should test to -20.

10) Fill the windshield washer reservoir.

11) Inflate tires to proper pressure and examine their tread. It's a good idea to carry two mounted spares—certainly one full-size spare besides the undersize spare that comes with a vehicle now. An extra tire can save you time and perhaps a long trip to town during a hunt.

These things can be a bother but are easily handled at home rather than on the roadside or in camp. It's a quick job to pack wheel bearings or replace them in the garage. If you burn one up and it seizes on the spindle—as happened to me in Wyoming once—you lose hunting time and pay whatever the local garage wants to charge.

As for carrying extra parts, don't expect the same good fortune that one Washington hunter had. His fan belt snapped on a mountain pass at midnight before opening day. A van pulled up behind him and the driver got out and asked what was wrong. The van was an auto parts truck with a rack full of fan belts.

Your binoculars need cleaning if they haven't been cleaned since they've been used. Swab each lens with lens tissue and a drop of lens fluid, then dry it with a clean tissue. Wipe the outside of the binoculars with a tack rag to remove dust. Check the center focusing adjustment for free play. Lubricate this and the hinge only if necessary and then very lightly with a teflon or graphite spray. Ocular focusing rings should not need lubrication; here you're likely to get spray or oil on glass. To keep binoculars clean on the hunt carry a vial of lens fluid and a few tissues in a dust-proof pouch. They work on scope lenses too.

I like to carry two folding knives. If one breaks or becomes dull I have another to finish whatever I'm doing. Before a hunt I sharpen each and oil the hinge. That's all.

Getting a rifle ready is more involved than most hunters think. If you've hunted with your rifle a long time you can skip some of the steps, but you shouldn't skip all of them. Even if you don't change or correct anything, checking your rifle thoroughly will give you confidence in it. Here's what I do:

First I take the rifle apart and clean it. The barreled action comes out of the stock; then I remove the trigger assembly and bolt, and disassemble everything I can with screwdrivers and punches. I soak each metal piece in bore solvent and wipe it dry. If there's any rust I remove it with a brass bore brush dipped in solvent. Wiped clean of dust, rust and solvent I put the rifle back together. As I do this I rub each piece with an oily rag. When it's

After zeroing, shoot other targets from hunting positions. Water-filled plastic milk jugs are fun, and about the same size as a deer's vitals.

a barreled action again I lubricate the trigger and bolt race with a Teflon or graphite spray or a touch of oil or grease.

If I have to do any stock work I do it now. There was a time when everybody was altering stocks, mainly because military rifles were being made into sporters and some factory sporter stocks weren't well adapted to scopes. But things have changed for the better and most modern sporting rifles have very shootable stocks. Yours may be too long or too short for you, but unless it's very long or very short it's probably not worth fooling with.

If a rifle doesn't fit you reasonably well it's smart to buy one that does; there are plenty of well-stocked rifles to choose from. If you must whittle, add a pad or do something else to the wood, be sure it will make your stock better before you start. If it doesn't you'll have cut the resale value of your rifle for nothing. It is un-British to adapt yourself to your gun, but it works most of the time.

The time to adjust the trigger is when the stock is off. I carefully check the pull for creep, weight and overtravel after I clean and reassemble the parts. I like my triggers to break sharply at just under two pounds, with no discernible creep and only enough overtravel to keep things working.

The stock goes on next. I wipe the guard screws with an oily rag before putting them into the lower receiver. If they bind as I insert them I take the metal out of the wood again and relieve the stock holes a little with a chain saw file. Screws that bear against stock wood impair accuracy and may cause the stock to split.

When the screws slide right in I start them in the receiver lightly with my fingers. If the rifle has a forearm screw I leave it out for the moment. Next I stand the rifle butt down on a carpet and tighten the guard screws not quite snug. Then I bounce the rifle a couple of times, firmly enough to seat the recoil lug back in its recess. Finally I snug the guard screws, the front first and then the rear, then turn both very tight, again front first. If there's a center guard screw I start it with the others but don't snug it till the others are tight. The forearm screw goes in last. Both it and the center guard screw I turn just snug, not tight. Both should start and turn easily. I correct any binding. Once in a while I check screw tension on my rifles. It changes as the stock shrinks and swells.

While my screwdriver set is out I check scope rings. Removing the scope to check bases will almost surely change its zero, so I don't do that. Though I use no locking compound on my screw threads I've not had a mount base loosen, ever. If the rifle is a new one with a set of open sights screwed on, I take them off now, plugging the holes with filler screws. Unless I plan to use iron sights I don't want them on the barrel or receiver.

Screwdriver bits must fit screws very well. If they do you can tighten each screw firmly without marring the head. If they don't you damage the screw and can't apply proper torque. It's possible to strip the flats on an allen-head screw and have to drill it out. To save yourself the trouble buy a gun screwdriver set like the one marketed by Brownell's. The bits are hard and correctly ground, and there's one for almost any screw you're likely to find on hunting rifles and scope mounts.

The next thing I check is the rifle's bore. I clean it thoroughly, first with a patch soaked in Shooter's Choice or Hoppe's solvent pushed through once from the breech. I use a rod guide to keep the rod centered in the bore and protect the chamber and throat. After removing the dirty wet patch at the muzzle I thread on a brass bore brush, also wet with solvent. With this I scrub the bore vigorously back and forth a half dozen times, following with dry patches until they come out clean. If I'm going to shoot the rifle right away I swab the bore with an oily patch then a dry one. If the rifle is to be left in the rack I stop with the oily patch.

Many shooters don't pay attention to the chamber, but the chamber is important. I wipe and scrub it just as I do the bore. A .45 pistol brush works well in most rifle chambers. Unlike the bore brush, it should not fit tightly. That's because it will have to reverse direction in the chamber. You have to dispense with the bore guide when cleaning a chamber, so I brush it just before I'm ready for dry patches in the bore. It's dried and oiled just like the bore. Before I shoot, though, I make sure the chamber is dry. You can shoot through an oily bore, but an oily chamber keeps the case from gripping the chamber on firing, increasing backthrust on the bolt. That's bad. A dry bore and chamber make for a more predictable first shot.

With the rifle clean and tight I wipe the scope lenses as I did my binocular lenses. Then I go to the range.

Ensuring An Accurate Shot

Whether handloads or factory ammunition, my cartridges are kept clean in a box or my leather belt pouch. Handling them with sweaty fingers stains the brass and eventually weakens them. Dropping cartridges in the dirt or carrying them loose in pockets can put grit on the bullets, scoring the barrel when you shoot. I feed all the cartridges I plan to hunt with through the magazine and chamber—not just cartridges out of the same box but cartridges I'm going to put in the rifle. A shoulder bulged by a seating die set too far down is no problem at the range; it can be a problem if you try to chamber it for a shot at a buck!

I shoot at 200 yards all the time. My rifles are sighted for that distance so it only seems reasonable. Besides, it's easy to shoot tight groups at 100 yards and easy to get complacent. Putting together a good 200-yard group is harder, so I work harder. Things show up at 200 yards that don't at 100. Still, 200 is close enough that bullet holes are easy to see. I shoot at six-inch white paper squares on plain pasteboard boxes. They work well for the low-power scopes I use, and bullet holes show up black in the paper or on the box.

You need sandbags to do a good job of sighting in or testing loads. Both butt and forearm of the rifle must be supported. For a right-hander, you control elevation by squeezing and relaxing your left-hand grip on the rear sandbag. You mustn't steady the rifle with your left hand or allow the barrel to touch anything. It's best to take the sling off, but you can lay it flat under the forearm. Keep the same points of contact between rifle and bags shot to shot.

If my rifle is sighted in, even roughly, I start shooting at 200 yards. If I've settled on a load I refine the sighting with that load by bringing the group centers exactly to my point of aim. This will take several sessions, because once a barrel gets warm it may give me a false group center—one that's not where the first shot from a cold barrel will be. So I fire several groups, cleaning the rifle between them, letting it cool and marking the first shot in each target. Comparing the placement of those first shots tells me if the rifle is shooting where I want it to. If there's more than a 1½-inch difference between the center of the group of first shots and the center of the group of subsequent shots I check the bedding or try a different load. I zero the scope with the first-shot group.

If I've just bought the rifle or mounted a new scope I'll not be sighted in that first trip to the range. To save ammunition when I sight in I put the rifle in sandbags, take the bolt out and move the gun around till I see my 200-yard white target in the middle of the bore. Then, without touching the rifle, I look through the scope. Probably the cross hairs are not quartering the paper. If not I turn the adjustments till it is, being careful not to bump the rifle. Then I peer down the bore to be sure.

This aligns the scope with the bore, something you can do with

Rifle practice, like reading and exercise, should be a year-round commitment. It's easier to maintain proficiency than to get it back in a hurry. Year-round shooting will help you hit when you must.

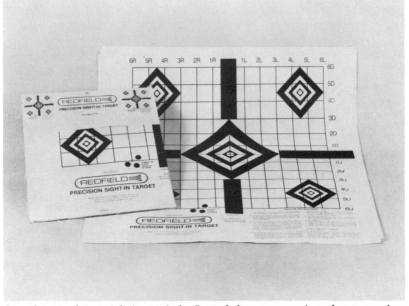

Some hunters do not sight in precisely. Sort-of-close accuracy is useless to a serious hunter. Shoot at targets you can see well and that help bring you to zero with tight groups.

a boresighter too. It won't be good enough for 200-yard shooting but will put you on the paper at 300 yards, and that's where I start. Shooting at a target the size of a quarter I move the scope dials after each shot; groups aren't important here. Usually after the third shot I'm within an inch of the target. Then I switch to my 100-yard bull's-eye: a three-inch white square. Again I adjust after each shot until I get one to print two inches high. That's the start of my first three-shot group. If it centers on the first hole or very close I swing the rifle to the 200-yard paper and shoot a three-shot group. This one should print in the middle. I adjust till it does. If I haven't picked a load to hunt with I don't fret about centering the group at 200 yards. All I want is for each shot to strike the box.

Choosing a load is an involved affair. There are too many choices of factory rounds and combinations of handloading components to shoot. You have to pick a few to try, then take the best of the lot. If you decide to shoot factory-loaded ammunition you've already narrowed things. When you're that far you simply select a bullet weight to give yourself a workable number of choices. You should shoot all that's available in one bullet weight.

Handloading gives you more possibilities than you can use. Bullet weight is a good place to start eliminating. Then you'd do well to choose a powder—after reading manuals that show which powders work best for your cartridge. Trying a half dozen bullets with varying powder charges is still time-consuming but usually worth the effort. To save a bit, don't bother with powder differences under three percent of maximum load levels. That is, if your .300 H&H Mag. is supposed to give its all with 70 grains of H4831 behind a 180-grain bullet, start loading at 66 grains (about six percent below maximum). Increase by two grains (three percent) to 68 and 70 grains as you monitor pressure signs and accuracy. By the time you've tried a couple of bullets in front of these charges you might easily eliminate one—probably the starting load. If the maximum charge consistently gives better results than the 68-grain load you might change to 69 and 70 grains for the remaining bullets.

In big cases with slow powders, magnum primers supposedly give better results than standard primers, but I've not been able to tell the difference. It's best to pick one brand of cases and one kind of primers and stick with that combination through your load development. For hunting ammunition there's little sense in trying to tune loads by changing cases or primers. If none of several reasonable loads gives you good accuracy you probably have a bedding problem or a poor barrel—assuming you shoot well enough to make tight groups.

You don't need a chronograph to see if your loads are potent, but chronographs are fun and tell you how consistent the loads are. It makes no difference whether your .270 Win. shoots 2,950 or 3,050 fps. A little extra speed makes some shooters excited. But loads that shoot accurately are the ones to use.

Once you've chosen a load you'll have to refine your sighting, making sure the rifle is zeroed at 200 yards. After that it's good to check its point of impact at 100, 300 and 400 yards. Shoot five-shot groups at each range. Take notes.

All this shooting off sandbags is a way to tune your rifle. You can't tune it any other way. But most of the shots you get at deer will be without a rest at unknown ranges. There will be wind and steep angles. You may be breathing hard; the deer may be running. You can't prepare for these things by shooting from a bench. Tuning your hand and eye is at least as important as tuning your rifle, but it's done differently.

One of the best ways to learn to shoot better is to buy an air rifle. I have one and I use it. It's an accurate .177 rifle from Beeman, and it weighs almost as much as my Model 70 Winchester. The stock is well-proportioned for a big adult, and the receiver sight I chose is good enough to use in matches. I bought a swinging metal disk for a target. All I have to do to practice shooting is step out the back door, insert a pellet and squeeze. The trigger is not all I'd like it to be, but it's OK and the rifle is accurate. If I miss, it's my fault. You can use a .22 rifle, but it's more expensive to shoot and you must have a solid backstop. My skirted pellets smash flat against a one-inch board. Shooting your deer rifle is a fine idea but you probably won't do it enough because of the cost and the trouble.

There are four recognized positions from which to shoot a rifle: Offhand, kneeling, sitting and prone.

Offhand. Offhand or standing is the toughest position, and should get most of your attention in practice. Mostly you shoot offhand when you can't get into any other position. Sometimes you have to shoot offhand because you can't see the game unless you stand up. It's a poor way to shoot. You're holding the rifle far from the ground with your feet the only contact with the ground. Your arms are straining to support the rifle in space while your back and legs must keep your body and the rifle still. There are loose joints and quivering muscles between the rifle and the ground. Blood belches through your veins while you try to time your trigger break with jumping crosswires.

You'll want to shoot a lot of offhand in practice, as little as possible in the field. To get the best offhand position you can, stand with your feet shoulder-width apart, angled 45 to 60 degrees from a line to your target. Stand erect, evenly on both feet, with just a bit more weight on the ball than on the heel. Lock your knees but relax your leg muscles. Because the rifle hangs out in front, pulling you forward, lean back a little, twisting your torso slightly to the left. With your trigger hand tug the rifle back into your shoulder; keep the right elbow level with that shoulder. Grip the forend lightly with your left hand and keep your left elbow bent at a comfortable angle almost directly under the rifle. The sight or cross hairs should rest naturally on target. Don't worry about all the jiggling going on. Everybody jiggles. If you have to force the sights to center, though, or if the target is not in the middle of those jiggles, move your whole body to correct your natural aim. No matter what position you shoot you must be comfortable, with the rifle swinging toward the target as if it had a brain.

When you're ready to shoot take two or three deep breaths and let the last leak slowly from your lungs as you begin your squeeze. Apply pressure to the trigger as the sights jiggle on target; hold the pressure as they jiggle off. The shot won't be a total surprise, but you shouldn't care when it comes because you're in control of the trigger and you won't let it break when the sights are off target. When the shot happens your lungs will be empty but not starved. If they become starved before the shot, start over. Follow through with each shot by remaining still for a second and calling the place you think you hit.

You can brace your rifle in the offhand position by using a hasty sling drawn tight against the triceps on your left arm. Snug it up with the heel of your left hand as you raise the rifle.

Kneeling. Kneeling is steadier than offhand because you're lower and there are three contact points with the ground: your left foot, right knee and right foot. Your left elbow rests on your left knee, braced. As in offhand, your torso and head should be erect, the left elbow just slightly left of plumb. The right elbow, though, is tucked down, well below shoulder height. Your tailbone rests on your right heel and should support at least half the weight of your torso. The vertical left shin supports the rest as your upper left arm leans on that knee. Your left elbow should be slightly in front of the left knee so elbow and knee joints aren't pressing like two balls against each other. Your left foot is flat on the ground but turned parallel to your right leg. Your right foot is curled, contacting the ground at ball and toes. Your upper left leg points close to the line of sight.

Sitting. Sitting is a very useful position. Well over half the deer I've shot have been from the sit. It is not the sitting position used in competitive shooting, where the legs are crossed and you get down very low and tuck your elbows in the hollows of your knees. That's a hard position to get into quickly even on level ground. On a hill it's not only hard to get into, it's hard to shoot from. The best sitting position for hunters is an open position, buttocks flat on the ground and legs jackknifed up in front. Here your ground contacts are your feet and bottom, which should roughly form an equilateral triangle. You lean over your knees and place your elbows just ahead of them so you have a flat contact point. Most of your weight is on your buttocks, but all the rifle's weight is on your legs. Your back is arched as you lean forward, your neck bent back slightly so you can aim.

Prone. Prone is the steadiest shooting position because it's the lowest. But it has limited use afield because your view is apt to be obstructed. Here you are belly down on the ground, your left elbow out in front and almost directly under the rifle. The right elbow forms a tripod of sorts, with the left elbow and your lower torso. Your right leg is drawn up slightly and cocked to roll the torso a little so you don't get pulse beats from your stomach disrupting your aim. Your left leg is extended at a comfortable angle. Both feet are turned outward, instep to the ground.

In offhand, kneeling, sitting and prone a tight sling is a great help in steadying the rifle. After it's adjusted and after you practice with it, a sling is easy to use. With the rifle grip in your right hand and the rifle pointing up and away from you in front, give the sling a half turn out. Then slip your left hand through the loop and slide it up your arm to just above the bulge of your triceps. As you swing your left hand out over the sling and onto the forend, and put the rifle butt to your shoulder, the sling snugs flat against your hand and pulls the rifle to you.

From a sitting position with a tight sling, you should be able to keep all your shots in six inches at 200 yards. That kind of accuracy will enable you to fatally hit any deer out to 350 yards.

A sling need not be attached to the rifle's butt for shooting, but it must be for carrying. Sling length and loop position are two things that need adjusting before you hunt. Leather dressing on the sling will keep it supple.

Rifle practice, like reading and exercise, should be a year-round commitment. It's easier to maintain proficiency than to get it back in a hurry. There are several ways to practice; those that emphasize shooting fundamentals in all positions are best. You don't have to shoot live rounds all the time. Dry firing will not damage most centerfire rifles and it's one of the easiest ways to practice. You can do it indoors and you can do it every day. There's no recoil or noise to disturb you. It helps you become familiar with your rifle. About a mile from my window is a big sign that makes a fine dry-fire target. Yours might be a brick or a rock. Every deer hunter should have one!

While you don't need dummy cartridges to dry fire, a few to run through the magazine from time to time are useful. Feeding problems won't appear in slow, careful loading at the range; they might if you have to bolt in a round quickly. Additionally, magazines feed differently full than if there's just one cartridge on top. Stuff some oatmeal in a handful of fired cases and seat your favorite bullets on top. Mark the cases with a felt pen. When you

Hunting in the off-season, like target shooting, keeps you in touch with your rifle, and it gives you the chance to test new loads. Coyote hunting might also put you into new and productive deer country.

have a few minutes, slip into your sling and run through a magazine, taking care with each shot but moving the bolt smartly.

Any time you can spend with your rifle in the field is bound to help you handle it more surely and shoot it better. Coyote hunting is particularly useful because it involves the same rough country you'll tramp for deer and the same unknown yardages. Like deer, coyote are wary animals, and you'll have to make shots under pressure—quick shots, long shots and running shots. Coyote hunting trains your mind as well as your shooting muscles. It teaches you to stay calm when you must.

The pressure or excitement generated by a buck against the cross hairs is what people call buck fever. It's really just a tension, an uncertainty, a feeling that this is perhaps the only chance I'll get and I want very much to make good on it but I don't know if I can. To get it over with, to rush the climax, hunters do silly things. They eject live cartridges, fire into the air, say bang to the animal, just stand there staring. If your practice involves some sort of pressure it can help you keep your head when a buck appears during season.

If you live where you can't hunt coyote you can substitute match pressure for the tension of hunting by joining a rifle club and shooting metallic silhouette. This game not only affords you great offhand practice, it teaches you about trajectory and wind. Distance to the farthest target is 547 yards—much farther than most hunters can justify shooting at a deer. The targets are animal-shaped, cut out of steel with no aiming point. They must be knocked down to count as hit. There's a time limit, too. Metallic silhouette shooting will get you used to your rifle and make you a better shot. On smaller ranges rimfire rifles can be used to shoot reduced silhouettes. The benefits are the same.

When you shoot targets by yourself it's best to use paper targets with small aiming points as well as life-size cardboard cutouts of deer with no aiming points. The small bull's-eyes—and they should be smaller than you can hit consistently—will make you concentrate on fundamentals: holding, breathing, squeezing and calling the shot. The paper records your hits, and that's important. Shooting at little cans in the grass is fun but you can't analyze what you did. There are no patterns to see, thus no mistakes to correct. People don't like to shoot at paper because there's no reaction to a hit and because every poor shot is there for inspection, forever, by anyone who cares to look. If you want to play with your guns, shoot cans. When you're serious about learning to shoot better, use paper.

Big cardboard cutouts of deer serve another purpose: they get you used to quickly choosing a small aiming point on a big object that has no visible aiming point. Lots of hunters miss deer because they shoot at the whole deer instead of a spot on the deer. This is particularly true of archers, but of riflemen as well. A hunter will suddenly see the buck over the tip of his arrow or the muzzle of his rifle or in his scope and without thinking release the arrow or press the trigger. The result is a miss or, worse, a crippled deer. To avoid that, shoot cutouts. Practice creating the spot in your mind, quickly. Call each shot relative to your aiming point and keep track.

Shooting at running game is hard to do consistently and a foolish thing to try if you're not good. To practice you might try shooting tires with cardboard inserts as they're rolled down a hill by your partner. Shooting running cottontail rabbits with a rimfire rifle or jack rabbits with your deer rifle is also useful. Knowing how far to lead is part instinct and part practice.

9

How To Hunt

A wash of cold was cascading from the rims. There wasn't much time to hunt, maybe just enough to shrug the pack, climb onto a bench and glass the west face. I unrolled and fluffed my sleeping bag so the down would loft, then hurried up the basin.

I bumped into the buck before the first bench, and he and the doe bounded off toward it. He stopped. I bungled the shot, flipped in another cartridge and killed him. There was no hunting here. I simply shot a mule deer that I happened to meet on a trail.

Some deer are killed this way, more are shot from roadsides, others are killed in grain fields from the porches of farm houses. Ranchers fixing fences shoot deer, as do loggers and firewood cutters. There are many ways to kill deer without hunting them.

But hunting is more than just getting meat or antlers or saying that you did. To hunt is to earn the chance to shoot. Here is how you can do that efficiently, with good prospects for success.

The Methods

You can hunt deer with people posted around likely cover while the rest walk into that cover and try to drive the deer out where they can be seen. Many whitetail are shot this way. But it's not so effective in most mule deer country where setting up the drive is time-consuming and exposes some of the hunters to the deer they want to fool. Brushy draws surrounded by open slopes are easy to drive, but usually there's considerable elevation to gain or lose while you're exposed. Small woodlots in blacktail range are good places to drive, as are blocks of second-growth between logging slashes. But the neat patches of timber that make whitetail drives popular in the East and Midwest are scarce in the West.

Besides, driving leaves you with little satisfaction. *You* aren't earning the shot. Whether driver or stander, you're depending on others. Even if a buck is pushed out of his bed and you kill him, you'll wonder if he would have been there to shoot without the other hunters. Would he have sensed you and moved away? Did he sense you and decide to stay hidden because running seemed risky? Driving can be a good way to kill deer but it lacks finesse.

Sometimes, hunting deer by yourself is the hard way to hunt, but it can be enjoyable whether or not you kill a deer. If you learn to hunt well by yourself you are truly a hunter. To be a hunter is really just that. The kills will come, harder at first than if you depended on others to help you. Each shot will be yours, each buck a prize to share with no one. The weather or terrain might foil party hunting, but you can still be successful on your own. You'll not depend on the schedules of others; your trips will proceed as you plan them, as you want them to go. A flat tire on someone else's pickup won't affect your deer hunt.

Most magazine articles about deer hunting tell you of two ways to hunt on your own: stand hunting (sitting still) or still hunting (moving slowly). It's OK to describe whitetail hunting this way, but mule deer country is more diverse and calls for a different, a more flexible approach. The best way to hunt mule deer on your own is to combine stand and still hunting, with glassing and stalking.

A few people have rattled mule deer in, but generally this is not as productive with mule deer as with whitetail. Rattling works best during the short rut season. It's ill suited to open country or where you want to stay a distance from the deer. In whitetail coverts you are with the deer, and any place you can be is likely a good place to rattle. In the mountains you may hunt where you don't expect to find deer, looking across a drainage or up a slope where you do. To rattle where deer don't normally go is foolish; to penetrate those areas that you could hunt from a distance to rattle will push deer out and away from you. Mule deer will leave cover if you disturb them. Still hunting justifies the risk of moving deer out. Rattling does not.

Let's hunt for a few minutes. We'll start before dawn, in

Sometimes, hunting deer by yourself is the hard way to hunt. But it can be enjoyable whether or not you kill a deer.

mountain country, from a camp high up. We could be in Colorado or Montana or Oregon. We might be at 6,000 feet or 10,000 feet. Based on the vegetation and sign you've determined that there are deer here, with good reason to stay. You've looked at the plants and water sources and trails before season, read the sign and doped the wind and figured out a plan. Now we hunt.

The camp is down from the rims, sheltered from weather and the eyes of deer. It's been a quiet camp, just us whispering and talking low. The fire was a luxury here, of little concern to the deer. Our clothes and bodies this morning are as clean as we can make them, and we'll take care not to push ourselves to a sweat as we climb.

We climb when the sky is still black, an iron gray to the east. There's no yellow up there, or pink or even a touch of white. The light is something that's leaking from far away, diffused thinly. If it were light enough to see cross hairs against the brightest part of the sky we would be too late.

But we're on time, with full canteens, loaded rifles and fanny packs plump with the needs of the day. Binoculars bang our chests a little, we've tightened the straps with a knot. All the glass is clean.

It's cold. The frost is thick on the ground. We shiver because our coats hang from our waists. In just a few yards we know it will be warm. Hills warm you quickly.

We climb into the thermal drag. There isn't much of it now, just a sense of settling. Last night it was strong. There's a trail that's hard to find but we don't use lights, preferring to go slow and stumble a bit. We thought about that, planned for it. We have the time.

It's an hour's climb, and just below ridgeline we rest. The iron gray had turned white, and then there was a pink streak and now there's a little yellow leaking up. The black has weakened even in the west, but the half moon is still bright. The stars have left us and you can see cross hairs in the sky.

Our breathing is back to normal. The wind is puffing at our bodies. We let ourselves shiver to dry any dampness, then don our coats. We won't be moving much for a while. We check the safeties, the glass. The rifles we've had on our shoulders are in our hands. We creep to the top and peer over. The bush on the crest, this bush we've chosen, will keep our heads hidden and cover us as we become part of the ridge.

It's hard not to look at the sky, it's so lovely. We'd be missing something if we didn't. So we do, briefly. Then we look down into the gut of the basin in front of us, into the dark timber that will again dilate our pupils so we can see detail. Before we raise our binoculars we look carefully without them, from near to far, from the basin head down. We look for movement, for off-white patches and solid blobs of darkness that are deer. We don't see any, not for sure.

Now we glass. Sitting on the ridge, we'd be skylined were it not for the bush at our backs. I look one way, you the other. We glass slowly, you in a grid pattern. I know the grid is the best way to glass but I don't do it because I don't like to. My way is like the chocolate swirl in an ice cream cone that's mostly vanilla. It's not a very neat pattern to watch, but I cover most of the ground and almost as well as you. Both of us stop moving our binoculars frequently, letting our eyes move in a field that's still. Then we shift the glass again, slightly. Our elbows are on our knees and it's pretty easy to hold the glasses steady with both hands.

In 15 minutes we're both tired and getting cold. The wind is puffing stronger and each puff is longer. The sun isn't up, but the sky is bright and its colors vibrant. You can see cross hairs in the trees. We lower the glasses and rest, then continue. It's easy to just glance at things or gaze. Our job is to inspect, scrutinize. That's work. Hunting is work. To hunt well you must work hard.

Another few minutes and the fire of the sun pierces a cut in the distant mountains. It will be a glorious day. I shiver with anticipation.

You say, "There's a deer."

It didn't just get there. It was there and we'd looked past it several times. It's far away, maybe 450 yards, feeding up from the bottom, near the basin head to our right. It's pretty much in the open and with glasses we can see antlers. It's not a big buck. You ask if I want to stalk him and I say no. You glass the buck again, then pick apart the surrounding cover, the bushes and little trees and big rocks.

"There's another one."

This one is a bigger deer. I can tell without looking at the antlers. His chest is deep and blocky and he looks more masculine than the yearling or two-year-old above him.

"You saw him, you take him." Nobody's cold now.

"It's too far. I'll stalk." There's no arguing. The time for being polite or talking about who is going to shoot what is before you see a deer.

You glass a little more to find landmarks. "I'll do this myself," you whisper. I nod as you drop quietly behind the bush and over the rim to the trail that threads the shaded side, the side we came up. I could signal directions, and make things easier, but easier isn't always better.

The deer move faster as the sun rolls up a mountain. They like its warmth but they want to bed. Still foraging, they walk slowly through the bushes, nibbling here and there. Their tails flick and their ears flip back and forth to catch the morning sounds. Once in a while they stop foraging to raise their heads and look. I see through the glasses that they sniff. I hope you have the wind.

You do, and you're trying to keep it. You move fast but quietly. You must get there before the deer decide to move with a purpose to bed. You've charted only their foraging route and will catch them only if they follow that route, and slowly. You are stalking blind because the ridge between you and the deer offers you protection from the wind. It screens you and muffles your sounds. When you come on the ridge again you'll shoot.

But the deer are alert to something: maybe you, maybe just the idea that it's time to bed. Both heads are up now, and they move purposefully, stiff-legged, away from the ridge, across the basin head, to the dense scrub on the opposite slope.

You see them as you top the ridge, and move in front of a bush, sit down and get into your sling. Your pulse is too fast yet and you wait as the taut sling battles the jiggling cross hairs. The deer are 300 yards or so but headed directly away from you. Now they're weaving among trees and rocks. When they stop the angle is wrong and they don't stop long. Everything is loose, sloppy. You could shoot and hit the big deer. But you don't feel that tight feeling, that feeling you're in control and can direct your bullet precisely. You don't shoot.

The sun's up when you return and I know before you tell me what happened because I saw most of it. We walk on a deer trail just below ridgeline on the sunny slope. We'll head down a bit, toward the timber, where in the shade of trees in small openings other animals might still be up and moving about. Because we glassed this well there's little chance another deer is in the upper part of this basin. The deer trail lets us walk quietly, where deer expect to hear little sounds and see movement.

One-quarter mile farther we're at the edge of the trees, glassing again. We eat raisins and bagels and drink some water. We let the sun loosen our muscles. In the canyon below the thermals are lifting. We can see that and feel it. Still hunting across the slope should be productive. We agree to separate.

I go low and you go high. Each step is slow, deliberate. I walk pretty evenly, with a short but definite pause after almost every step. You stop longer, less frequently. We go about the same speed. All the time we look. The cover here isn't thick. Still, a deer can hide in very little cover, and unless it thinks you've seen it, it will often stay motionless and let you pass. People think mule deer bounce out when you get close, because the deer that bounce out are the only deer they see. You remember the time on this very ridge I walked past a fine buck as he stood motionless. I saw his throat patch as I turned but kept walking so as to appear fooled. When I stopped I was ready to shoot and did.

You don't see the deer that bounces out. You know there's no sense in following. You wait a few minutes, counting so you don't cheat on the time, then move on. You must look more carefully. You do, and in one-half hour you see the horizontal belly line of a deer as you stoop to peer under a juniper. The horizontal lines of a deer are easier to see than the deer.

For many seconds you balance as you are, uncomfortable but wanting to find out what this deer is before it breaks. The wind comes then, canceling the thermal and splashing your scent to the deer. It crashes off and you see nothing but its tail.

We get together around lunch time on the ridge we'd climbed at dawn. It's a good place to meet, and an easy one in midday because you can glass the country. If time is lost getting together it's not so critical at noon—especially in a good glassing spot. We don't commit to meeting, ever, except at camp at night. There are too many things that can draw us apart during the day. Neither of us would compromise a hunt to get together. Loose arrangements are OK.

This time we saw few deer and had no shots. We kept to the trails, mostly with the sun behind us and the wind to our sides. We hunted good cover as best we could hunt. We learned a little more about the cover and the country and about looking for deer and walking slow. That will help us later, on other hunts.

Now we talk about the afternoon. You decide to explore, to hike a bit, glassing now and then likely bedding spots. I'll do the same in another drainage. We part.

Your pace is steady, a stride. It's fast but not quick. You're still careful where you step and stay aware of what's around you. The sun and exercise warm you quickly. You stop or slow down before you sweat. You walk just off ridgeline on deer trails, and stop next to a bush or tree to blend with it's vertical form. At each stop you glass, trying hard to concentrate. You drink a lot of water even when you're not thirsty.

About the time the sun turns red you've seen plenty of deer country and only one deer. But you saw that one, a little buck, unalarmed in its bed at the base of a cliff.

With all but west-facing basins in shadow now, you decide to move downslope to timber's edge to watch a stringer meadow with lots of trails crossing it. The seep at its base will attract deer. You sit down with your back to a tree just west of the slide. Thermals will switch soon, dragging down. You'll alert deer if you stay above the meadow. You can't see very far, but far enough in most directions to take advantage of what little light you'll have. Watching lots of country just before dark is silly because you'll have no time to stalk distant bucks and insufficient light to see beyond rifle range.

You're shivering by the time you leave. A doe and her fawn have drunk from the seep. That's all you've seen. It's a couple miles back to camp and you walk it as quickly as you can, using your flashlight in the timber. A stiff wind has come up and clouds have curtained the moon and stars.

You make it back to camp, eat a good supper and sleep.

In the morning there is snow, more than you'd have thought this early in the year. We get going at the same time and make the same hike up the ridge because we know it's a good spot. What we did or didn't see yesterday matters little. Sometimes you need faith, in yourself and in previous scouting and hunting trips that were productive. Unless we have reason to think the deer have moved we'll rely on what we know.

The snow is not heavy enough to have moved deer, at least not this early in the season. Later a light snow would signal migration. Now it's just snow. For us, though, it's a great option. Today we can track!

The glassing we did yesterday can't be done today because there's a cloud in the basin. In the dark we saw it and hoped for the sun. But the sky is overcast now. When it got light it did so suddenly, as it does on overcast days. Still the clouds stuck to the mountains.

We split up again. The inch of snow won't last if the sun comes out, but we can use it now. Better that we go far from each other so as not to cross tracks. I go into this basin, you head for the country you explored yesterday afternoon.

You move fast, along the ridge at first, looking with your binoculars into the basins on either side for deer. The places on rocks and trees where the snow has not stuck are dark, making the scenery speckled. It's hard to spot a deer in patchy snow because neither the white rump nor the brown body stand out. If you were glassing you'd take even more time and do it more slowly than you did yesterday. But now you are looking for tracks, keeping your eyes to the basins so you won't miss the obvious deer, the one that is moving.

You stop and take a compass reading, just in case the clouds move in. Then you glass a snowy slope below a saddle on a ridge that meets yours. A deer would be pretty obvious on this big white slide; but you're looking for something more specific. You're using the binoculars to find tracks in a place tracks are apt to be. Saddles are the easiest place to see fresh tracks in the high country, and they're one of the most likely places to find them.

Hunting in snow and heavy frost is productive because you can tell fresh tracks from old tracks. It's also easier to pick out deer against the white landscape.

You find them here. They're faint streaks from a distance. Had the snow been there a while there might have been places snow balls had tumbled down the slide. But this is fresh snow and still cold. In 15 minutes you're standing by the tracks.

They're well defined because the snow is not powdery. It was heavy as it fell, wet and sticky, and takes a print nicely. These tracks are big. There's only one set. The toes are blunt and the prints are well off centerline. While there are big does that travel alone and have hooves worn blunt by the rocks, the firm print of the dewclaws and the wide lateral spacing of the tracks makes you think this is a mature buck.

There is no way to tell the tracks of immature bucks from those of does, and sexing any track is risky. The mature mule deer buck is wide-chested and heavy, and often drags his feet. There are no drag marks here, but the snow is not deep enough. The other evidence suggests a big buck. You take the track into the basin.

Because the snow is new you know this is a fresh trail. If the snow stays the same temperature for several days it's hard to tell which tracks are fresh. You remember when I hunted where there were many fresh-looking tracks but few deer. The reason was that the snow had been the same temperature for six days. It had fallen late in the season after a very dry fall and about the time mule deer were rutting. Right after the storm deer had moved around, eating, migrating and mating. By the time I saw the tracks, the few deer that made them had moved to lower country.

You watch ahead as you walk just to the side of the track, careful not to spoil it because you may want to look at it again. Mule deer sometimes circle if they know they're being followed, walking back on the tracks they've made. Your boot prints there would make things hard to straighten out. Another reason you walk to the side is to avoid being spotted by the deer. The buck will probably keep alert to things behind him, especially what's happening on his trail.

You walk briskly at first because the buck is traveling at a fast walk, not foraging. His trail winds down the slope into thick timber, then back up into scattered bushes. It's a purposeful trail but not as straight-line and purposeful as a deer on the move to winter range. This is the kind of track a deer lays every night up here. Only now you can see it.

There's an anticipation in trailing a buck that's hard to understand by watching from a stand or still hunting. You know he's in front of you. You don't know where, but you know the

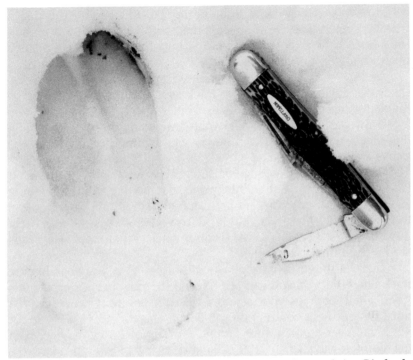

You cannot tell buck tracks from doe tracks if both are of normal size. Big bucks can leave tracks that are bigger than any doe's, and the prints are wide from centerline, suggesting a broader chest. The toes are often rounded, like these.

tracks will lead you to him. It's exciting! You feel that excitement now as you skirt a steep rim then plunge into the big timber opposite the saddle. He likes this drainage, you think.

The tracks are spaced closer now and you see where the deer has nibbled. You cross another set of tracks, and another. One looks as big as the set you're on and it's headed into the open country on the ridges. You'd like to take it, but jumping from one track to another is seldom a good idea. You refrain.

Soon you notice the track is leading you deeper into timber, across the basin, on an angle with the drainage. You stop for a compass reading, then go on. Another track joins the trail you follow. It was made by a smaller deer. Later it diverges. Now the prints are closer together and the trail twists. The timber is thick and you hope the buck has chosen another place to bed, a place you can survey before he knows you're there. With no wind today, a damp, steely cold hangs from the sky. If the wind were puffing you'd have to figure how to come in against it. With the tracks snaking here and there, it appears that the buck has started to look for a bed. If he's close, the wind is important. Until now you've ignored it.

As the buck has slowed you slow, peering through the trees, staying as far to the side of the track as you can without losing it. Suddenly there is a rockslide in front of you, an opening. You move forward cautiously. The trail straightens out and angles up the slide. You glass what rim you can see before you leave the trees. Then you climb.

Here the buck moves powerfully, with something in mind. It isn't a trot; the jagged rubble won't permit that. But something about the track tells you that he's alerted. You climb fast, right on the track because there's only a narrow path across the slide. On dirt again, the deer trots, confirming what you suspect. He heads across the slope. You follow.

There is rough country ahead and on impulse you abandon the track and climb. If you can see beyond the fingers coming off this basin's side perhaps you can spot the deer before it penetrates the thick new-growth conifers on the bench ahead.

You haven't much time, if any. For all you know the deer is in the conifers now. But if it was just a few yards ahead at the rockslide you may be close enough.

There's a rock above you, a big one. From it you can see. You're sweating in the cold, but there's a time to worry about sweat and a time to sweat. You climb faster, careful not to let your breath hit your binocular lenses. If they fog now you'll not have time to clear them.

Just below the rock you stop to catch your breath. No matter the time, if you can't hold your binoculars or rifle steady the deer is safe. Slowly you peek around the rock, trying to see deer on the fingers between you and the conifer bench a quarter mile away. There's still no wind, and while the clouds have inched up out of the basins they're still tight around the peaks, and the sky foretells more snow.

There's no deer in front of you. You make sure of that before turning to the opposite side of the canyon. When you do you see three deer right away. You can tell they're not big bucks by their body shape. In the binoculars and against the snow they become two does and a forkhorn. You look other places for deer, check the fingers in front again, then get out some peanuts and raisins. You drink too, more than you want because it's cold. After you're done you put your coat on to ward off the chill of your own sweat, then you glass the snow on either side of the conifers. You can see no tracks.

About the only thing left to do is descend the slope to the trail again and continue on. You don't like that idea because losing and gaining elevation is hard. Dropping to the track and stepping quickly along it you notice it turns down, toward the timber. The climb was for nothing! Now you wonder in disgust if one of the deer you saw on the other side of the canyon made these tracks. A doe or young buck after all that work! But you know you think that because you're tired, and you know that second-guessing has no place in hunting. A hunch works for you sometimes, but not a double mind.

The track stops short of the trees and winds along the foot of the slope, below the bench with the conifers. The deer is not trotting now; it's running! No doubt it saw you come out of the timber and start climbing. Then it came down behind a fold in the slope. Perhaps as you glassed it was watching from below—the only place you didn't look.

You run after this deer as best you can, slow to a brisk walk as the terrain gets tough. Beyond the bench the deer climbs again, slowing to that purposeful walk. The trail leads you over the rocks and through stunted aspens and low brush. You stop, look at your watch. Four o'clock! In an hour and a half it will be dark, and you're two hours from camp.

Before you abandon the track, though, you climb again, just above it, to look. This time there's nothing, even across canyon. Instead of dropping back down you angle up toward ridgetop. You'll walk the rim to camp. It's easier up there, and shorter. Half an hour later you crest the ridge.

On the other side is a basin, gloomy and rough-looking and turning darker with time. There is no sun but there's an evening look to things. You scan the basin without binoculars. This time you look down, and this time you see a buck.

He's not at the base of the slope, hundreds of yards off, but just below you, maybe 50 yards away. As you swing your rifle up he bounds downslope. The antlers are big and the back and neck are broad. He runs heavily. The cross hairs dance back and forth and you know it's hopeless unless he stops. You're too winded to shoot offhand at even a still target.

It's unlikely he'll stop, though. Mule deer often pause at the top of a hill or ridge. As long as they're above you they seem to think distance a safe barrier. But deer—and other big game animals—seem more frightened of things above them and charge frantically into cover without stopping. This deer looks as if it will do that too.

But you'll be ready if he does stop. You scramble downhill to a little rock ledge, where you slide into a sitting position. You'd like to use the sling but there's no time. And even now you find the slope too steep; you can't point downhill! The buck bounds under another rim and you can't see him anymore. Then, to your left, you hear something move.

Again, from what seems to be the air itself, a deer bounds into view. It's another deer, another mature buck. You find him in the lens and can't stay with him. He moves at a trot now, over the rocks and through a copse of aspen. On the other side he stops. His head is hidden and he must think his body is too. But you have the last ribs where your cross hairs meet, and the rifle stops wiggling long enough for the shot.

The deer is moving again, but out of control. You can't get the second shot but the first looked good. There's the clatter of rolling rocks, and when that stops you move ahead cautiously. Below, you spot a leg, and you know the deer is dead.

It's a fine buck but not the one you tracked all day. If you had followed the trail you abandoned, you'd have found it stayed at the same elevation, went around a point and angled up the back side of the ridge—up to where you flushed the first buck. When that buck had sensed you in the bottom he had changed direction but not destination. Instead of climbing the ridge and exposing himself to get to the next canyon, he had stayed low, working his way around the point. The fact that there had been another buck on the back side of the ridge when he got there was coincidental. It was a good thing for you, though.

So even this buck, taken with a good shot after a hard day's hunt, was as much a victim of chance as of your prowess! But that's OK, because you hunted persistently and as well as you could. You made some mistakes but did several things right. You hunted several ways in two days, adapting your style to times and conditions. You played a hunch on occasion and varied your pace as you thought best. On the track you tried to imagine where the buck was going, what he was doing and what he was thinking. You didn't follow procedures but did things that other hunters do to get a shot at a deer.

You can do those same things in the desert or on the prairie or in the wet woods hunting blacktail. You've shown how to adapt strategies to weather and terrain. Adapting to different habitat is just as easy.

There's a lot about hunting that you learn only by doing. You don't have to kill to learn—in fact, you may learn most when you don't kill, because then you spend more time in the field. Learning means that you stay alert and keep your mind open to new thoughts. It's a good idea to have a notebook of things you want to remember. Mine is a six- by nine-inch spiral notebook that cost 49 cents. It is the best bargain in hunting equipment I've found. Like a diary, it must be used to be useful.

Techniques To Remember

During the past several years I've developed a list of ideas that work for me. I suspect many will work for you. Some won't, perhaps, because you choose to hunt black-tailed and mule deer differently. But you might use these ideas to start a notebook of your own. When I started hunting, I wish I would have had a list like this. They aren't as fun to read as stories about someone's hunt, but they're the germ of what you can do to better your own skills.

1) Hunt the best times in areas you know best.

2) Be where you want to be in the morning one-half hour before you can shoot.

3) Time your hunt so you have no more than one-half hour walk in the dark back to camp.

4) Take several compass readings in new country or when tracking.

5) Wear wool mittens or gloves to keep your hands nimble for shooting in cold weather. Never allow your trigger hand to get stiff!

6) Occasionally check safety, floorplate latch, scope and binocular lenses.

7) Exhale through your nose, keep breath off your binoculars.

8) Never set your rifle out of arm's reach.

9) Drink more water than you want to.

10) Be alert. When you find yourself not alert, rest.

11) Hunt all day if you can hunt well all day. Time in the woods helps you get deer. Skill and time are what you have to give.

12) On days you think the hunting is poor or when you can't concentrate on your hunting, explore new territory. Hunt it, but be

satisfied if all you get is a good idea of how you can hunt it again. You should always be expanding your hunting grounds, but not at the expense of prime-time hunts in familiar deer habitat.

13) Mule deer use their eyes most at long range, their ears at middle distances, their noses close up. Close up, all the senses work well. The closer you get the more careful you must be.

14) Never look a deer in the eye at short distances, even if you believe you're hidden. Staring directly at the eye of a deer looking at you will prompt him to run away.

15) Hunt with the sun to your back if at all possible.

16) Never skyline yourself on a ridge. A bush behind you is almost as effective as one in front, because it breaks up your outline. Crest out next to a bush or tree or rock or in a sharp depression—not in an open saddle. Sometimes, especially at dawn and dusk, it's a good idea not to move at all. When you sit, break your silhouette with cover. It needn't be much, and is as effective behind you as in front.

17) Deer can see your breath, just as you can see theirs, in the cold.

18) Deer carefully monitor those things closer than 100 yards away. Within that ring deer perceive any threat as immediate. Their reaction depends on the cover.

19) Walk softly; mule deer have good ears and hear vibration in the ground. Wear jogging shoes where you can.

20) Walk on trails; step over things, not on them. Be quiet!

21) You can't be silent, but you can imitate the noise of animals moving through cover. The noise you make should sound like the noise a deer makes in the places deer expect to hear deer.

22) Hunt in the rain. Gentle rain puts deer at ease, and they'll forage actively in a light rain or mist. The rain confines your scent and muffles your noise.

23) Hunt in light snow. It also muffles noise.

24) When tracking, stay with one track in the snow unless you come across one as promising and definitely more recent.

25) Don't bother still hunting in dry, crunchy conditions or on a crusted snow. It's a waste of time.

26) Stop if you make an unnatural noise still hunting. Either wait several minutes before continuing or abandon the covert.

27) Move across wind or into the wind, but don't worry about shifty mountain breezes that blow from all directions. Worry won't change them, and even a strong prevailing wind can curl down into timber and onto the off side of ridges, splashing scent all over.

Sometimes, especially at dawn and dusk, it's a good idea not to move at all. When you sit, break your silhouette with cover. It doesn't need to be much, and is as effective behind you as in front of you.

Sometimes things jutting into the wind can cause a reversal at ground level, where you are.

28) Pay attention to thermals. The deer do. Thermals start rising about one-half hour after the sun hits the ground and fall at night near sunset. There may be a sudden and strong wash of wind downslope at the evening shift, but in the morning thermals will rise gently. Sudden wind puffs at sunrise are not thermals, though they may be caused by temperature changes in the air. Prevailing winds cancel thermals, and there's no thermal drift on cold, overcast days.

29) Think of wind as liquid the deer can taste 200 yards away.

30) Deer travel nose-to-wind when they can but run away from danger without regard to wind initially. While trailing deer I often have the wind to my back. I don't know if they intentionally run with the wind so they can tell what's following them.

31) Still hunt in good cover that hasn't been disturbed, with the wind in your face, as if you were stalking a deer. If you don't think there's one in front of you, why bother to hunt the cover at all?

32) Hunt cover that looks difficult and has lots of bushes and good escape routes. If it looks tough to you, it has to other hunters and the deer are likely there, avoiding you all.

33) Assume a mature mule deer buck will hold like a whitetail in heavy cover. Hunt slowly and look.

34) Hunt unlikely cover: fence rows and weed patches on the plains and any other little place that looks too small or isolated to hold deer but that has enough cover to conceal one. Water and forage and thermal protection must be close by. If pressure is heavy deer shift to places hunters don't look, no matter that such places aren't typical or customary.

35) Very rough or steep terrain is a poor bet unless deer have been heavily pressured. If you can walk or climb without using your hands it's not too rugged for deer; if you have to use your hands it probably is. Deer don't like to work hard to move around; you'll find them where the terrain is easy but the plants and topography afford cover.

36) In mountain country big bucks like to summer on ridges, but there are does on the ridges too, and some mature bucks down low near farm ground.

37) High ridges attract deer in the summer because there's little vegetation for insects to breed in and there are cool breezes to keep flies away. In cool fall weather, high sunny slopes are warmer than basins that act as a thermal sink.

38) While deer generally like to see from their beds, you can find bucks on flats in tall sagebrush and in standing grain.

39) In canyon country or on the plains, look for deer at the heads of wooded draws, not down in the gut.

40) Late in the season, but before winter migrations, look for mountain deer halfway between the bottom and top, where hunting pressure has been lightest.

41) Logging slash is a good place to find deer if it has ample leaves, needles and twigs. In winter deer stay close to logging operations, even when the saws are running, and move into the slash as soon as the loggers leave at night. The rest of the year deer move away from active logging, foraging instead in quiet, abandoned cuts.

42) Black-tailed deer like wet places much better than mule deer. You can find them in the swampy skirts of coastal rivers, as well as hillside logging cuts and second-growth timber.

43) Snow will move deer if it's deep enough to hamper movement—a foot or so. A late storm after a dry fall will move deer even if snowfall is light. Deer forage heartily before a storm, and if they migrate they migrate after it. Prolonged snowfall can prompt migration during the storm.

44) Deer will move to winter range before any snow if the snows come very late. Migration is gradual this way, unlike migration after a heavy snow. Big bucks are sometimes the last to come down, but does can also stay high late in the year.

45) Look for bedded bucks in burns, on ledges with bushy cover or young trees, in thick sagebrush on hilltops and in tangles of cover on slopes. They like to bed where they can watch their backtrail, see most approach routes and have good wind coverage.

46) Glass any area worth glassing twice as long as you think you should—especially during times deer move.

47) Brace your binoculars whenever possible.

48) Glass from the edges of openings before you enter them. Cross openings quickly.

49) When glassing, look for rectangular brown blobs, patches of off white, shiny things, straight vertical and horizontal lines. Ears and eyes and back- and belly-lines show up most in brush; full bodies, legs and rump patches show up in the open.

50) In open country, first quickly glass close, so you don't miss a deer in rifle range. Then quickly glass far away. Next, carefully glass far away, working a grid pattern. Rest often, looking for deer with your eyes unaided as you do.

This buck's ears are telling him about sounds behind him. He's lying in a position where he can watch his back trail and catch scents from places he can't see or listen to.

51) Look lower than you think you should in cover. Investigate any movement. Never second-guess what you think you saw.

52) Listen. You can hear deer move as they forage or travel or even sneak if ground litter is dry. In rut listen for the clacking of antlers as bucks spar or fight. When you hear a deer bounce, look immediately for an opening to shoot. A deer that has bounced even once is committed to run.

53) Once a deer has moved, snorted or made some other commotion deliberately, it assumes you have seen or heard it and will always move off.

54) When you see a buck, look at the antlers first and decide immediately if you want to shoot. Then concentrate only on your aiming point. If you don't have one, watch his ears and eyes and the muscles in his hams but keep the crosswires where you expect to see the shoulder or ribs.

55) In early season big bucks stay alone or in bachelor groups.

56) Mature bucks think only of themselves in escape, though bucks running together may stay together if the escape route of the buck in front is good. A mature rutting buck with a doe will split from the doe in escape, though the two will likely reunite as soon

In pressured areas, mature bucks prefer to sneak away rather than bounce or dash from cover.

as they feel safe again. Yearling bucks follow the lead of older companion bucks or does.

57) Mature bucks run low and heavily. Young deer bounce. Stotting is more common in young deer. Listen for the clatter of brush on big antlers.

58) Mature bucks like to sneak, not run. They make better use of cover in escape than do young deer and does.

59) Assume a buck will stop. Shoot before he does only if you have a very good position, angle and opportunity.

60) Don't shoot at a stotting deer.

61) Shoot from the sit with a sling. Make yourself do it, even if time is short. It will calm you down. You might relinquish a shot now and then, but you should never miss.

62) Shoot only at a spot on the animal; know the bullet path through the deer before you shoot.

63) Shoot when you are certain you'll kill with that one shot.

64) Don't shoot at a buck standing your side of another deer. Bullets that pass through kill and cripple.

65) Once you've fired, keep shooting until the deer is down.

66) If you kill a deer far away keep the crosswires on it for a few seconds before moving in. Mark the spot first!

67) A deer poorly hit will head for heavy cover and water. It's best to trail slowly, after a wait of one-half hour. The deer may stop soon, even if it's lightly wounded. But surely it will watch its back trail and may hook off the trail before lying down so it can better see you. If you bump the deer once it will be much harder to see a second time.

68) If you don't get a shot, mark the last spot you saw the deer and its direction of travel. Try to think of its destination. If the deer is in open country and goes behind a ridge or hill you may see it again. Stalk it slowly and glass very carefully. If the deer goes into a big block of timber or tall brush you'll need snow to track and find it again.

69) Deer that think distance or topography will keep them safe are vulnerable. Not many of these deer survive.

70) If you have the track, pursue a buck as long as you can. Mule deer and blacktail can be approached again and again.

71) Run after a flushed buck if in a short distance you might be clear for a shot. If the buck stops making noise, stop until you hear him again.

72) Think positively, appreciate the hunt. You are allowed to think of it as lots of work but not as a job. You have no mission, no one to please but yourself.

73) Keep an open mind. Deer don't live by rules, and what you observe at one time may be of little use to you later. Learn as much as you can and remember what you learn. Be willing to forget what you remember if it proves useless.

There are other items in my notebook. Some are elementary, but I write them down because I don't think about them enough. Other entries are blunt chidings. You probably don't need them; I deserve them and would kill more deer if I heeded them. Still others are observations about particular deer and particular country, things to remember in this drainage and reminders of the bucks that outsmarted me and how they did. That sort of thing is useful.

How It All Works

There's more to be learned from failing to kill a deer than from a successful shot. When we're successful we tend to be smug, less interested in how we could have done better.

There was the time, for instance, when I'd hunted the rubbly burn on the steep west face of a familiar ridge. I'd seen a couple of bucks, but they were yearlings. It was a hot day in early October and by noon I was trudging along a deer trail, being noisy and going too fast. Three deer bounded out of a fir thicket above me. I didn't want the buck so I just watched them crash off downhill. Then I resumed walking.

Out onto an open rockslide I tramped without glassing, and only good fortune kept the big buck still until I could see it. He was standing above me, about 150 yards away. It had probably been with the deer I'd seen just moments before but had split with them and sneaked uphill. I just happened to see the buck at the top of this rockslide.

I shot that deer, one of the biggest I've ever killed. My hunting partner thought that was really something, to have taken so fine a buck—and at midday. My wife liked the antlers too. All that made me feel very accomplished, but actually the buck was doing what he should have done and I was behaving like a raw beginner, marching along the trail. I stumbled into this buck.

Not that marching is always the wrong thing to do. In fact, the beginner's luck that people talk about is often not luck at all. It's the result of beginners acting in a way that deer don't expect. The more raw the recruit, the more likely he'll bumble into a deer. The hunters who have it tough are those who behave like the deer expect them to but are not disciplined, fit or stealthy enough to see the deer first.

Doing something unorthodox in the woods is sometimes a good idea. I try new techniques all the time. But it's important to be honest with yourself. If you kill a deer while being careless, as I did on that old burn several years ago, admit it. If you've deliberately broken rules and fooled a deer that expected you to follow them, that's different. You've learned something.

Because method follows predictability, any method you use to hunt deer is fallible. Deer are predictable only to a degree, and you'll be successful only to the degree that you depend solely on method. Methods that have worked for you and for me are still worthwhile because deer will behave more or less the same this season as they did last. Still, some deer are not vulnerable to method. They have learned to predict *us* and have become unpredictable themselves.

Last fall I was hunting elk in thick north-slope fir and larch when I flushed a huge buck mule deer. He got up at only 10 or 12 yards and lunged away, his thick, powerful shoulders and haunches driving him quickly out of sight in the black timber. Stout and muscular though he was, he artfully dodged deadfalls and standing trees. His wide, heavy antlers looked as if they would wedge him fast, but they didn't. In a second he was gone.

I hunt that ridge quite a bit. I'd never seen that buck before. Earlier he may have been higher, in the rock rubble and stringer meadows where you might spot him from a distance. But then again he may have been a timber buck, not following the rule that says mule deer like open ridges. He couldn't see very far from his north-slope bed. He didn't have to, though, because he'd found that almost nobody hunted that thick cover. He had figured out hunters and their method. He was all but invulnerable to someone with traditional ideas.

It's best to stay with simple plans. Elaborate ones seldom work. The more there is to go wrong, the more goes wrong. Deer need catch only a little mistake to get the better of you, and sometimes you don't even have to make a mistake—the wind or luck can scuttle your hunt. Occasionally, though, an involved scheme will work. It did for me on a blacktail hunt some time ago.

There was mist on the river, then rain as the sky turned from black to gray and the fissures in the clouds became plain. It was a typical coastal Oregon morning in December: quiet, close and wet. I couldn't see very far. The leaves dripped water in the woods behind me and the Willamette gurgled along to my right. In front there was a little patch of alfalfa.

The buck came through the alfalfa alone. He was a yearling in a cheery mood. He kicked and frolicked and only stopped to eat once. He was very fat. He was moving from the woods beyond the alfalfa to the timber by me. He saw me too late.

But I didn't shoot. Actually, I felt somewhat ashamed of even being there, of intruding. His energy was an inspiration. Here was I, drab and squat in the mist, a wet lump tuned to kill.

He passed me in long bounds. I heard his hooves tick once or twice and that was the end of it.

I got up and moved back into the woods. The mist swirled around me and the dripping was so loud and constant it sounded like applause. I made no noise at all in the sodden alder leaves.

Not far along the trail I flushed two deer that bounded off toward the river. They separated. One, I thought, is surely a buck. But they were alert now, in thick river-bottom tangles of blackberry, alder and willow. If I followed them the wind would be to my back. I had no chance at all.

Two alternatives came to mind. One was to abandon that covert. Another was to circle it and come in from the opposite direction, crosswind and along the river. The deer would probably still be close; my idea was to intercept them in the middle of the cover. Though it sounds simple enough, this was a sophisticated plan for me. It would be a tough job because the deer knew I was about and would be watching for me. Additionally, the brush was so thick I'd have little chance of seeing them first.

But the rain and river would help me. The deer could swim across the river but probably wouldn't. If they did I'd hear them. The river and the alfalfa limited their options and would discourage them from leaving cover unless I got quite close.

It took a long time to circle and find a deer trail that led me in the direction I wanted to go. There wasn't much distance to cover, but I had to go slowly to be sure I saw everything. I'd have just one chance.

The plan worked. I saw the ear of a doe first, only the ear. But as I watched there was suddenly a head. It hadn't moved; I'd just recognized it late. I eased the binoculars up and tried to see through the wad of twigs and vines and big branches comprising this covert. The doe's head was motionless, her nose up and pointed my way. What little breeze there was told her nothing.

I glassed till my arms ached. Then I glassed some more. I paid attention to the area around the doe, though it was only my hunch that the deer would get back together. Maybe the other wasn't a buck after all....

I lowered the binoculars and brought the rifle up. The 2½x Alaskan gave me a bigger field and better perspective, though detail suddenly sank back into the bristly wad of brush. I was ready to spook the doe and get this over with, when a little patch of white caught my eye. It was the throat of a fine buck. My only clear shot was to the face, but the range was short. I triggered the .308 Win. and the buck dropped instantly.

Here was strategy that worked. The premise was sound, the route a good one, my still hunting pretty professional. Still I was lucky to see the doe's ear. Both deer had seen and recognized me well before I'd seen them. They'd stayed where they were because it was a secure place and I wasn't close enough to be distinct in the mist or, given the dense cover, to justify bolting. Many things could have gone wrong but nothing did.

Sometimes even the simplest plan goes awry. On a steep north slope at timberline, seeps from the base of the rim were feeding

Often assumed to be open-country animals, mule deer are spending more time in the timber. Big bucks, especially, like to hide there.

lush stringer meadows between the rockslides. With plenty of stunted lodgepole, I couldn't see far on a clear day. This particular day was heavily overcast with thick clouds hiding the peak. By the afternoon I was still hunting a deer trail that looped about the slides and hillocks along the base of the rim.

Almost ready to turn back, I climbed to the top of a finger ridge and hunkered in the cover of a pine to glass one last meadow. The wind was coming up, the light fading and snow starting to fall when I spotted a doe mule deer about 130 yards away. I got into my sling and watched her through the scope. Through the curtain of snow I saw behind her the head and antlers of a buck. It wasn't a big buck, but it was late in the season and I wanted to shoot one.

With the .30-06 steady, I moved the cross hairs into the grass where the deer's chest should be, waited till I was certain of my hold, then shot. I was confident, and watched unalarmed as the buck jumped to his feet and bolted downhill. It was to be expected. I pocketed the empty. The snow got heavier. The doe lay still, looking my way. I stood up and walked toward her.

Suddenly the buck reappeared, running away, angling upslope. That worried me. I fired twice. The first shot missed to the left as the buck bounced right. I waited with the second and triggered it just as the deer crested another finger between two trees and went out of sight. It was a good hit.

First I tracked the buck downhill from his bed to be sure there weren't two bucks. There weren't. I followed his trail as it angled up toward that next finger. There was a little blood but not as much as I'd expected, and the deer's behavior had told me the first hit was not good. I felt bad about that, disgusted with myself.

The snow was falling in big wet flakes by now, so fast I could see only 20 yards. The tracks in the old snow were plain but filling fast. Darkness had come with the snow.

At the place I'd heard my third shot hit there was considerable blood under the trees, and the tracks cut sharply downhill. I knew the deer was dead, or would be very soon, but I couldn't wait. In the open the snow was covering the blood and tracks so quickly I would lose the trail if I didn't follow it right away. I slipped on a snow-covered rock and fell, brushing away the snow. The rock was bright red.

At the bottom of a rock slide I heard the buck crash into the timber. When I entered the trees there was no more light to shoot. Soon I lost the trail. My tiny flashlight was of no use in the storm. I climbed out of the trees. It was night. The snow was still coming.

I couldn't see the tracks I'd just made. Though I was familiar with the ridge, I lost my way coming off the mountain, missed the road my pickup was on and walked all the way to the valley floor, getting out of the woods at about 10 o'clock. I went back up the mountain the next morning to track and recover my buck. Six inches of fresh snow had obliterated the signs of the hunt. I found nothing.

To blame that on the snow would be wrong. Any time you make a shot it should be quickly fatal. Mine wasn't, and it just happened that unexpected weather kept me from claiming the deer. I made the first mistake. Had I made it a few minutes earlier I'd not have lost the buck, but you mustn't assume you'll have the chance to correct your mistakes. The only way to be sure you don't forfeit a chance at a deer is not to make mistakes.

But we all make mistakes, and even if we didn't we'd not kill deer every time out. The same luck that helps you shoot a deer can keep you and the deer apart. It's difficult to say when that happens, because the deer you don't see may be slipping through the timber or walking through the clearing you just glassed. Sometimes you know when you came close because the tracks are there. Or maybe you saw movement or heard something. It's frustrating when you do everything right, except the whim of a buck leads him away from you, and away from a shot.

But part of good hunting practice is taking advantage of luck when you can. It's anticipating typical and atypical behavior. It means you have set your standards of fair chase and keep to them, accepting graciously defeat by sour luck and cagey deer, but also being aggressive, probing for an advantage, turning bad luck into good and watching for the unexpected change that will better your position. You're keen on the scent but aware of what's going on around you.

I was trailing a deer along timberline just below the crest of a ridge. I was moving fast because the deer was. I knew it was a buck because I'd seen it, and knew that if I scrambled I could shoot it as it rounded a certain rim. Beyond that was timber and there the deer would lose me.

The track led through prime mule deer bedding at a prime time, but I was so intent on the track I hardly glanced to the side as I barreled along, sweating in the 20-degree air. A movement 10 steps away made me look up to see a buck rocketing from a small clump of whitebark pine. His antlers were huge! He ran downslope toward timber, clattering over the rocks, kicking up frozen clods of

The author took this buck at midday while sneaking through bedding cover on an Oregon rim.

dirt. As an afterthought, it seemed, he stopped short of the trees and looked back. I fired. The bullet from my 7 x 57 Mauser killed him instantly.

I wasn't very smart there, committing myself so completely to one set of tracks that I neglected to watch for others. Had I not come so close to the big buck he'd have lain still and let me pass. As narrow-minded as I was at the time, he could have done that anyway, right where he was. I would not have seen him. I killed him because he gave me an uncommonly good opportunity when I was all but oblivious to opportunity. The only thing I can say for myself is that I made a reasonably good offhand shot while panting for breath and mumbling to myself how silly I'd been for racing through such cover. It would have been better for me to compromise, to go a little slower and be more aware.

Sometimes, though, you must commit. Sometimes you'll have a shot only if you pursue it with all your energy. Sometimes you can't afford to distribute your efforts but must channel them. Knowing when to do this is as important as knowing how.

Late one season, with ankle-deep snow on the slopes, I climbed for a morning into country I hadn't hunted. It was an exploring trip because I thought most of the deer to be on lower benches. But as I got into clumps of conifers just below the rims, with wind-scoured glades between them, I found deer tracks. They were all filled with blown snow, though most looked only hours old. Instead of following any I still hunted the trees from clump to clump. The wind, I thought, would keep the deer in shelter.

Skirting the low side of a thicket of pine, I flushed a deer that crashed out the top. I had no chance for a shot, but I recognized the blocky form and muscular stride of a mature buck. As he flashed through an opening I glimpsed big antlers. The deer ran into a draw, down its brushy middle toward heavier timber. There was little chance I'd see it again.

The afternoon was about half spent and snow was starting to fall. Instead of backtracking along the rims I decided to parallel my trail just inside the timber below me. That way, if the buck hadn't gone too low I might push him upslope into the open.

I walked fast because the sky was getting dim and the snow falling harder. My only chance at a buck would be at the one I'd jumped. There was not enough light to hunt slowly.

The deer had stopped at timber's edge, and I flushed it but didn't see it. I followed its track along the top side of the woods and flushed it again. I ignored all other tracks.

The snow was coming so hard I couldn't see well. I was walking so fast there'd be no chance of catching the deer in the trees without spooking it first. I was out of time.

Climbing again, I left the trees and headed for the ridge. Panting and sweating, my only light was on the open slopes, and that was fading quickly. To hunt now was to race with the deer and the sun, both invisible. The more country I saw the better my chance of seeing the buck.

Now the wind came harder, driving the snow almost flat across the ridge. The light was almost gone when I glassed for the final time the black line of timber below. It was hard to hold the binoculars steady. In the blurred field, suddenly and like a ghost, he was there. His gray muzzle and russet coat, the thick, chocolate antlers—what a deer! But I couldn't hold the rifle still. Hitting would have been easy enough, but a killing hit was hard to guarantee. Knowing he was ready to bolt I flipped the rifle up, looped the sling on my arm and sat down all at once. As the rifle pulled the sling tight, cross hairs appeared out of the storm and settled on the treeline. Against the shadows, missiles of snow shot one after another across the scope field. That was all.

10

Shooting Deer

When the cross hairs settled down to a kind of sporadic bump I pulled the trigger. The buck jumped and ran; and then I heard the hit. But he kept running and caught up with the does. They crested the ridge and went behind it. I fumbled another cartridge into the single-shot rifle. My hands were stiff in the cold.

I followed the deer as fast as I could, but he was through the next basin by the time I got to the ridge. I felt bad about my judgment and my shooting, worse about the hit. It had been solid, destructive—I could tell by the sound. But the buck was still moving.

By the time I'd scrambled across the scree to the next ridge the sun was on it. I glassed quickly. There was more timber in this basin and surely the deer would go there. I would lose the track in the trees; there had been no blood for half a mile.

I strode ahead, not hunting but looking far to the front. I listened for rolling rocks, watched for movement among the stunted pines. The trail turned down into a cleft that gaped at denser timber below. I stopped for a last look at the top.

Rocks rolled and a buck raced into view on the rim above me. I sat down and let the sling drop because there was no time. Just a moment and he'd be gone again. Antlers flickered through the shadows against the rock wall. Behind a tree, out. Behind a rock, out again. When he rounded a snag I swung with the point of his

"There are no lucky shots," says the author pictured here with another nice mule deer. "You determine when and if a bullet leaves the muzzle. No one else does and luck has no part in it."

shoulder and fired as he sped into the shadows.

For several seconds there was no noise. Then a rock rolled, and another. Then the deer shot out of the rocks, pinwheeling through the air and landing hard on the scree. He slid quite a distance downslope and there was lots of dust. After it settled, though, he didn't move.

I was fortunate to have killed that deer. I'd judged the distance poorly during the first shot, and though my hold was good the bullet hit low, angling forward but not into the lungs. My last shot was good but it shouldn't have been necessary.

You have to do many things well to find a deer to shoot. You have to be a little lucky too. Once you find a deer there's no more luck. What you make of the shot is your doing only. A good shot means you have done everything right. There's no alternative. When you make a poor shot you've done something wrong.

When crosswires bounce this way and that and your rifle fires as they pass your target you might think you were lucky. If the next time the shot goes where you don't want it to you feel unlucky. But if you can't control the crosswires you do control the trigger. You can pull it or not pull it. You determine when and if a bullet leaves the muzzle. No one else does and luck has no part in it.

The first thing to stop thinking about when you think of shooting deer is luck. There is no such thing when you shoot.

It follows, then, that there are no lucky shots. I've heard some people talk about lucky shots and you have too. One hunter I know killed a deer at very long range by hitting it in the neck with a .35 Rem. bullet. He had no scope and had to elevate the muzzle until the deer was all but covered by the front sight. Another hunter shot a buck at 150 yards with a shotgun slug—the last in his gun—after he'd missed the buck four times close up. Again the gun was pointed pretty high. These are typical of lucky shots. They're shots that we don't make very often.

But really they're not lucky shots. The fellow with the .35 Rem. was just hoping the bullet would kill the deer. Surely he was not aiming at the neck. He could as well have hit the deer in the foot. Given his ability to see iron sights and hold the rifle still and shoot tight groups at 300 yards it's unlikely he could repeat the hit. The deer is dead and it's dead because this hunter shot it, not because it was unlucky or the hunter was lucky. That every shot is mechanical means luck has no part in it. That this man can't control the mechanics of each 300-yard attempt with his .35 Rem. means he will miss the vitals of most of the deer he shoots at out there. That's poor shooting.

The same is true for the fellow who shot the deer with a slug. He hit and he killed. The deer is dead. But his shooting was 20 percent effective. You can't count only the hits.

Where To Shoot Deer

The best aiming point on a deer standing broadside is about one-third of the way up from belly-line tight behind the shoulder. Find the intersection of lines drawn vertically through the elbow joint between the ulna and humerus and horizontally through the point of shoulder between humerus and scapula. If you hit that point you will center the lungs with your bullet, killing quickly and humanely and wasting little meat. The lungs are big vitals and easily destroyed by expanding bullets. If you miss low there's a good chance you'll hit the heart. If you miss high, the spine; if behind, the liver, if in front, the scapula. All are serious or fatal wounds.

Heart shots are OK if you don't like to eat heart and are content with an aiming area one-quarter the size of the lungs. Deer usually stagger or run a few yards after a lung hit; heart shots prompt a frantic dash, often farther.

Hits to any major bone should keep the deer from moving off, or at least moving very fast. But when a bullet hits bone it blasts bits of bone and bullet through a lot of meat, ruining it. If you hit the forward part of the spine you will kill the deer, but shots to other big bones are not fatal unless they destroy vital organs. You'll likely have to shoot the deer again.

Some hunters like to shoot deer in the neck. That's not a very good idea because the only part of the neck immediately vital is the spine and close-lying carotid arteries. I've shot deer in the neck. When I hit the spine the deer died right away. When I didn't it usually stumbled or fell and then regained its feet and was off. Then I had to shoot again, quickly and at a running target. Lots of deer are lost each year because hunters assume one that drops to the shot will stay down. A deer that falls immediately is one to watch because almost certainly your bullet went near the spine. If it shattered the spine the buck will not get up. But if it just clipped a spinal process the deer will be on its feet as soon as the shock wears off.

The brain is a poor place to shoot a deer. A brain shot is immediately fatal and destroys no meat, but the bullet makes a mess of the head, ruining the skull for scoring or mounting. Sadly, shooters least qualified to shoot at small targets shoot at heads. The results are deer with jaws and noses shot off and eyes torn out and ears and throats mangled. When you must kill a starving deer with a hammer because it has no jaw, you'll feel the same as I do about hunters who shoot heads.

Sometimes you won't have a good shot at the lungs and must take another shot or wait till you see what you want to see. The decision, when that happens, is part of your shot. I've killed deer with shots to other vitals, but seldom. If at all possible I shoot for the lungs. Hit the lungs and the deer is dead within seconds and shouldn't move more than 50 yards. I don't have to fool with a blood trail or bone splinters in my meat, and I never need to shoot twice.

Most of the time you'll find your shots are broadside or quartering. That's fine. If there's an angle, remember that the lungs have depth and you're aiming for the center. Think of them as a basketball. If the deer is quartering to me I hold on the near shoulder. You have the bone problem then, and you can opt to wait. It is not a good idea to try to slip a bullet past bone—that's like trying to miss a branch. Your attention must be on what you want to hit, not what you want to avoid hitting.

For head-on shots a center chest hold is deadly. Deer quartering sharply away can be shot through the last ribs, the bullet knifing toward the point of the off shoulder. I usually pass up deer facing directly away from me.

A bullet to the base of the tail will shatter the spine and anchor the deer for a killing shot. It destroys a lot of meat, though, and the spine is a small target. If you miss you destroy a ham but likely won't stop the deer from running away. If the bullet breaks a hip the deer can't run but it can still move, just as it can with a broken shoulder. Shots to immobilize game are usually poor ones. At best you'll waste a quarter of meat; at worst you'll lose the animal. Bullet damage to major bones is nearly always fatal.

Except for the hard quartering shot through the rear of the ribs it's best to keep your bullet out of the stomach and intestines. Shots there are messy, and meat that isn't tainted by the bullet will probably be when you gut the animal. You can kill deer facing directly away with a shot between the hams, but a little error to the side tears a ham and opens it to gut contents blown about by the expanding bullet. A shot to the paunch from the side is fatal, but unless there's snow you might lose the deer. A hit in the paunch leaves little blood on the ground and won't prevent escape. Starvation or peritonitis kill if internal bleeding doesn't. Conscientious hunters keep their shots well forward.

No matter how good you feel about a shot it's wise to quickly chamber another round, just in case. I open my bolt right away. If by then the deer behaves as I predict I'll pick out the empty with my fingers and pocket it, chamber another round. All the time I'm watching the deer. If it goes out of sight I at once pick a couple of landmarks to lead me to it. Usually it goes down before I lose sight of it. Then I watch it through my scope to make sure it's dead, choose landmarks and get out of my sling.

Angling slightly away, this buck presents the perfect shot. A hit just behind the near foreleg and one-third of the way up will destroy both lungs, and break the far humerus.

If I called a poor shot or the deer acts as if it weren't hit well I use the ejector, bolting in another cartridge and shooting as soon as I can.

Once a deer is hit it is your responsibility to recover it. To do that you may have to take shots you'd pass up on an uninjured deer. I do. Just last year my partner and I, hunting parallel along a slope, spotted two bucks moving away. I couldn't see Vern and didn't know then if he had seen the deer. I did know that he was below me, well out of my line of fire. I sat down, settled the crosswires on the buck in front and shot. The deer collapsed.

The other buck jumped ahead and ran uphill. I followed it with my scope. Vern fired and missed, then hit. But the bullet landed too far back and the buck kept going. It was closer to me now than it was to Vern, not giving him much of a shot. I knew the hit was fatal and decided to shoot to finish things. My first bullet at the bounding deer was ill-timed; it went high as the buck came down. The second shot was better and the deer crumpled and died. I'd not have shot at that buck but for Vern's bullet. After a deer is hit a clean, precise shot is less important than stopping the deer.

Deer react predictably to bullets most of the time. A deer shot in the brain or in the spine forward of the shoulders will drop so fast you may not see it go down. If you hit the spine near the shoulders or the scapula close to the spine the deer will buckle in the shoulders, dropping right away, often throwing its head back. Should you shatter the spine in the middle of the back the deer will go down squarely but often keep its head up. It will usually try to regain its feet and may drag itself with its front legs. A buck shot in the rear part of the spine will act the same way, but when he falls his back end will drop first.

A shoulder shot that doesn't damage the spine may still put a deer down. Almost always it will send the deer to its knees. A hit through heavy bones in the rear quarters will cause those quarters to drop. It's pretty easy to tell when you hit a leg low because it will be visibly broken. A broken leg doesn't stop a deer or slow it down enough for you to catch it. On one hunt I saw a young mule deer shot that had a bullet in its foot. The foot was broken and festered and the buck too thin to winter.

Any hit to major bones will sound solid and hard. If the bone is close to the skin, like the scapula, you may hear a crack when the bullet strikes. A deer has to be about 100 yards away before I hear a hit. Closer than that and the sound of the shot drowns the hit.

Hits in the fleshy part of the neck sound muffled, like hits too far back but not as sodden. A neck-shot deer pitches forward, may or may not fall depending on how close the bullet comes to the spine and how destructive the bullet is. If the deer falls it will get right back on its feet again and run. You must shoot again. A hit in the jugular vein will give you a nice blood trail but will not quickly kill the deer. Ruining the trachea or esophagus does nothing but invite infection.

When your bullet lands too far back you may hear the brittle snap of a rib but will always hear a thud. Deer hit in the gut jump forward at once, often kicking at their stomach with their hind feet. They usually run low and heavily and sometimes stop to look back after an initial sprint. Once in a while a fast bullet that opens violently will kill instantly with a hit in the paunch. But most of the time you must shoot again, and quickly.

Deer hit in the heart almost always run. Sometimes they run in a straight line, sometimes in circles. One blacktail buck I shot jumped around like a bucking horse for a few seconds after the hit. Deer can go quite far after a heart shot mainly because they run frantically and fast. If they line out, those few seconds they live may be enough to put them out of sight. In Africa I heart-shot a duiker, a frail antelope about one-tenth the size of a mature mule deer. My rifle was a .300 H&H Mag. The little buck ran well over 100 yards before falling down.

While the lung shot is most effective, it's hard to predict what deer will do when hit in the lungs. Most of the deer I've shot there have scrambled a short distance and died. A few have run frantically as if heart-shot. Some will simply drop. Once in a while a lung-shot deer will stagger or walk slowly in a circle. The result is always the same, provided you use a bullet designed for deer. A lung hit sounds as final as it is: a solid pop.

Sometimes you can't tell where you've hit a deer. One might stand still after the hit, giving you no clue. Another might do something you don't expect it to. Several bucks I've shot in the lungs have kicked as though paunched. Recoil can block your vision just long enough that you can't see a reaction. Or the deer might be in brush where it's hard to see what happens. For this reason it's important that you call your shots, that you be sure when you fire your reticle is where you want it.

Deer that are already moving when you shoot don't always register a hit. A sudden sprint usually means a hit, but you can't know where. If the deer changes direction or stumbles or switches its tail or lowers its head, you have probably struck. It's a good idea to keep shooting at running deer until they fall down. Not only because it's hard to tell where your bullets go, but because running deer absorb shock and a bullet's destruction much better than deer shot undisturbed.

Be deliberate but fast with follow-up shots. You practiced bolt manipulation for this very possibility. If the deer is far away and you question the range pay special attention to dust and snow kicked up by your bullets. Bullet strikes tell you all you need to know about range if your hold is good. If it isn't they tell you nothing.

When a deer is climbing away and you have time for several clear shots, hold your fire for a moment. Bullets hitting around it will keep the deer on the move. A sudden silence may cause it to stop offering you the only shot you should need. Better that you take one good shot than shoot holes in the hillside.

If the deer goes down on your first shot or lunges out of sight stay where you are for a moment, with your rifle ready. You're probably in the best place for another shot should one be necessary. Pick two landmarks to guide you to the deer. When I was young, I once spent 20 minutes looking for a deer that dropped to my shot in shin-high wheat stubble only 160 yards out. Who could help but find a deer there, I thought.

If you didn't see the deer fall but are certain of your hit, mark the spot where you last saw the deer. After waiting a few minutes, approach the spot. You'll probably find the deer within a few yards of where you lost sight of it.

A rifle bullet kills by destroying vital tissue. It transfers a lot of energy to do this but it cannot knock a buck down. One shooter wanted to find out about this and fashioned a heavy steel plate with handles on one side. He shot at the plate with a .458 Winchester rifle. The softnose bullets did not penetrate. Encouraged, he braced himself behind the plate as he supported the weight of it on the thin edge of a board in front of him. A friend, who was also a good shot, then fired at the plate. There were about 5,000 foot-pounds of energy smashing into the plate with that bullet, but the fellow behind it was not even rocked off balance.

Next to knockdown power, hydrostatic shock is the cracker-barrel choice for much talk and no answers. A lot of fluid in a deer has to move out of the way rather quickly to let the bullet through. When it doesn't move quickly enough—it can't, really—the bullet sends it packing. The explosive force of a bullet displacing fluid is easy to see. Fill a gallon milk jug with water, cap it, then shoot it with a softnose bullet. Fluid under such sudden and terrific pressure can do a lot of damage to tissues. Maybe this is hydrostatic damage. It certainly can kill deer if it happens in the lungs or other vital organ.

Besides this damage the bullet also rips a path, destroying the organ. Splinters of bone and bullet fragments acting as secondary missiles cause more damage. When vital organs no longer work the deer dies. Shock, strictly defined, is a result of damage, not a primary cause of death.

Finding Hit Deer

If you make a poor hit and can't immediately cover your error with a lethal shot you must know how to trail. There's not much to it; it's a simple thing. What's hard is becoming good at it. Trailing deer is like walking a tightrope. The fundamentals are easy; proficiency takes work.

The stories about primitive hunters tracking game in rocks or sand strike me as fictitious. I like to track and have done enough of it to feel good about my skill. Then in Zimbabwe I watched Philip,

Anything you can use to steady your rifle is worth using. A stump is a good choice. Otherwise, the author would use the sling.

a Matabele tracker, follow the trail of a sable in sand. The bull hadn't been shot so there was no blood. The tracker had only my word that the sable had been there that morning at all. In the dry sand, pocked with the prints of hundreds of sable, kudu, eland, impala and lesser antelopes, the tracks of the bull looked just like all the others: caved dimples with no form, size or direction. In one-half hour of pretty fast walking though, Philip brought me to the sable. It broke fast through thick thorn and offered no shot. That didn't matter to me; I had been impressed as I'm seldom impressed. Here was a *tracker*. He had stayed on the tortuous trail of this one animal in places where trailing seemed difficult without considering the distraction of other prints. He'd done it fast but as casually as you or I might follow a park path.

Philip got his training as a cowherd, tending cattle that roamed randomly through unfenced bush. Cows are as valuable in his culture as they are hard to keep track of. Young Philip often had to trail a cow through the tracks of cattle belonging to other people. He got good at it because the alternative was to lose cattle, a serious fault. When he trailed that sable he was doing something he'd done nearly every day for most of his life.

Since then I've not told anybody I know how to track game.

Compared to what Philip had to tackle, most deer tracking jobs are preschool. We have trouble with them because we're not good trackers. Our eyes have been abused by computer screens and fine type. We see little detail and what we see we don't recognize. The obvious things escape us.

The first thing to learn about tracking is that everything on the trail matters. You must see everything before you choose to discard any of it. You discard thoughtfully what you can't use, then let the things you retain lead your feet. The trail should pull you. All you do is sift information. If you do that well you'll find tracking fun and productive.

Hit deer don't always head for water and if they do it might be water you don't know about. Plunging to the nearest creek, hoping the deer will be there, is all wrong. If the deer is losing a lot of blood it will want to drink. But maybe it will go to a small seep, a familiar place. Deer drink most of the time at little places.

Go first to where the deer was standing when you shot. It is important that you do this, even if the deer was far away when you lost sight of it. The place where the bullet struck should tell you about the kind of wound you've inflicted, and that will tell you what you must do next.

When a bullet hits it always cuts hair. It may not make the deer bleed outside, but you should find hair. If the bullet did not exit there won't be much hair, and it will be very close to where the deer was standing. A bullet that exits is big and ragged, and will cut more hair and may throw it far from the deer. I've seen big clumps of hair blown 15 feet from an animal's off side.

Hair will confirm a hit. So will blood, but you don't need blood. Fat or hair or bone fragments can plug an entry hole, and if the hit is high the curve of the body will keep the blood from dropping before it's absorbed by and coagulates in the hair. If you see no blood at the place the deer was shot you might still find some down the trail. It might be that the only blood you find is right where the deer was hit.

The color and consistency of blood can tell you about your hit. Bright frothy blood means a lung shot, and your trail won't be long. Lung-hit deer continue to bleed as they run, each gasp spraying the blood to the side. There's usually blood high on the bushes next to the trail, especially on the side of the bullet's exit. Lung blood is bright, sometimes almost pink, because it's oxygenated.

Heart and arterial blood is bright, but not foamy. If there's a lot of blood far from the track it's likely you clipped an artery. Arterial blood is under high pressure and if your bullet severed a carotid, brachial or femoral artery—or the aorta or other major pipe—the deer will quickly bleed to death.

Venous blood is darker because it is returning to the heart and lungs for more oxygen. Venous blood is also under less pressure than arterial blood and leaks instead of squirts from a ruptured vessel. A deer can run far with damage to even big veins.

Paunch hits are easy to identify because the blood is very dark and usually mixed with material from the stomach or intestines. Paunched deer don't bleed very much outside because inner matter is forced into the bullet holes. Inside, though, gut wounds can bleed profusely. If bleeding doesn't cause death, peritonitis will. A deer hit in the gut will seek water right away but can travel far before becoming too weak to stand.

Deer hit in the liver are hit fatally but can run a long way. Liver blood is very dark.

Bright, random spots of blood tell of a muscle wound. One to the quarters will show up in the track as a misplaced hoof or a drag mark or skidding in places the deer would normally be sure-footed. Muscle wounds are not lethal. But the bullet causing the wound can penetrate to the vitals or shatter a bone, driving shrapnel and bone splinters in all directions, severing arteries and puncturing vital organs. Muscle wounds that aren't serious bleed sporadically but for a long time on the trail.

Blood spilled on thick dust is quickly absorbed and turns black under a hot sun. Blood on rocks turns black rather quickly, but because it isn't absorbed is much more visible if you see it while it's still red. Rough tree bark soaks up blood. Grass stems and the leaves of bushes show blood well, and sun-bleached logs show blood best of all. It's easy to see blood in snow; snow makes a little blood look like a lot and can make you think the deer is bleeding to death when it isn't. You needn't follow blood in snow once you can recognize the track of a crippled deer. It's better to follow tracks as long as you're sure you're on the right trail. If the deer stops bleeding you will have to follow its tracks anyway and you should know them well.

Once you determine where your bullet landed pay no attention to the amount of blood you see on the ground. If the deer bleeds to death it will still lie at trail's end. Besides, blood lost outside has no fixed relationship to total blood lost. Most deer that lose enough blood to die lose most of it internally.

A deer has about an ounce of blood for each pound of body weight. A 200-pound buck has about 200 ounces of blood—about 12½ pounds or 12½ pints. That deer will die if it loses a third of its blood, or roughly four pints. Four pints of blood spilled on the ground is a lot of blood, more than most hunters ever see. It is 25,600 drops of blood from an eye-dropper with an inside diameter of .30 inch, the size of a rifle bullet on entry. Even if only a small part of the blood is spilled on the trail you'll have to count a lot of drops before you can reasonably expect to find the deer dead from hemorrhage.

If you destroy the heart or lungs of a deer so that blood cannot circulate the deer will die before it loses a third of its supply. A lung-shot deer may drown in its own blood. One hit in the heart may drop because oxygenated blood is no longer being pumped to the brain.

A deer can live about three minutes with no oxygen. Suppose for a moment that it can run one minute. While deer can sprint at 45 mph, in most places they run no faster than 35. In one minute a deer racing away at 35 mph will cover over 1,000 yards. That means that even if you've placed your shot well you should be prepared to follow the buck one-quarter mile. Of all the mistakes hunters make tracking deer the most common and tragic is not staying with the track long enough.

Perseverance is more important, even more so with a poor hit. I've found deer that have been shot and left to die because the shooter had neither the skill nor ambition to follow. That is wasteful, cruel and unnecessary. No matter how developed your skill as a tracker, you must persist. Pulling a trigger is easy; with it comes the responsibility to follow hit deer until following is impossible.

How soon you should start trailing is arguable. If I think the hit is good I trail right away. I walk slowly so I'm ready if the deer isn't badly hurt and gives me another shot. If the hit looks to be a poor one it's best to wait a bit before taking the trail to let the deer bed close by. Once bedded, an injured deer gets stiff. Bleeding will weaken it. Then you can approach it slowly. The same deer, charged with adrenalin and closely followed, may run far and lead you where you can't follow.

Some hunters like to chase even poorly-hit deer right away because they think the shock of the bullet will wear off if they wait and give the deer time to rest. No doubt this is true. But if shock is the only damage and there is no internal bleeding it probably

Approach downed deer at the ready. Hits to the spine, neck muscle or antler may drop a deer, but it may not be a fatal shot.

doesn't matter when you follow because the deer will be alert and hard to approach anyway.

If there is rain or snow coming, or anything that will make trailing harder, take the track right away, no matter the hit.

When I trail a deer—injured or not—I walk to the side of the track so I can retrace it later if I must. Sometimes it will cross other deer tracks and confuse me. I've spent a lot of time on my knees looking for bent grass, dislodged pebbles, a dimple in a talus slide. Just before a deer beds it often hooks around to the bed so it can see anyone on its track. I approach good bedding spots carefully, sometimes marking the trail then circling away from it and downwind so I can inspect the thicket or ledge from a place the deer wouldn't expect me.

If you don't find the deer by dark you can choose to sleep on the trail or come back the next morning. Better to do either than press on in the dark. Hurrying in rough country in poor light is inviting an accident. When you hurry you miss things; instead of observing things you rush by them. You may lose the track, may even walk by a dead deer without seeing it. Because deer are active at dusk you'll likely see some as you follow the one you hit. You won't know whether to shoot or not.

Just after the sun had settled behind the hills one evening I spied a blacktail buck moving through some willows on the far side of a river. I waited till the shot looked clear then took it. The deer jumped and kicked at its belly and ran from the willows into dense blackberries. I chambered another cartridge and crossed the river to where the buck had been.

The willows were thicker than I'd thought. With the fire of a sunset in my eyes I'd badly misjudged what was between me and the deer. My position was steady and the range less than 100 yards, but from what I'd seen, I suspected I'd hit it in the paunch. I found tracks in the mud and followed them. I lost them on high ground but discovered blood on blackberry leaves.

I tried to walk into the blackberries but couldn't. They were too thick. They tore my hands and face and hooked my shirt, holding me back. As I fought the barbs one place another branch would wrap around me and fasten its claws. I crouched, shielding my face with my elbow, and waddled forward like a duck. A deer burst through the tangle in front of me almost close enough to touch. As it turned directly away I had a shot. I declined it.

In a moment the blackberries were again a solid wall, the deer having plunged through them like a porpoise cleaving the surface of the ocean. Then I lost the trail. There was no more blood at all. I got down on hands and knees and started making circles around the last blood. Because I couldn't follow deer paths while I made circles I came against blackberries vines so tightly woven even a wren would have had to pick its way through. Soon I was down on my stomach, probing for an opening in the vines and disgusted that I'd taken the shot in the first place.

It got dark. I forded the river and went home.

The next morning I was back, now convinced that the deer I'd jumped had been the injured buck and that the shot I'd refused would be the only one I'd have. Without blood I couldn't trail.

On my belly again I was quickly soaked with dew. But as I pushed against the blackberries to the side of the track I found some to give way, opening to me a tunnel. I crawled in. It was a little corridor—a foot wide and a couple high. It wasn't a trail in the way you'd think of one, just a channel of thick brush in a patch of very thick brush. I forced my way along it on my knees and found the deer dead only 30 feet from where I had been the evening before. The buck had made a sharp turn into the tunnel, squeezing through like a rabbit. If I'd shot the other deer or not returned in daylight I'd not have found this buck.

Trailing, like shooting, is best done deliberately. If you shoot that way you won't have to trail often.

What To Do With A Dead Deer

Last fall I was still hunting along a ridge near the head of a basin when I saw a hunter's tracks fresh in the snow in front of me. I changed course but soon heard shots so close I decided to look. In a few moments I came upon two hunters about to dress a small mule deer buck. They had shot at it several times but had hit it only once.

The buck was thin. There was a bullet wound in one foreleg and his right antler had been injured at the base. That antler had grown tight to the side of his head, down to his mouth. Next to the mouth there was still velvet on the tines. He couldn't eat or walk very well and probably wouldn't have lived the winter.

The hunters weren't too proud of him and told me they would turn the deer in to the local warden. They didn't think it fit to eat. I wondered then why they'd shot it but didn't say so. I watched as they unsheathed knives big enough to prune fruit trees.

They put the deer on its back, head uphill, and one of them sawed through the belly hair to the skin. He was a little careless there and nicked an intestine. Foul-smelling fluid oozed out. After that he worked quickly, ripping the belly skin from anus to the base of the neck. Then he used the big knife like a machete to split the pelvic girdle. Warming to his job, he attacked the ribs on the side of the sternum, hacking through them to open the chest cavity. Everything inside was then dumped outside, the stubborn parts pulled. He was done in a few minutes. Grabbing the buck by its one normal antler he dragged it down the hill, his partner following with the rifles.

These fellows started field-dressing the right way, with the deer on its back and head uphill. But they finished crudely. It was a messy job done with the wrong tools and techniques.

You don't need a big knife to dress a deer. I like one with a blade no longer than three inches. It should be a reasonably narrow blade with either a straight back or conservative drop point. It must be as sharp as sharp can be. Folding knives that lock are easier to carry than fixed-blade knives. I've dressed a lot of deer with ordinary pocket knives.

Some books go into great detail about taking care of dead deer. Telling what to do is a bit like describing how to ride a bicycle, in that there's more to the telling than the doing. Here's the way I do it. After a few deer you'll have your own method.

Where the terrain permits I lay the deer almost level. I hunt steep places so I've used rocks as chocks to keep the deer from rolling or sliding, the antlers as props to keep it on its back. Cutting the legs off at hocks and knees prevents them from flopping around and pulling the deer over. I cut the hocks low to keep the hamstrings intact and make the quarters easy to handle later. Because deer are always sliding when I want them to stay put I habitually work from the rear, with my knees against the hams to keep them spread and to hold the deer in one place. I pinch up a little belly skin just forward of the penis and stab through it, knife blade up.

I extend this slit to the base of the sternum in front, then along the side of the penis to the anus in back. I try to cut only the skin, leaving mesenteric tissue intact the first pass. I always cut with the blade up, pulling up from underneath so the hair doesn't dull my blade. I shield bulging organs from the knife point by keeping a finger on either side of the blade, the palm of my right hand up. After the skin has been slit the length of the paunch I slit the layers underneath, taking care not to puncture the stomach or intestines. Spilled paunch contents almost always taint meat. If the bullet tore

Field dressing mule deer and blacktails is like learning to ride a bicycle: you learn only by doing. Use a small, very sharp knife. Cut from the inside, shielding the entrails so you don't slice them. You don't need to sever any bone.

the innards or if I make a mistake with the knife I work quickly to get the insides rolled out on the ground where they can leak without ruining meat.

Usually my bullet hasn't touched the gut, and I have plenty of time to work. While the intestines steam I core the colon, inserting my knife at the side of the anus and cutting around it. It's good to have the rump just a bit off the ground for this job. As the rear of the colon comes free I cut deeper, working around it and forward through the pelvic cavity. When I can go no farther I paw the intestines out of the way in front of the pelvis and finish the job from there. I cut the penis close to the anus, slicing it and the testicles free of the paunch and tossing them aside. Now what is inside the deer will easily come out.

Sometimes I scoop it out so I don't get dirt in the paunch cavity. On snow or clean grass I roll the deer on its side and pull the intestines and other organs free, cutting mesenteric tissue as need be. I always save the liver, severing connections carefully because it's easy to nick an intestine here. The colon comes out

Core the colon and pull it forward so you keep the entrails intact. Roll them out, cutting the esophagus and trachea far to the front. Separate the liver and pull the heart out later.

forward. Some hunters tie it closed at the rear so it doesn't spill pellets on its way out. I don't bother, just clearing the channel of pellets afterward. They don't touch meat.

Now I reach forward of the paunch, cutting around the diaphragm. Usually this uncorks a wash of blood as lungs pulped by the bullet rush to the rear. That's OK. The deer is on its back and the blood will go out through the pelvic tunnel. I cut free the rest of the lungs, then the heart, saving it. With my hand I sweep blood out of all the little pockets collecting it so it doesn't pool. If there's snow I wipe the insides clean with it. Then I lift the front of the deer and let it drain a few moments.

If I'm to leave the deer I use sticks to prop it up in front, open between the ribs and off the ground in several places along the back to cool. On sunny days or when it's raining or snowing I first move the deer under a tree or into the shadow of a rock. I leave the heart and liver in the snow, on a rock or in the open paunch of the deer.

Most deer I shoot I bone out to pack out. I've dragged them

over snow, and that works well if you have a trail. I've carried them in halves, unskinned, and don't like that method. Once a partner and I packed a deer six miles with its feet tied together over a pole like you see Indians doing in history books that tell of the Pilgrims and the first Thanksgiving. I was thankful I didn't have to carry that deer any farther.

If you have snow or wet grass and smooth, open ground that is level or slopes down from where you are, dragging is a pretty good way to bring a deer home. I hardly ever shoot deer where conditions are this nice, so I don't drag deer very often. Even in the best conditions big bucks pull hard after a mile or so. On bare ground or through timber with deadfalls it's foolish to drag. The hide will be ruined and you'll work much harder than you must.

I don't skin a deer until I have the packframe ready. The skin keeps the animal clean and scavengers from finding it quickly. I skin with the same little knife I use for gutting deer. I start at the hock and knee joints and run the blade point up under the skin on the insides of the legs to pelvis and sternum. Then I work with the knife under the hide around the hind legs, stripping them and peeling the hide down each ham. If I don't want to save the cape I extend the paunch slit all the way up the sternum and neck to the base of the jaw. As I did at the rear, I peel the skin off ribs and neck down to the back, spreading it flesh-side up on either side of the deer to keep hair from touching the meat.

When only a small strip of hide along the back remains attached I roll the deer on its side, still resting on the hide, and cut the back free. Next I cut the head off by working the knife blade between two vertebrae, then twisting the head by the antlers.

If you decide to cape the deer you must skin differently. The inside leg cuts are the same, but in front do not bring them in to the center of the sternum. Instead angle the cuts to the rear to meet about six inches behind the leg. At that spot begin a cut through the hide around the deer. For a proper shoulder mount you'll need all the hide forward of that cut.

Once you've made this cut around the ribcage skin you can either skin the back part of the deer or cape it first. The deer should be on its back no matter what you decide. To cape, peel the leg and shoulder skin down toward the backline as you would if skinning the front quarters. But don't make any cuts in the brisket or throat. When you've gone as far forward as you can, roll the deer on its side and cut a straight line from the center of the back of the skull along the top of the neck between the shoulders to the circumferential

Wipe the body cavity clean or wash it with cold water and dry it. Keep the carcass cool and dry. Cover it if you must to prevent dust and flies from entering.

cut you made around the ribs. Peel and slice the neck skin down to the throat on each side. The cape should now be free to the back of the head.

Next make a short cut from the front end of the neck incision to the base of each antler. With the knife blade cut around the burr of each antler work the skin forward on the skull. At the sides of the head cut the ears off inside, being careful to sever only cartilage. The head will be cased like a mink.

Pull the skin forward on the head as you would a sock you wanted to take off inside out. Cut as you need to, with short strokes. Face skin is thin and the hair is short; a slit here is hard to patch. When you reach the eyes be especially careful to save the lids. Get down deep into the preorbital cavity with your knife point. The lips and nose should have some fat and cartilage left on the flesh side when you're done. It's better to flesh delicate parts later than cut things close when removing the cape.

You won't know exactly what to save and what to leave with the skull the first time. You'll make mistakes. After showing a taxidermist your first cape you'll know better how to cape. It's one of those things you must do to understand. The first time save anything that has color, and more skin behind the shoulders than you think necessary. Roll up the cape flesh-side in and put it in a game bag or pack pocket or tie it like a rolled roast to the bottom of your packframe. Don't drag or hang a deer that you want to cape. Keep the cape dry and clean.

Boning is simple. You just cut the meat off the bones. Cut it in the biggest chunks you can pack easily, to waste as little as possible. Be sure to get the backstraps on either side of the spine below the saddle inside the deer. These two tenderloins are best taken as long ropes of meat, cut free from the spine and ribs at roughly right angles. Get all the neck you can, and the meat between the ribs. Leave all fat and the gristly ends of the shank meat. The more time you have to bone the more meat you'll get and the less you'll have to pack off the mountain and discard later. Boning takes quite a while, but it's something you'd have to do anyway at home.

If the weather is warm let the buck cool thoroughly before you bone it. If you have to carry warm meat many miles in your pack it can spoil. On most hunts I like to leave deer overnight to cool. If the weather is very cold, though, it's best to bone before the deer gets stiff. I remember a very big buck I had to leave overnight in severe cold before boning. The meat came off in little chips, as if I was carving hard soap. I could work only a few minutes at a time before my hands would get numb.

Boned meat is best put in muslin sacks, then in your pack. Except in very cold weather it will bleed through the sacks into your pack. The blood will wash right out with cold water when you get home. My old pack has carried so many deer I no longer use muslin, just stuffing the meat into the pack pockets. It's a red pack, the right color for this kind of thing.

The way to get tasty venison is to shoot each deer in the lungs, field dress it promptly, make sure it cools right away and keep the meat cool, clean and dry. Treated well, venison is as fine a fare as beef and better for you because it's leaner. Poorly-handled venison tastes bad. People say it's gamey. The truth is, game meat is good meat. Bad flavor is sometimes caused by things the deer eats, but usually by improper field care.

Meat is heavy stuff, and a big load won't fill your pack. You'll have plenty of room for camp on top. About a third of a deer's weight is usable boned meat; 70 or 80 pounds would be an average for mature mule deer where I hunt.

To remove the skullcap with the antlers you'll need a small saw. Without the saw you must carry the head. To comply with regulations you may have to leave the eyes attached to the skull cap or pack out the head. Once my partner and I went with two other hunters on a backpack hunt. All of us shot deer. No one had brought a saw. We packed out camp, four deer and four deer heads. A saw weighs less than a head and will cut wood too.

I usually discard the hide on a backpack hunt because it is heavy and I don't use it. If you aren't too far from a road or can drag your deer out it's best to save the hide, being careful when skinning so that you don't nick it. After it's off you can flesh it with your knife, scraping off the fat, meat, sinew and mesenteric tissue.

Next salt it with a pound of table salt, rubbing that into the flesh side vigorously by hand. Roll it up and keep it cool. In a couple days drain it of the water the salt has drawn out. Resalt it and roll it up again and put it in a garbage bag and then in your freezer. It will store well for several weeks. While you can keep it longer than that, any hide is best tanned promptly. You can salt and store capes the same way, but lips and ears have to be turned if you're storing one for more than a couple weeks.

The Missed Shot

The most common cause of missed deer is shooter incompetence. In fact, there aren't many factors that prevent a bullet from going where we want it to that we don't control or can't accommodate. Excuses wear thin fast on people who know about shooting.

But there are things besides the fundamentals of holding the rifle and triggering the shot that affect that shot. The most important are wind, distance, shooting angle and target movement.

Wind. Wind is a powerful force affecting all bullets. From the front or rear, normal wind has the opposite affect of what most people think. Head winds lift bullets, tail winds depress them. While you might think head winds would slow the bullet and tail winds push it, there's not much of either going on. A bullet speeds along at over 100 times the velocity of strong wind and any difference in velocity caused by the wind pushing or pulling it is slight. The drag caused by air friction, wind or no wind, is already 56 times the force of gravity.

But wind as pressure does affect bullets. You won't see how at deer-shooting ranges with deer rifles and ammunition, but on the

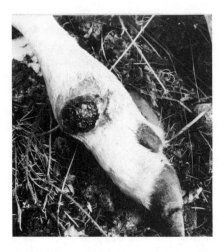

All good hunters are good marksmen, and all good marksmen use good judgment. Some dolt shot this deer in the foot.

target range with an accurate rifle you'll find bullets hitting high in a headwind, low in a tailwind. This is because a bullet launched roughly tangent to the earth is launched nose up from a barrel. If it weren't it would drop below the target. Unlike an arrow with its weighted tip, a bullet retains this nose-up attitude throughout its flight. Wind scooting under the bullet tip from the front lifts it. At the same time there's low pressure on the top-side of the bullet behind the tip. The opposite happens if the wind is from the rear. It bears on the bullet's top; low pressure is now under its nose.

But that won't bother you much when hunting. A side wind is the one to watch. Its affect is most severe at right angles to your bullet's path, less as the angle increases or decreases. How far the wind shoves your bullet depends not only on the wind but on the bullet—its speed, shape, weight and ballistic coefficient. Fast bullets spend less time in the air than slow ones and the wind has less time to work on them. But velocity is most important as it affects lag: the velocity lost between muzzle and target. Bullets with less lag are less affected by the wind. A high-speed .22 long rifle bullet has more lag than a .22 match bullet. Though the .22 long spends less time in the air it is more easily pushed by the wind.

Bullet rotation speed and direction matter too. A 9 o'clock wind, you might think, would push bullets to 3 o'clock. It pushes my target bullets to 4 o'clock. A reversal shoves them to 10 o'clock.

Heavy bullets are less affected than light ones, all things the same. But a modest wind the other day drifted my 300-grain .375 H&H Mag. bullets six inches from 200 yards. The shape and ballistic coefficient of a bullet are important because they determine how well a bullet resists any force working to change its speed or direction.

You can calculate what affect wind will have on your bullet. One formula is $D = RW/C$. D is the deflection in minutes of angle. R is the range in 100s of yards. W is wind speed in miles per hour. And C is a constant for a given bullet at a known velocity. For most western deer cartridges, this constant is 10 ($C = 10$). A .30-caliber, 150-grain flatbase bullet fired from 300 yards ($R = 3$) in a 20-mph wind behaves like this: $D = 3(20)/10 = 6$ MOA or 18 inches at 300 yards.

Another way to calculate wind drift is $D = W(T\text{-}Tv)$ where D is deflection in feet, W is wind speed in feet per second, T is time of flight and Tv is time of flight in a vacuum.

In the field you won't have time for paperwork so must learn to judge what you see and correct quickly for what you predict the wind will do to your bullet. You can't see the wind, but you can see the movement of grass and trees and you can feel the wind on your face. Wind under 3 mph hardly drifts smoke. At 5 mph it moves thistledown. At 10 mph it unfurls flags, bends grass and blows leaves. At 20 mph it straightens flags. We lean into wind blowing 25 mph, and at 30 mph we head for shelter. You don't have to know the numbers to shoot successfully in wind if you shoot a lot in wind; but they'll help you if you want to calculate wind drift or read what other people have to say about it.

Reading mirage is a worthwhile skill. Mirage is the shimmering you see in a warm day if you look down a railroad. You can see it dance in your scope at a target range or if you're hunting prairie dogs. The earth is radiating heat too fast for the air to absorb it gracefully, as a tea kettle emits steam too fast for the air to soak it up. When you take the kettle off you can't see any more steam, but the water that's left is still there.

Mirage isn't wind and it doesn't affect your bullet. Strong mirage can affect what you see as your target. The best thing about mirage is that it shows you immediately what the wind is doing. It flattens out as the wind speeds up, bubbles and rolls as it slacks, boils straight up if it dies. Like waving grass, it's close to the ground, where you want to know about wind. There's little mirage in most places come deer season because cold cancels it. But you can learn about wind by shooting in mirage in summer.

A problem with shooting in wind, especially at long range or small targets where little errors count, is that to do well you must aim where you don't want to hit. That bothers some shooters. To hit you must do it, though, sometimes quickly. You must treat the wind as real because it will affect your bullet. That you can't see it doesn't matter. Neither does it mean you can't beat it. Wind is like liquid. If you think about it like that you can dope it.

One day when there was very little wind I cleanly missed a mule deer buck facing me at just a bit over 400 yards. I'd favored the windward side but not enough. He stood still and from my rest on a rock I fired again, striking him in the heart. He lurched and stumbled, charged into a patch of timber and died. I'd held a foot off his left side, 20 inches above where the bullet hit. Another time I shot a buck at about the same range in very strong wind. This buck was broadside. I held nearly a foot in front of his nose and hit his heart. I'm not a heart-shooter at long range; these bullets were for the lungs, but hit a tad low.

When you sight in a deer rifle it's best to do it in calm weather. A target shooter must use prevailing conditions for his zero because he has little time to shoot several shots. To zero for calm would mean a correction for each shot. Besides, a calm condition is pretty temporary most days and usually signals a reversal. It's safer to shoot targets sighted for prevailing wind. On the hunt you must know your rifle is sighted for no wind so you can accommodate any or shoot with a center hold in a lull. You'll usually have but one shot and won't care what the wind has done in the last half hour or what it will do in the next.

Wind makes your bullet hit where you aren't looking. Gravity and wind both tug your bullet from your line of sight and compel you to adjust that line to more closely correspond with the bullet path. We build in some adjustment for gravity when we sight in because gravity is a constant. Wind is not so we must compensate for wind on the hunt by holding off target.

Distance. The trajectory of bullets from modern deer cartridges like the .270 Win. is flat enough over normal hunting ranges that you seldom need to hold high. You can sight in for very long range and never have to hold high, but that means you'll shoot over closer deer unless you hold low. Most hunters think it's OK for a big game bullet to hit within three inches of where they want it to, so they sight in to put the bullet three inches above the line of sight at the apex of the trajectory. That way they take advantage of all the point-blank range they can: about 250 yards for the .270. Oddly, many hunters then shoot over deer beyond 100 yards, probably because even a modest 200 or 250 yards looks farther than it is and they think they must hold high.

There are shooters too who think that because the cartridge they use has a belt or was recommended by some gun guru that its bullet doesn't drop at all. They shoot right at any deer they want to kill, not knowing the range or caring about it. They miss a lot of deer and break some legs. They don't think about gravity at all or read ballistics tables that would tell them a 150-grain, .30-06 bullet drops nearly two feet from line of bore at 300 yards and almost six feet at 500.

To hit deer between your muzzle and 250 yards you must know how to shoot and accomplish well what you know. With the .30-06 you can hold the same for long distances and short if the deer shows you its whole ribcage; the long distances only magnify errors. Zeroing at 200 yards you've put sightline at an angle to boreline, so instead of dropping 17 inches from where you're looking at 250 yards the bullet falls only three.

Beyond 250 steps, though, you'll have to compensate a bit or miss your target by more than three inches. To do that you must know the range. Many shooters who memorize ballistics tables can't tell how far away a deer is in the field. It helps you little to know how far your bullet will drop at 400 yards if you don't know how many yards it is to the deer you're aiming at. The longer the range the harder it is to estimate and the more critical it becomes because a bullet falls in a parabolic curve, more sharply as it travels farther from the muzzle.

You've read of buffalo hunters shooting bison at long ranges with slow bullets shaped more like soup cans than rockets. Some of these stories are lies. Of the rest, those that aren't innocent exaggerations are true because a bison is a big target and the hunters had plenty of time and perhaps a practice shot or two. They often shot many animals from one place and knew by the previous hits where to hold. They were good at judging yardage because they made their living doing that and most of the time they shot in country that made judging yardage easy. Still, their bullets were dropping fast when they did hit bison. An error in range estimation of 50 yards at 1,000 yards could mean a miss! The bullet would drop several feet in the last 50 yards.

Judging range well is something you learn by pacing off every shot you take, by practicing with your rifle at long distances in the off season, by pacing after guessing how far they are. Pretty soon you think of range when you look at something and your guesses are better.

How you judge range is impacted by how you see the deer and its surroundings. Big flat areas make deer seem closer than they are. A canyon or broken country between you and the deer makes it seem farther. In good light deer are well-defined and appear close. At dawn or dusk, when it's raining or snowing or when there's fog, close deer look far away. An exposed deer looks bigger and closer than a deer partly in shadow or obscured by branches. A deer on its feet seems closer than one in its bed. Looking up or down can fool you; things below look closer than things above. And what you want to see is often what you perceive. If you want to see a deer within range badly enough the next one will be, no matter the yardage.

You can use your sights and scope to estimate range. The bead on one of my iron-sighted rifles subtends six inches at 100 yards. A dot in one of my scopes covers three inches, like the tip of the post above the horizontal wire in another. The duplex crosswire in another has a thin portion below the intersection that's seven inches tall. Because I know a mature mule deer buck has a chest 18 to 20 inches deep I can estimate range close enough for a hit just looking at my sight or reticle against the deer.

I try to keep my shots at deer within 400 yards. To 250 yards I can hold center. If the deer looks a bit farther than that I hold at the top of its shoulder. Whether it's 275 or 300 or 325 yards away doesn't matter because my bullet will kill whether it drops four inches or six or eight. If I think the deer is at the edge of my range, almost 400 yards, I lift the crosswires just over its back. At 400 yards there's daylight half the depth of the deer's chest between my horizontal wire and the deer's back.

I don't shoot farther than 400 yards because I don't like to miss and like even less to cripple. Besides range estimation there are other factors to worry about: wind, the accuracy of your rifle, your own holding and shooting skill, the possibility of a follow-up shot, the problems of calling your shot, tracking and even finding a dead deer in rough country.

With a good scope you can see a deer that is too far to hit with the best of rifles. The best of rifles will group within the vitals of a deer farther than you can accurately estimate range. Good shooters are not the ones with the most long-range kills but those who kill at every range they shoot.

Shooting Angle. Our perception of distance is part of the reason we miss shooting uphill and down. Because only the horizontal part of a bullet's flight is affected by gravity we must know not only the distance to the deer but the angle and how much to subtract for the vertical component not affected by gravity. If you shot a bullet straight up it would eventually fall back to earth because air friction and gravity are pulling it. But it would not arc because if there were no wind there would be nothing affecting its original direction. The bullet would fly straight; only its velocity would be affected by gravity. If you were to bore a hole through the earth and shoot into it, again perpendicular to a line tangent to the earth's surface, the same thing would happen. The bullet would fly straight, to be dragged down eventually by air friction and gravity.

When you shoot at a deer at an angle to horizontal, think about the bullet's path as the hypotenuse of a right triangle. The horizontal part of its flight then becomes one leg and the vertical part another leg. The horizontal leg is the important one.

Suppose you wanted to shoot a deer 500 yards away. This is too far for an accurate shot, but it makes the illustration easy. If the deer were at about the same elevation as you, you'd hold for 500 yards and hit. But what if the deer were uphill at a 30-degree angle? At this long range you know miscalculations can mean a miss or crippling hit because the bullet is arcing down pretty steeply. What range would you hold for?

If you held for 500 yards you'd miss high. The correct hold is for 430 yards. Here's why: If the hypotenuse of a right triangle with one 30-degree angle is 500 the leg adjacent to that angle will be 430. The bullet will travel 500 yards, but gravity will only affect it's 430-yard horizontal travel.

If the shot angle were 60 degrees you'd calculate the length of the short leg of the triangle, here 250 yards. You'd hold for 250 yards and hit. If the shot angle were down instead of up you would hold this way too. Gravity has virtually no effect on the vertical component of an angled shot at hunting ranges so it does not matter whether you shoot up or down. Only the horizontal distance counts. Now, there is some difference in points of impact between bullets fired horizontally at 430 yards and those fired at 500 at a 30-degree angle. The bullet traveling 500 yards is in the air longer so must battle friction and gravity longer. It hits lower but not enough lower to notice with most hunting rifles.

Practice shooting uphill and down, at long ranges if you can.

Running deer are hard to hit well. Better that you don't shoot than cripple a deer. Shoot only if you've practiced on moving targets, have the lead figured and are sure you can hit the imaginary basketball in the deer's chest.

While most of the shot angles you have at deer will be so gentle you can ignore them, you'll likely find someday that you want to shoot at a buck far away and well above or below you. Then you must know quickly how much to compensate for the angle.

　　Target Movement. Shooting running deer is similar to shooting deer at long range or steep angles: You can calculate lead easily at a desk but the shot must be taken quickly. You won't have time for numbers but must rely on a kind of instinct you've developed with lots of practice. What looks right in the scope is what you'll use. Practice is what tells you how to recognize the right lead.

　　I've shot few running deer because I don't like to shoot fast or offhand and most running shots must be taken fast and offhand. Of the running shots I've tried I've made as many as most hunters would: not enough. I killed a running blacktail buck very close once with some quick shots from an iron-sighted Winchester 94, a whitetail at 90 yards with an open-sighted .303 British SMLE.

With scoped bolt rifles I shot a bounding mule deer buck 200 yards away, another much closer streaking across a shale slide. There have been a few others. For every well-placed shot I missed or hit poorly enough times I was too embarrassed to keep track. Shooting running deer is hard to do. Doing it well, with finesse and a 90 percent kill ratio is very hard.

Deer don't run as fast as most people think. They run from 18 to 25 mph when jumped in heavy cover and scrambling to get away. A deer walks about the same speed we do, three mph, and trots about seven mph. The high bounding or stotting gait of mule deer is pretty slow at 10 to 15 mph. A lower bounce speeds things up. A scared deer in the open can sprint 45 mph.

You might think that because deer go slower than we think we lead too much. Apparently that's not the case. At least that's what most nimrods say. I've missed forward at least as much as I've missed behind because shooting deer in the paunch is very distasteful to me. But a miss is a miss and merits no medals no matter where the bullet goes.

The hardest shot at deer is at stotting deer. Not only must you think about lead but about up and down movement as well. Deer will also change directions when stotting. A different direction at each bounce leaves you guessing where to hold because the deer's direction affects the angle of the shot and that affects lead. I don't shoot at stotting deer unless they're very close and going almost directly away and I haven't time to think twice and do the smart thing and decline the shot.

Deer walking or trotting are pretty easy to kill if they're in easy range say 200 yards, and you're in a good position to shoot. If your 140-grain .280 bullet starts out at 2,900 fps it will be going just over 2,400 fps at 200 yards. The mean velocity, then is 2,650 fps, but average velocity is less because the bullet spends more time traveling at the lower speeds. If the average velocity is 2,600 fps the bullet gets to a 200-yard target in .23 seconds. A deer walking three mph moves about one foot in the time the bullet takes to reach it at 200 yards. If you hold on the forward edge of the chest and sustain your lead by moving the rifle with the deer you'll kill. A trotting deer requires roughly twice that lead at 200 yards.

If the deer is running you must swing well in front of it. A buck running 21 mph is moving three times as fast as a trotting deer and you must lead it three times as far. That's six feet, or five feet in front of its chest. That's more than a deer length and a lot of space to see behind your vertical wire. Beyond 200 yards bullet velocity

A stotting buck is especially hard to kill because you must figure vertical as well as horizontal lead. Stotting deer can change direction quickly.

drops quickly and leads for running deer get big. Next time someone tells you of the sprinting buck he clobbered at 400 yards, ask him how he measured the 30-foot lead required.

Because many deer run away at an angle and not directly across your front, you'll have to think of these angles as you would think of oblique wind or elevated shot angles. If a deer is running away from you at 21 mph and is 100 yards out but angling at 45 degrees you must know instantly the deer is covering three feet while your bullet travels 300, but that only 1½-foot lead is called for. As with wind speeds, you needn't have a lot of numbers in your head once you've developed a feel for shooting running deer and can recognize the right sight picture. But calculating bullet travel times and deer speeds is good because it makes you think of lead deliberately. Your lead will be right or wrong, and you have very few inches for error.

A few factors make shots at running deer even harder: A buck you want may be in a herd or running with another buck. As they cross in stride your bullet may hit the wrong deer or pass through the right one and cripple another. If the deer you want is moving uphill or down you must lead vertically as well as horizontally. That's very hard. In timber you must think of the trees, find an opening, swing with the deer at the near edge of the opening and trigger your shot immediately. If instead of big trees there's light brush it's sometimes best to forget about the twigs and shoot the deer as you would a grouse, quickly. Shots at running deer in thick places are almost always close so you needn't lead much or even at all. But brush will blur your sight picture; and the deer will change direction to go around trees and jump above your crosswires to clear deadfalls. Your field of view is small close up and usually you have little time.

Shooting running game is like shooting standing game in that you must fire at the right time and without disturbing your aim. In thickets you shoot quickly if you shoot at all, sometimes so quickly you don't remember aiming. Some people call this snap-shooting. It's the same method used by trick shooters like Annie Oakley, Ad Topperwein, Ernie Lind. It is useful when time and range are short. It is not easy to learn. It is as disciplined a shooting style as any—aim, trigger control and form are all there. If you simply throw your rifle up and pull the trigger you are not snapshooting in the legitimate sense of the word. Anyone can do that. Snapshooting is like shooting skeet but is more demanding because you're directing a bullet, not a cloud of shot. I'm not a good snapshooter. I'm too slow and deliberate. So I decline shots other shooters would take. I admire shooters who routinely make those quick shots, who are good snapshooters.

Frequently you'll have enough time to shoot running mule deer that you can sit down and get your sling on. Maybe you'll have only enough time to sit down. Surely you will have time to position your body and trigger carefully for one shot. That's all you must do. Regardless of your position you must be "open" to the deer and flexible enough that you can swing with it. You can be open in any position. Once, on a hill too steep to sit on, I threw myself prone and made a fine shot on a buck running up the slope 200 yards above me. Another time I was readying for a long shot when a buck sprinted past me at 50 yards. I killed it with one shot, prone.

But prone is a poor position to shoot running game from because it's too rigid. Sitting allows you some movement, as does kneeling. I don't like to shoot running deer kneeling because the natural wobble of the cross hairs is horizontal. When you swing you accentuate that, but must control it at the same time you're trying to establish lead. It's very hard. Offhand is best suited to shots at running deer, and the swinging motion smooths out some of the blips you see when you try to hold the cross hairs still.

Being open to the deer so you can easily swing with it means having your body pointed right. When standing, your feet should be pointed so you are most comfortable where you expect to make the shot. That means you'll have to twist your torso a bit to pick up the deer in your scope and start your swing. What is true for your feet offhand is true for your legs when sitting and kneeling and your entire body when prone. The reason high positions are better for shots at running game is that the higher you are the less locked you are to the ground.

Having your body aimed the right way is vital to the shot. Keeping the rifle moving is too. If you shoot with a still rifle you have to think about your reaction time, trigger time, lock and ignition time to calculate lead. You can't. Only lock and ignition times are constant. The time it takes you to realize that you must pull the trigger varies. The time it takes your finger to move the trigger varies. All the while the running deer is covering ground. If you shoot with your rifle moving the same apparent speed as the deer you can forget about everything save the flight time of your bullet.

It's a good idea never to shoot moving game with your rifle still, even if there's just a small opening in the trees you're waiting for it to cross. Swing with the game and fire the shot in the opening and keep swinging. If you don't keep swinging after the shot you'll have the same problems golfers do if they don't follow through. Even snapshooters swing. Like aiming, it is part of what you must do to hit moving targets.

11

Understanding
What's To Come

Because almost everybody enjoys deer hunting or at least seeing
deer, it's easy to get support for managing deer. But there's
some disagreement on how to do that, and programs that make
sense now may not in five years.

The one thing that everyone agrees on is the need for active
management. Deer won't do well left alone. We have changed
their environment to the point that natural support and control
mechanisms no longer work. Predators and disease still kill deer
but seldom limit populations.

Man is part of nature. Whether that's an outdated view or an
undeserved compliment matters little. What matters is that the
world changes as man changes it. No other creature has such
influence. Deer have adapted to those changes so even when we
don't act, when we "let nature take its course," nature functions
unnaturally. To leave wild things alone is to make them the wards
of other people.

Habitat is a critical concern because we use land. Unlike deer
we don't just wander over it, sleep on it and browse its shrubs. We
claim it, tame it. We make it over so it does what we want it to do.
Some areas are protected by us from us, so that other life can exist.
Wilderness helps some animals more than others. It is as close as
we get to leaving natural things alone. The establishment of
wilderness boundaries and regulations is a form of active

management. Mule and black-tailed deer live in some wilderness, but they get along fine elsewhere. Most western deer live on public and private land that is profoundly affected by humans.

Since 1950 nearly 5 million acres of chaparral and pinon/juniper range has been treated chemically or mechanically to improve its value for cattle. West of the Rockies, roughly 200 million acres are under some form of agriculture. Deer can live with cattle and they like the crops planted on what was once their range. But rangers don't like deer in their haystacks or nibbling their green wheat. Orchard owners don't want them near fruit trees. Game agencies are sensitive to these conflicts. They manage deer to avoid such conflicts.

Lots of good deer range is located on public land: about 55 percent of the western rangeland and 62 percent of the western forest. Even here, though, deer must compete with cattle. Ranchers pay a lower fee to run cattle on public land than they would on private. Because it is not their land, some let it deteriorate. Overgrazing is common, ruining the range for deer and other wildlife. Timber cutting on national forests changes habitat. But if done with deer in mind it can actually improve the deer habitat. In some areas strip mining for gravel, coal, uranium and oil shale destroys the habitat. Montana has over one million acres of important mule deer range on top of coal reserves. In Colorado 34,000 acres were disturbed by mining in 1978.

Forest roads make deer accessible to hunters. Highways claim not only the right-of-way but land developed on either side. They become barriers to deer travel, and can be a major cause of mortality. In 1940 roads in the U.S. had 302 billion miles of vehicle use; by 1970 they were getting 1,121 billion miles. In 36 states surveyed in 1975 over 146,000 deer were reported killed on roads.

Reservoirs inundate a lot of land, some of it valuable to deer. In the Upper Colorado basin 200,000 acres of mountain brush and desert shrub used by mule deer have been flooded. In Washington 94 hydroelectric projects are expected to cover 426,000 acres.

What we do with land isn't too surprising when you think of who we are.

We are nearly 240 million people adding 7,000 more of us each day. There are 67 of us for every square mile in the U.S. To make homes and work for us we have put 34,000 square miles under asphalt since 1960. We pave 11,200 miles each year so we can roll to where we go, use 450 billion gallons of water each day.

In some areas, deer fence is used to keep deer out of orchards, grainfields and haystacks—and off highways. Building deer numbers is relatively simple. Sustaining them at the habitat's carrying capacity is harder. Resolving conflicts between deer and people is hardest of all.

We spread 285,000 tons of pesticides annually, generate 156 million tons of garbage.

When Columbus "sailed the ocean blue in 1492," there were 250 million acres of tallgrass prairie in the U.S. Today we have less than five million. Back then, there were 215 million acres of wetland; today less than half remain. The wildlands we've kept are being used more and more. From 1965 to 1978 the number of visitor-days each year on national forests rose from 125 million to 163 million.

Each year nearly two million people hunt mule deer in our western states, shooting over one-half million deer. Poachers kill many more. Studies to determine how many more are inconclusive, but estimates run high. In a New Mexico poaching simulation the public witnessed 43 violations but reported only one. Illegal kill in that state may equal legal kill. An Idaho study determined 8,000 deer were poached there annually.

What we do on the land can affect deer as much as what we do with it. A hiker who picks up a fawn, a woodcutter who drives a buck from its cover, a farmer who lacerates a bedded doe with his mower are as much a threat to deer as a rifleman. Dogs that run loose in winter kill deer. As a wildlife control agent in Washington, I found it hard to convince people that their dogs would or could kill deer. One big German shepherd belonged to a convent. The ladies were shocked when I showed them the mangled remains of the deer and the blood on their dog's throat. In crusted snow even smaller dogs can and will kill deer. Like coyote, they run on the surface, chasing a deer that breaks through at every bound. The dogs are well fed, usually; the deer are weak from winter's pinch.

Game agencies aren't in the business of making deer. A larger population is sometimes a management objective, but sometimes it's not. Giving hunters good hunting, keeping landowners happy, keeping deer habitat in good condition and keeping license money coming in to support deer management is a hard job. In addition to society's demands, managers must consider nature's own demands on the land. State game agencies must buffer deer management for that winter storm, the fire in winter range or drought. Naturally, hunters want to shoot deer. We want to shoot big deer, and see big deer next year. We want to hunt a long time each season, move about as we please and meet few other hunters. Much of managing deer is managing deer habitat and people.

There's talk now about high-quality hunting, the kind that

Fitted with a radio collar, this fawn will tell biologists about deer movement, foraging habits and perhaps mortality.

gives you a fine outdoor experience and the chance to shoot a big buck. It's the kind of thing that costs a lot. But few people want to or can afford to pay for that. To have big bucks in a herd managers must let little bucks grow old. That means protecting them. Managers must also manage for fewer deer because while they get old and big the bucks must eat. The same forage that supports several yearling bucks will feed only one big buck.

The legal minimum of a fork or visible antler is standard in all mule deer states. Antler point restrictions are reserved for special hunts or management units. They are popular in some areas, tolerated in others. Point restrictions can make for healthier herds because they allow more mature bucks to compete for breeding privileges. They reduce kill figures and hunter success.

According to most of the hunters I talk with, hunters who want to see more deer, shooting does is a bad thing. But some hunters must apply for antlerless tags because the tags are always oversubscribed. There's really nothing wrong with shooting does, provided the age and sex composition of the herd is known and there's an objective. While each buck can breed several does, there can be too many does for the few bucks in a heavily-hunted area. Balancing the sex ratios keeps some natural selection in the herd.

Some hunters who wouldn't shoot a doe will shoot a small four-point buck standing by a legal deer with spike antlers. If you're managing for big bucks, this isn't a good thing. Better that you shoot the spike because it is probably genetically inferior. Normal yearling mule deer have forked antlers. If you shoot the four-point you are probably killing a two-year-old buck with the potential to be a great big buck that you'd give your pet rifle to see some opening day. There's no trophy value in the four-point now, but some hunters would shoot the bigger deer without a thought. They are sometimes the same ones who complain that there are no great bucks to shoot anymore, who urge predator control and winter feeding to boost deer numbers.

Predators, mostly lions and coyote, have been shot under bounty with poor results. The best-known debacle occurred on the Kaibab Plateau in the 1920s. Lions were shot hard and the deer prospered. In a short time the deer had stripped their range of forage. A couple tough winters decimated the population.

Predators are hard animals to study because they are secretive and range widely. Their effects on deer depend on the season and deer condition. Little conclusive work has been done on predation, and what evidence there is suggests that predators promote healthy

Feeding deer during a particularly tough winter can sustain a good population. But regular feeding artificially boosts deer numbers beyond what is good for the herd or its habitat.

deer herds. They have a small impact on deer numbers in most places. If they affect population structure it is for the good, killing the easiest prey, the weakest animals.

Winter feeding is like predator control in that we can see results right away. And yet neither feeding nor predator control does much for deer populations. Coyote increase where there are fewer coyote than the prey can support. Deer fed this year have to be fed next year. If there isn't enough natural forage to support them now, more than likely there won't be later. Feeding helps deer survive. It also helps them reproduce by keeping them strong and healthy. That puts greater strain on the habitat, which makes feeding more important. In some places, the habitat will support deer most of the time, and feeding in a severe winter can prevent a crash. Feeding can also draw deer away from farms where crop damage is a problem. Regular feeding is expensive and seldom thought of as a good long-term management practice.

In most places there are plenty of black-tailed and mule deer to hunt. What most hunters want now is a better hunt.

When you can talk intelligently of local deer management, let your desires and opinions be heard. Write your state game commission and management agency. While you may not be a biologist, you can affect deer and deer hunting where you live. Show your concern, and share your ideas in a polite, professional way.

If you're interested enough in deer and deer hunting to read this book this far you're surely ready to explore further what kind of deer management is going on in the area you hunt. You can get that information from your game agency. There you can also get a management plan for the area you hunt and learn why it is written as it is. You'll learn about your local deer population by talking with the people who have to manage them.

Good hunting.

Appendix A:
Government Agencies

Bureau of Land Management, Washington, DC 20240, (202)343-5717.

U.S. Forest Service, P.O. Box 2417, Washington, DC 20013, (202)447-3957.

U.S. Geological Survey, National Center, Reston, VA 22092, (703)860-7000.

Alaska Department of Fish and Game, P.O. Box 3-2000, Juneau, AK 99802, (907)465-4100.

Alberta Department of Energy and Natural Resources, Main Floor, North Tower, Petroleum Plaza, 9945-108 St., Edmonton, Alberta T5K 2G6, (403)427-3674.

Arizona Game and Fish Department, 2222 W. Greenway Rd., Phoenix, AZ 85023, (602)942-3000.

British Columbia Ministry of Environment and Parks, Parliament Bldgs., Victoria, British Columbia V8V 1X5, (604)387-9731.

California Department of Fish and Game, 1416 Ninth St., Sacramento, CA 95814, (916)445-3531.

Colorado Division of Wildlife, 6060 Broadway, Denver, CO 80216, (303)297-1192.

Idaho Fish and Game Department, 600 S. Walnut, Box 25, Boise, ID 83707, (208)334-3700.

Montana Department of Fish, Wildlife and Parks, 1420 East Sixth, Helena, MT 59620, (406)444-2535.

Nevada Department of Wildlife, Box 10678, Reno, NV 89520, (702)789-0500.

New Mexico Game and Fish Department, Villagra Bldg., Santa Fe, NM 87503, (505)827-7899.

Oregon Department of Fish and Wildlife, 506 S.W. Mill St., Portland, OR 97207, (503)229-5403.

Utah Division of Wildlife Resources, 1596 W. North Temple, Salt Lake City, UT 84116-3154, (801)533-9333.

Washington Department of Wildlife, 600 N. Capitol Way, Olympia, WA 98504, (206)753-5700.

Wyoming Game and Fish Department, Cheyenne, WY 82002, (307)777-7631.

Appendix B:
Recommended Reading

Accurate Rifle (The), by Warren Page, Alfred A. Knopf, New York, NY, 1973.

Advanced Hunting on Deer and Elk Trails, by Francis Sell, Stackpole, Harrisburg, PA, 1954.

American Rifle Design and Performance, by L.R. Wallack, Winchester Press, New York, NY, 1977.

Antler Development in Cervidae, edited by Robert Brown, Caesar Kleberg Wildlife Research Institute, Kingsville, TX, 1983.

Book of the Rifle (Jim Carmichel's), by Jim Carmichel, Outdoor Life Books, New York, NY, 1985.

Colorado's Biggest Bucks and Bulls, by Jack and Susan Reneau, Colorado Big Game Trophy Records, Colorado Springs, CO, 1983.

Deer Hunter's Guide (The), by Francis Sell, Stackpole, Harrisburg, PA, 1964.

Deer Hunting Book (Outdoor Life's), edited by Chet Fish, Harper & Row, 1974.

Game Loads and Practical Ballistics for the American Hunter, by Bob Hagel, Alfred A. Knopf, New York, NY, 1978.

Guns, Loads, & Hunting Tips, by Bob Hagel, Wolfe Publishing, Prescott, AZ, 1986.

Hatcher's Notebook, by Julian Hatcher, Stackpole, Harrisburg, PA, 1962.

How to Bag the Biggest Buck of Your Life, by Larry Benoit, The Whitetail Press, Duxbury, VT, 1975.

How to Find Giant Bucks, by Kirt Darner, Walsworth Publishing, Marceline, MO, 1983.

Hunting Rifle (The), by Jack O'Connor, Alfred A. Knopf, New York, NY, 1977.

Hunting Trophy Deer, by John Wooters, Winchester Press, New York, NY, 1977.

Loading manuals by Hodgdon, Hornady, Nosler, Sierra and Speer have more than just data now. There's lots of good technical information on rifles and ammunition.

Mule and Black-tailed Deer of North America, edited by Olof Wallmo, Wildlife Management Institute, University of Nebraska Press, Lincoln, NE, 1981.

Pet Loads (Ken Waters'), by Ken Waters, Wolfe Publishing, Prescott, AZ, 1979.

Records of North American Big Game, by the Boone and Crockett Club, Boone and Crockett Club, Alexandria, VA, 1981.

Scopes & Mounts (Gun Digest Book of), by Bob Bell, DBI books, Northfield, IL, 1983.

Whitetail!, by George Mattis, Stackpole, Harrisburg, PA, 1969.

White-tailed Deer - Ecology and Management, edited by Lowell Halls, Wildlife Management Institute, Stackpole, Harrisburg, PA, 1984.

Index Of Rifle Calibers

Index